Famous Documents & Speeches
★ ★ ★ ★ ★ of the ★ ★ ★ ★ ★
CIVIL WAR

Famous Documents & Speeches
★ ★ ★ ★ ★ *of the* ★ ★ ★ ★ ★
CIVIL WAR

Edited by **BOB BLAISDELL**

DOVER PUBLICATIONS, INC.
Mineola, New York

Bibliographical Note

Famous Documents and Speeches of the Civil War is a new work, first published by Dover
Publications, Inc., in 2006.

Library of Congress Cataloging-in-Publication Data

Famous documents and speeches of the Civil War / edited by Bob Blaisdell.
    p. cm.
    ISBN 0-486-44851-7 (pbk.)
    1. United States—History—Civil War, 1861–1865—Sources. 2. Speeches, addresses,
etc., American. I. Blaisdell, Robert.

E464.F36 2006
973—dc22

2006050006

Manufactured in the United States of America
Dover Publications, Inc., 31 East 2nd Street, Mineola, N.Y. 11501

Contents

Contents vii

Note

IN *The Rebellion Record* (1861–1868) Frank Moore (1828-1904) tried to catch the Civil War in its complexity as it was happening, "in a digested and systematic shape, a comprehensive history of this struggle; sifting fact from fiction and rumor; presenting the poetical and picturesque aspects, the notable and characteristic incidents, separated from the graver and more important documents,"[1] just as we, more than seven score years later, continue to try to sort out what the Civil War was and meant. There may be no better way to understand it than going back to the beginning of the war and watching it document itself. In Frank Moore's twelve volumes of 10,000 double-columned 1,000-word pages, he gamely tried to keep pace—fielding literature from everywhere North and South—newspaper articles, official records, testimony, diaries and letters, poetry, rumors, anecdotes, jokes.

"The editor," Moore writes of himself in New York in 1861, "aiming at entire partiality, has collected, *from every quarter,* whatever appeared to be of general interest, in any way connected with the great topics of the day, or likely to elucidate, in the slightest degree, the questions at issue, or the spirit and temper of the people, whether loyal or otherwise. Thus it will be found that a very considerable portion of the volume is occupied with 'secession documents,' or articles from the 'secession' press, reprinted *verbatim,* without alteration, or comment. Every individual who has spoken or written with effect on either side, or 'on the fence,' has been placed 'on record,' and his utterances are here electrotyped for the benefit of future generations."[2]

---

[1] Frank Moore. Preface. *The Rebellion Record*. Volume 1. 1861. iii.
[2] *Ibid.*

I have limited this selection to those "utterances" in Moore's primary interest and place of importance, the "Documents" that comprise the bulk of each volume, and have allowed traditional Civil War history, with its mythologizing and simplifying and complicating and irradiating factors at work, to suggest the selections, notwithstanding a few irresistible accounts that should be better known. Few of the authors are obscure; most are by the most prominent men of the war—the generals, the officers, the presidents, the congressional leaders. For the budding or life-long Civil War amateur, Moore's volumes are a gold mine.

More than half of the documents and speeches included here come from Moore's first ten volumes, but most are available from other sources. I have eschewed memoirs and historical reconstructions, not because of their lack of rigor or precision (some are of course more accurate and comprehensive than those by contemporary eyewitnesses), but because of all the possible strategies for arranging such a collection, I found that the eyewitness-participant accounts seem most vivid and least after-the-fact clever and wise. The warriors at Manassas Junction and Gettysburg felt as if they were part of something very important, as indeed they were—but they did not know yet how it was all going to come out, and usually they could not yet be aware of the *other* accounts. Their concentration is on the present, and we see and feel their causes for alarm, relief, joy, and horror that the ravenous reading public in the United States and Confederate States shared.

I have tried not to alter the punctuation except for needless periods in closings of correspondence and have only occasionally added paragraph breaks to provide the reader with ledges on which to perch and muse. Each selection is complete, as found in Moore, or complete as found in other sources of contemporary documents, most notably the U. S. Government's *The War of the Rebellion: A Compilation of the Official Records of the Union and Confederate Armies* (1880–1901). Despite Moore's good example of discrete silence, I have provided brief notes on the relevance of each passage, but there are books about almost every incident included here and about almost every author or subject.

The best collection of documents that is built in the mode of Moore's work and which I have consulted and benefited from is Henry Commager's 1,200-page *The Blue and the Gray: The Story of the Civil War As Told by Its Participants* (1950; rev. 1982). The best source for materials in the *Official Records* are the hundreds of unwieldy, idiosyncratically arranged volumes themselves. The next best is Cornell University's "Making of America" website <http://moa.cit.cornell.edu/moa/>, which provides the *Official Records* on-line.

I have benefitted from documents and accounts suggested by my friends Daniel Evan Weiss and Ian Frazier and my father, F. William

Blaisdell. Columbia University's Butler Library has made my job of finding source books relatively easy, and I thank its librarians for preserving and making accessible thousands of Civil War publications. Finally, I am grateful to my great-great-grandfather, Solon Greenleaf Blaisdell (1834–1897), Company F, Twelfth Regiment, New Hampshire Volunteers, for carrying in his chest pocket the diary and photographs of his wife that dulled the impact of a Confederate bullet on June 3, 1864, at Cold Harbor.

—Bob Blaisdell

Bibliography

Asa W. Bartlett. *History of the Twelfth Regiment: New Hampshire Volunteers in the War of the Rebellion.* Concord, New Hampshire: Ira C. Evans. 1897. [HTR]

Frederick Douglass. *Douglass' Monthly.* Rochester, New York. April 1862. [DM]

Mary Anna Jackson. *Life and Letters of General Thomas J. Jackson.* New York: Harper & Brothers. 1891. [TJJ]

Robert E. Lee. *Recollections and Letters of General Robert E. Lee.* New York: Doubleday, Page, and Co. 1904. [REL]

Abraham Lincoln. *Letters and Telegrams: Gasparin to Meade.* New York: Current Literature Publishing Co. 1907. [ALLT]

Abraham Lincoln. *Great Speeches.* Edited by John Grafton. New York: Dover. 1991. [ALGS]

Frank Moore. *The Rebellion Record.* Volumes 1–10. 1861–1866. [RR]

William R. Plum. *The Military Telegraph During the Civil War in the United States.* Chicago: Jansen, McClurg, and Co. 1882. [MT]

William T. Sherman. *Memoirs of General William T. Sherman*, Vol. 2. New York: 1913. [MWTS]

The War of the Rebellion: A Compilation of the Official Records of the Union and Confederate Armies. Washington: Government Printing Office. 1880–1901. [OR]

For the notes on the documents, the most helpful reference book has been Mark Mayo Boatner's *Civil War Dictionary* (1959); I have also borrowed occasionally from my own *The Civil War: A Book of Quotations* (Dover, 2004) for summaries of events and sketches of participants.

"Sovereignty of South Carolina"
The Address of the People of South Carolina, Assembled in Convention, to the People of the Slaveholding States of the United States
(December 21, 1860)

[RR–I:396–401]

South Carolina had threatened secession for many years and, finally, after Abraham Lincoln's election in November, went through with it, leading the secession movement. "A geographical line has been drawn across the Union, and all the States north of that line have united in the election of a man to the high office of President of the United States whose opinions and purposes are hostile to Slavery," wrote the authors of "The Declaration of Causes Which Induced the Secession of South Carolina."[1] After South Carolina, ten other states "went South," into a new confederacy.[2]

The South Carolina politicians in Charleston who drafted "Sovereignty of South Carolina" justified their decision to secede by a presentation of the history of the United States. The North—that home of "negro fanaticism"—had trampled on South Carolina's rights, just as Great Britain had done to its colonies in the eighteenth century. South Carolina was seceding, its slaveholding legislators wrote, without any irony, because "We prefer . . . our system of industry, by which labor and capital are identified in interest, and capital, therefore, protects labor, by which our population doubles every twenty years; by which starvation is unknown, and abundance crowns the land; by which order is preserved by an unpaid police, and the most fertile regions of the world where the Caucasian cannot labor are brought into usefulness by the labor of the African, and the whole world is blessed by our own productions. All we demand of other peoples is to be let alone to work out our own high destinies."

---

[1] *The Rebellion Record:* I. Doc: 3.
[2] The states seceded in this order: South Carolina (Dec. 20, 1860); Mississippi (Jan. 9, 1861); Florida (Jan. 10); Alabama (Jan. 11); Georgia (Jan. 19); Louisiana (January 26); Texas (Feb. 1); Virginia (April 17); Arkansas (May 6); North Carolina (May 20); Tennessee (June 8).

IT IS now seventy-three years since the Union between the United States was made by the Constitution of the United States. During this period their advance in wealth, prosperity, and power, has been with scarcely a parallel in the history of the world. The great object of their Union was defense from the external aggressions of more powerful nations, now complete, from their mere progress in power. Thirty-one millions of people, with a commerce and navigation which explores every sea, and of agricultural productions which are necessary to every civilized people, command the friendship of the world. But, unfortunately, our internal peace has not grown with our external prosperity. Discontent and contention have moved in the bosom of the Confederacy for the last thirty-five years. During this time, South Carolina has twice called her people together in solemn convention, to take into consideration, the aggressions and unconstitutional wrongs, perpetrated by the people of the North on the people of the South. These wrongs were submitted to by the people of the South, under the hope and expectation that they would be final. But these hopes and expectations have proved to be void. Instead of being incentives to forbearance, our submission has only instigated to new forms of agression and outrage; and South Carolina, again assembling her people in convention, has this day dissolved her connection with the States constituting the United States.

The one great evil, from which all other evils have flowed, is the overthrow of the Constitution of the United States. The government of the United States is no longer the government of confederated republics, but of a consolidated democracy. It is no longer a free government, but a despotism. It is, in fact such a government as Great Britain attempted to set over our fathers, and which was resisted and defeated by a seven years' struggle for independence.

The Revolution of 1776 turned upon one great principle, self-government and self-taxation, the criterion of self-government. Where the interests of two people united together under one government, are different, each must have the power to protect its interests by the organization of the government or they cannot be free. The interests of Great Britain and of the colonies were different and antagonistic. Great Britain was desirous of carrying out the policy of all nations toward their colonies, of making them tributary to their wealth and power. She had vast and complicated relations with the whole world. Her policy toward her North American colonies was to identify them with her in all these complicated relations, and to make them bear, in common with the rest of the empire, the full burden of her obligations and necessities. She had a vast public debt; she had a European policy and an Asiatic policy, which had occasioned the accumulation of her public debt, and which kept her in continual wars. The North American colonies saw their interests, political and commercial, sacrificed by such a policy. Their interests required that they should not be identified with the burdens and wars of the mother country. They had been settled under charters, which gave them self-government, at least so far as their property was concerned. They had taxed themselves, and had never been taxed by the government of Great Britain. To make them a part of a consolidated empire, the Parliament of Great Britain determined to assume the power of legislating for the colonies in all cases whatsoever. Our ancestors resisted the pretension. They refused to be a part of the consolidated government of Great Britain.

The Southern States now stand exactly in the same position towards the Northern States that our ancestors in the colonies did towards Great Britain. The Northern States, having the majority in Congress, claim the same power of omnipotence in legislation as the British Parliament. "The general welfare," is the only limit to the legislation of either; and the majority in Congress, as in the British Parliament, are the sole judges of the expediency of the legislation this "general welfare" requires. Thus, the government of the United States has become a consolidated Government, and the people of the Southern States are compelled to meet the very despotism their fathers threw off in the Revolution of 1776.

The consolidation of the government of Great Britain over the colonies was attempted to be carried out by the taxes. The British Parliament undertook to tax the colonies to promote British interests. Our fathers resisted this pretension. They claimed the right of self-taxation through their colonial legislatures. They were not represented in the British Parliament and therefore could not rightfully be taxed by its legislature. The British government, however, offered them a representation in Parliament; but it was not sufficient to enable them to protect themselves from the majority and they refused the offer. Between taxation without any representation and taxation without a representation adequate to protection, there was no difference. In neither case would the colonies tax themselves. Hence, they refused to pay the taxes laid by the British Parliament.

The Southern States now stand in the same relation towards the Northern States in the vital matter of taxation, that our ancestors stood towards the people of Great Britain. They are in a minority in Congress. Their representation in Congress is useless to protect them against unjust taxation; and they are taxed by the people of the North for their benefit, exactly as the people of Great Britain taxed our ancestors in the British Parliament for their benefit. For the last forty years the taxes laid by the Congress of the United States have been laid with a view of subserving the interests of the North. The people of the South have been taxed by duties on imports, not for revenue, but for an object inconsistent with revenue—to promote, by prohibitions, Northern interests in the productions of their mines and manufactures.

There is another evil in the condition of the Southern towards the Northern States, which our ancestors refused to bear towards Great Britain. Our ancestors not only taxed themselves, but all the taxes collected from them were expended among them. Had they submitted to the pretensions of the British government, the taxes collected from them, would have been expended in other parts of the British empire. They were fully aware of the effect of such a policy in impoverishing the people from whom taxes are collected, and in enriching those who receive the benefit of their expenditure. To prevent the evils of such a policy was one of the motives which drove them on to Revolution. Yet this British policy has been fully realized towards the Southern States by the Northern States. The people of the Southern States are not only taxed for the benefit of the Northern States but after the taxes are collected, three-fourths of them are expended at the North. This cause, with others, connected with the operation of the General Government, has provincialized the cities of the South. Their growth is paralyzed whilst they are mere suburbs of Northern cities. The basis of the foreign commerce of the United States are the agricultural productions of the South; yet Southern cities do not carry it on. Our foreign trade is almost annihilated. In 1740 there were five shipyards in South Carolina to build ships to carry on our direct trade with Europe. Between 1740 and 1779 there were built in these yards twenty-five square-rigged vessels, besides a great number of sloops and schooners, to carry on our coast and West India trade. In the half century immediately preceding the Revolution, from 1725 to 1775, the population of South Carolina increased seven-fold.

No man can for a moment believe that our ancestors intended to establish over their posterity exactly the same sort of government they had overthrown. The great object of the Constitution of the United States, in its internal operation, was, doubtless, to secure the great end of the Revolution—a limited free government—a government limited to those matters only which were general and common to all portions of the United States. All sectional or local interests were to be left to the States. By no other arrangement would they obtain free government by a Constitution common to so vast a Confederacy. Yet by gradual and steady encroachments on the part of the people of the North, and submission on the part of the South, the limitations in the Constitution have been swept away, and the government of the United States has become consolidated, with a claim of limitless powers in its operations.

It is not at all surprising, whilst such is the character of the government of the United States, that it should assume to possess power over all the institutions of the country. The agitations on the subject of slavery in the South are the natural results of the consolidation of the government. Responsibility follows power; and if the people of the North have the power by Congress "to promote the general welfare of the United States" by any means they deem expedient—why should they not assail and overthrow the institution of slavery in the South? They are responsible for its continuance or existence, in proportion to their power. A majority in Congress, according to their interested and perverted views, is omnipotent. The inducements to act upon the subject of slavery, under such circumstances, were so imperious as to amount almost to a moral necessity. To make, however, their numerical power available to rule the Union, the North must consolidate their power. It would not be united, on any matter common to the whole Union—in other words, on any Constitutional subject—for on such subjects divisions are as likely to exist in the North as in the South. Slavery was strictly a sectional interest. If this could be made the criterion of parties at the North, the North could be united in its power, and thus carry out its measures of sectional ambition, encroachment, and aggrandizement. To build up their sectional predominance in the Union, the Constitution must be first abolished by constructions; but, that being done, the consolidation of the North to rule the South by the tariff and slavery issues, was in the obvious course of things.

The Constitution of the United States was an experiment. The experiment consisted in uniting under one government different peoples, living in different climates, and having different pursuits of industry and institutions. It matters not, how carefully the limitations of such a government be laid down in the Constitution, its success must at least depend upon the good faith of the parties to the constitutional compact in enforcing them. It is not in the power of human language to exclude false inferences, constructions, and perversions in any constitution; and when vast sectional interests are to be subserved, involving the appropriation of countless millions of money, it has not been the usual experience of mankind that words on parchment can arrest power. The Constitution of the United States, irrespective of the interposition of the States, rested on the assumption, that power would yield to faith—that integrity would be stronger than interest; and that thus the limitations of the Constitution would be observed. The experiment has been fairly made. The Southern States, from the commencement of the government, have striven to keep it within the orbit prescribed by the Constitution. The experiment has failed. The whole Constitution, by the constructions of the Northern people, has been swallowed up by a few words in its preamble. In their reckless lust for power, they seem unable to comprehend that seeming paradox that the more power is given to the General Government the weaker it becomes. Its strength consists in its generality and limitations.

To extend the scope of its power over sectional or local interests, is to raise up against it opposition and resistance. In all such matters, the General Government must necessarily be a despotism, because all sectional or local interests must ever be represented by a minority in the councils of the General Government—having no power to protect itself against the rule of the majority. The majority, constituted from those who do not represent these sectional or local interests, will control and govern them. A free people cannot submit to such a government. And the more it enlarges the sphere of its power, the greater must be the dissatisfaction it must produce, and the weaker it must become. On the contrary, the more it abstains from usurped powers, and the more faithfully it adheres to the limitations of the Constitution, the stronger it is made. The Northern people have had neither the wisdom nor the faith to perceive that to observe the limitation of the Constitution was the only way to its perpetuity.

Under such a Government there must, of course, be many and endless "irrepressible conflicts" between the two great sections of the Union. The same faithlessness which has abolished the Constitution of the United States, will not fail to carry out the sectional purposes for which it has been abolished. There must be conflict; and the weaker section of the Union can only find peace and liberty in an independence of the North. The repeated efforts made by South Carolina, in a wise conservatism, to arrest the progress of the General Government in its fatal progress to consolidation, have been unsupported, and denounced as faithless to the obligations of the Constitution by the very men and States who were destroying it by their usurpations. It is now too late to reform or restore the government of the United States. All confidence in the North is lost in the South. The faithlessness of half a century has opened a gulf of separation between them which no promises or engagements can fill.

It cannot be believed, that our ancestors would have assented to any union whatever with the people of the North, if the feelings and opinions now existing among them, had existed when the Constitution was framed. There was then no tariff—no negro fanaticism. It was the delegates from New England who proposed in the convention which framed the Constitution, to the delegates from South Carolina and Georgia, that if they would agree to give Congress the power of regulating commerce by a majority, they would support the extension of the African slave trade for twenty years. African slavery existed in all the States but one. The idea that they would be made to pay that tribute to their Northern confederates, which they had refused to pay to Great Britain; or that the institution of African slavery would be made the grand basis of a sectional organization of the North to rule the South, never crossed their imaginations. The union of the Constitution was a union of slaveholding States. It rests on slavery, by prescribing a representation in Congress for three-fifths of our slaves. There is nothing in the proceedings of the convention which framed the Constitution, to show that the Southern States would have formed any other Union; and still less that they would have formed a Union with more powerful non-slaveholding States having a majority in both branches of the Legislature of the government. They were guilty of no such folly. Time and the progress of things have totally altered the relations between the Northern and Southern States since the Union was established. That identity of feelings, interests, and institutions which once existed, is gone. They are now divided between agricultural and manufacturing, and commercial States—between slaveholding and non-slaveholding States. Their institutions and industrial pursuits have made them totally different people. That equality in the Government between the two sections of the Union which once existed, no longer exists. We but imitate the policy of our fathers in dissolving a Union with non-slaveholding confederates, and seeking a confederation with slaveholding States.

Experience has proved, that slaveholding States cannot be safe in subjection to non-slaveholding States. Indeed, no people ever expect to preserve their rights and liberties unless they are in their own custody. To plunder and oppress where plunder and oppression can be practiced with impunity, seems to be the natural order of things. The fairest portions of the world have been turned into wildernesses, and the most civilized and prosperous communities have been impoverished and ruined by antislavery fanaticism. The people of the North have not left us in doubt, as to their designs and policy. United as a section in the late Presidential election, they have elected as the exponent of their policy, one who has openly declared that all the States of the United States must be made free States or slave States. It is true, that amongst those who aided in his election, there are various shades of anti-slavery hostility. But if African slavery in the Southern States be the evil their political combinations affirm it to be, the requisitions of an inexorable logic must lead them to emancipation. If it is right to preclude or abolish slavery in a Territory, why should it be allowed to remain in the States? The one is not at all more unconstitutional than the other, according to the decisions of the Supreme Court of the United States. And when it is considered that the Northern States will soon have the power to make that Court what they please, and that the Constitution never has been any barrier whatever to their exercise of power, what check can there be in the unrestrained counsels of the North to emancipation? There is sympathy in association, which carries men along without principle; but when there is principle, and that principle is fortified by long-existing prejudices and feelings, association is omnipotent in party influences.

In spite of all disclaimers and professions, there can be but one end by the submission by the South to the rule of a sectional anti-slavery Government at Washington; and that end, directly or indirectly, must be the emancipation of the slaves of the South. The hypocrisy of thirty years—the faithlessness of their whole course from the commencement of our union with them show that the people of the non-slaveholding North are not and cannot be safe associates of the slaveholding South under a common government. Not only their fanaticism, but their erroneous views of the principles of free government, render it doubtful whether, separated from the South, they can maintain a free government among themselves. Brute numbers with them is the great element of free government. A majority is infallible and omnipotent. "The right divine to rule in kings" is only transferred to their majority. The very object of all constitutions, in free popular government, is to restrain the majority. Constitutions, therefore, according to their theory, must be most unrighteous inventions, restricting liberty. None ought to exist, but the body politic ought simply to have a political organization, to bring out and enforce the will of a majority. This theory may be harmless in a small community having identity of interests and pursuits, but over a vast State—still more over a vast Confederacy, having various and conflicting interests and pursuits—it is a remorseless despotism. In resisting it, as applicable to ourselves, we are vindicating the great cause of free government, more important perhaps to the world than the existence of all the United States. Nor, in resisting it, do we intend to depart from the safe instrumentality the system of government we have established with them requires. In separating from them we invade no rights—no interest of theirs. We violate no obligation or duty to them.

As separate, independent States in convention, we made the Constitution of the United States with them; and, as separate independent States, each State acting for itself, we adopted it. South Carolina, acting in her sovereign capacity, now thinks proper to secede from the Union. She did not part with her sovereignty in adopting the Constitution. The last thing a State can be presumed to have surrendered is her sovereignty. Her sovereignty is her life. Nothing but a clear, express grant can alienate it. Inference should be dumb. Yet it is not at all surprising that those who have construed away all the limitations of the Constitution, should also by construction, claim the annihilation of the sovereignty of the States. Having abolished barriers to their omnipotence by their faithless constructions in the operations of the General

Government, it is most natural that they should endeavor to do the same towards us in the States. The truth is, they having violated the express provisions of the Constitution, it is at an end as a compact. It is morally obligatory only on those who choose to accept its perverted terms. South Carolina, deeming the compact not only violated in particular features, but virtually abolished by her Northern confederates, withdraws herself as a party from its obligations. The right to do so is denied by her Northern confederates. They desire to establish a despotism, not only omnipotent in Congress, but omnipotent over the States; and as if to manifest the imperious necessity of our secession, they threaten us with the sword, to coerce submission to their rule.

Citizens of the slaveholding States of the United States, circumstances beyond our control have placed us in the van of the great controversy between the Northern and Southern States. We would have preferred that other States should have assumed the position we now occupy. Independent ourselves, we disclaim any design or desire to lead the counsels of the other Southern States. Providence has cast our lot together, by extending over us an identity of pursuits, interests and institutions. South Carolina desires no destiny separated from yours. To be one of a great slaveholding confederacy, stretching its arms over a territory larger than any power in Europe possesses—with population four times greater than that of the whole United States, when they achieved their independence of the British empire—with productions which make our existence more important to the world than that of any other people inhabiting it—with common institutions to defend, and common dangers to encounter—we ask your sympathy and confederation. Whilst constituting a portion of the United States, it has been your statesmanship which has guided it in its mighty strides to power and expansion. In the field, as in the cabinet, you have led the way to its renown and grandeur. You have loved the Union, in whose service your great statesmen have labored, and your great soldiers have fought and conquered—not for the material benefits it conferred, but with the faith of a generous and devoted chivalry. You have long lingered and hoped over the shattered remains of a broken Constitution. Compromise after compromise, formed by your concessions, has been trampled under foot by your Northern confederates. All fraternity of feeling between the North and the South is lost, or has been converted into hate, and we of the South are at last driven together by the stern destiny which controls the existence of nations.

Your bitter experience of the faithlessness and rapacity of your Northern confederates may have been necessary to evolve those great principles of free government, upon which the liberties of the world depend, and to prepare you for the grand mission of vindicating and reestablishing them. We rejoice that other nations should be satisfied with their institutions. Self-complacency is a great element of happiness with nations as with individuals. We are satisfied with ours. If they prefer a system of industry, in which capital and labor are in perpetual conflict—and chronic starvation keeps down the natural increase of population—and a man is worked out in eight years—and the law ordains that children shall be worked only ten hours a day—and the sabre and bayonet are the instruments of order—be it so. It is their affair, not ours. We prefer, however, our system of industry, by which labor and capital are identified in interest, and capital, therefore, protects labor, by which our population doubles every twenty years; by which starvation is unknown, and abundance crowns the land; by which order is preserved by unpaid police, and the most fertile regions of the world where the Caucasian cannot labor are brought into usefulness by the labor of the African, and the whole world is blessed by our own productions. All we demand of other peoples is to be let alone to work out our own high destinies. United together, and we must be the most independent, as we are the most important amongst the nations of the world. United together, and we require no other instrument to conquer peace than our beneficent productions. United together, and we must be a great, free and prosperous people, whose renown must spread throughout the civilized world, and pass down, we trust, to the remotest ages. We ask you to join us in forming a Confederacy of slaveholding States.

—*Missouri Republican,* Dec. 29, 1860

First Inaugural Address,
President Abraham Lincoln
(March 4, 1861)

In Washington, D. C., Abraham Lincoln, inaugurated as the sixteenth president of the United States, greeted the looming crisis with calming and lengthy legal reasoning: "One section of our country believes slavery is right, and ought to be extended, while other believes it is wrong, and ought not to be extended. This is the only substantial dispute." The address satisfied neither secessionists nor abolitionists, but it clearly outlined the present and future. At his second inaugural in 1865, Lincoln remarked of this first address: "Then a statement, somewhat in detail, of a course to be pursued, seemed fitting and proper."

Fellow-citizens of the United States:

IN COMPLIANCE with a custom as old as the Government itself, I appear before you to address you briefly, and to take, in your presence, the oath prescribed by the Constitution of the United States to be taken by the President, before he enters on the execution of his office.

I do not consider it necessary, at present, for me to discuss those matters of administration about which there is no special anxiety or excitement. Apprehension seems to exist among the people of the southern States, that, by the accession of a Republican Administration, their property and their peace and personal security are to be endangered. There has never been any reasonable cause for such apprehension. Indeed, the most ample evidence to the contrary has all the while existed, and been open to their inspection. It is found in nearly all the published speeches of him who now addresses you. I do but quote from one of those speeches, when I declare that "I have no purpose, directly or indirectly, to interfere with the institution of slavery in the States where it exists."

11

I believe I have no lawful right to do so; and I have no inclination to do so. Those who nominated and elected me, did so with the full knowledge that I had made this, and made many similar declarations, and had never recanted them. And, more than this, they placed in the platform, for my acceptance, and as a law to themselves and to me, the clear and emphatic resolution which I now read:

"*Resolved,* That the maintenance inviolate of the rights of the States, and especially the right of each State to order and control its own domestic institutions according to its own judgment exclusively, is essential to that balance of power on which the perfection and endurance of our political fabric depend; and we denounce the lawless invasion by armed force of the soil of any State or Territory, no matter under what pretext, as among the gravest of crimes."

I now reiterate these sentiments; and in doing so, I only press upon the public attention the most conclusive evidence of which the case is susceptible, that the property, peace, and security of no section are to be in anywise endangered by the now incoming Administration.

I add, too, that all the protection which, consistently with the Constitution and the laws, can be given will be cheerfully given to all the States when lawfully demanded, for whatever cause, as cheerfully to one section, as to another.

There is much controversy about the delivering up of fugitives from service or labor. The clause I now read is as plainly written in the constitution as any other of its provisions:

"No person held to service or labor in one State under the laws thereof, escaping into another, shall, in consequence of any law or regulation therein, be discharged from such service or labor, but shall be delivered up on claim of the party to whom such service or labor may be due."

It is scarcely questioned that this provision was intended by those who made it for the reclaiming of what we call fugitive slaves; and the intention of the lawgiver is the law.

All members of Congress swear their support to the whole Constitution—to this provision as well as any other. To the proposition, then, that slaves whose cases come within the terms of this clause "shall be delivered up," their oaths are unanimous. Now, if they would make the effort in good temper, could they not, with nearly equal unanimity, frame and pass a law by means of which to keep good that unanimous oath?

There is some difference of opinion whether this clause should be enforced by national or by state authority; but surely that difference is not a very material one. If the slave is to be surrendered, it can be of but little consequence to him or to others, by which authority it is done. And should any one, in any case, be content that this oath shall go unkept, on a merely unsubstantial controversy as to how it shall be kept?

Again, in any law upon this subject, ought not all the safeguards of liberty known in the civilized and humane jurisprudence to be introduced, so that a free man be not, in any case, surrendered as a slave? And might it not be well at the same time to provide by law for the enforcement of that clause in the Constitution which guarantees that "the citizens of each State shall be entitled to all previleges and immunities of citizens in the several States?"

I take the official oath to-day with no mental reservations, and with no purpose to construe the Constitution or laws by any hypercritical rules. And while I do not choose now to specify particular acts of Congress as proper to be enforced, I do suggest that it will be much safer for all, both in official and private stations, to conform to and abide by all those acts which stand unrepealed, than to violate any of them, trusting to find impunity in having them held to be unconstitutional.

It is seventy-two years since the first inauguration of a President under our national Constitution. During that period fifteen different and very distinguished citizens have in succession administered the executive branch of the government. They have conducted it through many perils, and, generally with great success. Yet, with all this scope for precedent, I now enter upon the same task for the brief constitutional term of four years, under great and peculiar difficulties.

A disruption of the Federal Union, heretofore only menaced, is now formidably attempted. I hold that in the contemplation of universal law and of the Constitution, the Union of these States is perpetual. Perpetuity is implied, if not expressed, in the fundamental law of all national governments. It is safe to assert that no government proper ever had a provision in its organic law for its own termination. Continue to execute all the express provisions of our national Constitution, and the Union will endure forever, it being impossible to destroy it except by some action not provided for in the instrument itself.

Again, if the United States be not a government proper, but an association of States in the nature of contract merely, can it, as a contract, be peaceably unmade by less than all the parties who made it? One party to a contract may violate it—break it, so to speak; but does it not require all to lawfully rescind it? Descending from these general principles we find the proposition that in legal contemplation the Union is perpetual, confirmed by the history of the Union itself.

The Union is much older than the Constitution. It was formed, in fact, by the Articles of Association in 1774. It was matured and continued in the Declaration of Independence in 1776. It was further matured, and the faith of all the then thirteen States expressly plighted and engaged that it should be perpetual, by the Articles of Confederation, in 1778. And, finally, in 1787, one of the declared objects for ordaining and establishing the Constitution, was to form a more perfect Union. But if the destruction of the Union by one or by a part only of the States be lawfully possible, the Union is less than before, the Constitution having lost the vital element of perpetuity.

It follows from these views that no State, upon its own mere motion, can lawfully get out of the Union; that resolves and ordinances to that effect are legally void; and that acts of violence within any State or States against the authority of the United States, are insurrectionary or revolutionary, according to circumstances.

I therefore consider that, in view of the Constitution and the laws, the Union is unbroken, and, to the extent of my ability, I shall take care, as the Constitution itself expressly enjoins upon me, that the laws of the Union shall be faithfully executed in all the States. Doing this, which I deem to be only a simple duty on my part I shall perfectly perform it, so far as is practicable, unless my rightful masters, the American people, shall withhold the requisition, or, in some authoritative manner, direct the contrary.

I trust this will not be regarded as a menace, but only as the declared purpose of the Union that it will constitutionally defend and maintain itself.

In doing this there need be no bloodshed or violence, and there shall be none unless it is forced upon the national authority.

The power confided to me, *will be used to hold, occupy, and possess the property and places belonging to the Government,* and collect the duties and imposts; but beyond what may be necessary for these objects there will be no invasion, no using of force against or among the people anywhere.

Where hostility to the United States shall be so great and so universal as to prevent competent resident citizens from holding the Federal offices, there will be no attempt to force obnoxious strangers among the people that object. While the strict legal right may exist of the Government to enforce the exercise of these offices, the attempt to do so would be so irritating, and so nearly impracticable withal, that I deem it better to forego for the time the uses of such offices.

The mails, unless repelled, will continue to be furnished in all parts of the Union.

So far as possible, the people everywhere shall have that sense of perfect security which is most favorable to calm thought and reflection.

The course here indicated will be followed, unless current events and experience shall show a modification or change to be proper; and in every case and exigency my best discretion will be exercised according to the circumstances actually existing, and with a view and hope of a peaceful solution of the national troubles, and the restoration of fraternal sympathies and affections.

That there are persons, in one section or another, who seek to destroy the Union at all events, and are glad of any pretext to do it, I will neither affirm or deny. But if there be such, I need address no word to them.

To those, however, who really love the Union, may I not speak, before entering upon so grave a matter as the destruction of our national fabric, with all its benefits, its memories, and its hopes? Would it not be well to ascertain why we do it? Will you hazard so desperate a step, while any portion of the ills you fly from, have no real existence? Will you, while the certain ills you fly to, are greater than all the real ones you fly from? Will you risk the commission of so fearful a mistake? All profess to be content in the Union, if all constitutional rights can be maintained. Is it true, then, that any right, plainly written in the Constitution has been denied? I think not. Happily the human mind is so constituted, that no party can reach to the audacity of doing this.

Think, if you can, of a single instance in which a plainly-written provision of the Constitution has ever been denied. If, by the mere force of numbers, a majority should deprive a minority of any clearly-written constitutional right, it might, in a moral point of view, justify revolution; it certainly would, if such right were a vital one. But such is not our case.

All the vital rights of minorities and of individuals are so plainly assured to them, by affirmations and negations, guaranties and prohibitions in the Constitution, that controversies never arise concerning them. But no organic law can ever be framed with a provision specifically applicable to every question which may occur in practical administration. No foresight can anticipate, nor any document of reasonable length contain, express provisions for all possible questions. Shall fugitives from labor be surrendered by national or by State authorities? The Constitution does not expressly say. Must Congress protect slavery in the Territories? The Constitution does not expressly say. From questions of this class, spring all our constitutional controversies, and we divide upon them into majorities and minorities.

If the minority will not acquiesce, the majority must, or the government must cease. There is no other alternative for continuing the government but acquiescence on the one side or the other. If a minority in such case, will secede rather than acquiesce, they make a precedent which in turn will ruin and divide them, for a minority of their own will secede from them, whenever a majority refuses to be controlled by such a minority. For instance, why may not any portion of a new confederacy, a year or two hence, arbitrarily secede again, precisely as portions of the present Union now claim to secede from it? All who cherish disunion senti-

ments, are now being educated to the exact temper of doing this. Is there
such perfect identity of interests among the States to compose a new
Union as to produce harmony only, and prevent renewed secession?
Plainly, the central idea of secession is the essence of anarchy.

A majority held in restraint by constitutional checks and limitations
and always changing easily with deliberate changes of popular opinions
and sentiments, is the only true sovereign of a free people. Whoever
rejects it, does, of necessity, fly to anarchy or to despotism. Unanimity is
impossible; the rule of a majority, as a permanent arrangement, is wholly
inadmissable. So that, rejecting the majority principle, anarchy or despotism in some form is all that is left.

I do not forget the position assumed by some that constitutional questions are to be decided by the Supreme Court, nor do I deny that such
decisions must be binding in any case upon the parties to a suit, as to the
object of that suit, while they are also entitled to very high respect and
consideration in all parallel cases by all other departments of the government. And while it is obviously possible that such decision may be erroneous in any given case, still the evil effect following it, being limited to
that particular case, with the chance that it may be overruled and never
become a precedent for other cases, can better be borne than could the
evils of a different practice.

At the same time the candid citizen must confess that if the policy of
the government upon the vital questions affecting the whole people is to
be irrevocably fixed by decisions of the Supreme Court, the instant they
are made, as in ordinary litigation between parties in personal actions, the
people will have ceased to be their own masters, unless having to that
extent practically resigned their government into the hands of that eminent tribunal.

Nor is there in this view any assault upon the court or the judges. It
is a duty from which they may not shrink, to decide cases properly
brought before them; and it is no fault of theirs if others seek to turn
their decisions to political purposes. One section of our country believes
slavery is right, and ought to be extended, while the other believes it is
wrong and ought not to be extended. This is the only substantial dispute.
The fugitive slave clause of the constitution, and the law for the suppression of the foreign slave trade, are each as well enforced, perhaps, as
any law can ever be in a community where the moral sense of the people imperfectly supports the law itself. The great body of the people
abide by the dry legal obligation in both cases, and a few break over in
each. This, I think, cannot be perfectly cured, and it would be worse in
both cases after the separation of the sections,than before. The foreign
slave trade, now imperfectly suppressed, would be ultimately revived,

without restriction, in one section; while fugitive slaves, now only partially surrendered, would not be surrendered at all by the other.

Physically speaking we cannot separate. We cannot remove our respective sections from each other, nor build an impassable wall between them. A husband and wife may be divorced, and go out of the presence and beyond the reach of each other, but the different parts of our country cannot do this. They cannot but remain face to face; and intercourse, either amicable or hostile, must continue between them. Is it possible, then, to make that intercourse more advantageous or more satisfactory after separation than before? Can aliens make treaties easier than friends can make laws? Can treaties be more faithfully enforced between aliens than laws can among friends? Suppose you go to war, you cannot fight always; and when, after much loss on both sides, and no gain on either, you cease fighting, the identical questions as to terms of intercourse are again upon you.

This country, with its institutions, belongs to the people who inhabit it. Whenever they shall grow weary of the existing government, they can exercise their constitutional right of amending, or their revolutionary right to dismember or overthrow it. I cannot be ignorant of the fact that many worthy and patriotic citizens are desirous of having the national constitution amended. While I make no recommendation of amendment, I fully recognize the full authority of the people over the whole subject, to be exercised in either of the modes prescribed in the instrument itself, and I should, under existing circumstances, favor, rather than oppose, a fair oppertunity being afforded the people to act upon it.

I will venture to add, that to me the convention mode seems preferable, in that it allows amendments to originate with the people themselves, instead of only permitting them to take or reject propositions originated by others not especially chosen for the purpose and which might not be precisely such as they would wish either to accept or refuse. I understand that a proposed amendment to the Constitution which amendment, however, I have not seen, that has passed Congress, to the effect that the Federal Government shall never interfere with the domestic institutions of the States, including that of persons held to service. To avoid misconstruction of what I have said, I depart from my purpose not to speak of particular amendments, so far as to say that, holding such a provision to now be implied constitutional law, I have no objection to its being made express, and irrevocable.

The chief magistrate derives all his authority from the people, and they have conferred none upon him to fix the terms for the separation of the States. The people themselves also can do this, if they choose, but the Executive, as such, has nothing to do with it. His duty is to administer the present government as it came to his hands, and to transmit it unimpaired by him to his successor. Why should there not be a patient confidence in the ultimate justice of the people? Is there any better or equal hope in the world? In our present differences is either party without faith of being in the right? If the Almighty Ruler of nations, with his eternal truth and justice, be on your side of the North, or on yours of the South, that truth and that justice will surely prevail by the judgment of this great tribunal, the American people. By the frame of the Government under which we live, this same people have wisely given their public servants but little power for mischief, and have with equal wisdom provided for the return of that little to their own hands at very short intervals. While the people retain their virtue and vigilence, no administration, by any extreme wickedness or folly, can very seriously injure the Government in the short space of four years.

My countrymen, one and all, think calmly and well upon this whole subject. Nothing valuable can be lost by taking time.

If there be an object to hurry any of you, in hot haste, to a step which you would never take deliberately, that object will be frustrated by taking time; but no good object can be frustrated by it.

Such of you as are now dissatisfied still have the old Constitution unimpaired, and on the sensitive point, the laws of your own framing under it; while the new administration will have no immediate power, if it would, to change either.

If it were admitted that you who are dissatisfied hold the right side in the dispute, there still is no single reason for precipitate action. Intelligence, patriotism, Christianity, and a firm reliance on Him who has never yet forsaken this favored land, are still competent to adjust, in the best way, all our present difficulties.

In your hands, my dissatisfied fellow-countrymen, and not in mine, is the momentous issue of civil war. The government will not assail you. You can have no conflict, without being yourselves the aggressors. You have no oath registered in Heaven to destroy the government, while I shall have the most solemn one to "preserve, protect, and defend" it.

I am loath to close. We are not enemies, but friends. We must not be enemies. Though passion may have strained, it must not break our bonds of affection.

The mystic chords of memory, stretching from every battle-field and patriot grave, to every living heart and hearthstone all over this broad land, will yet swell the chorus of the Union, when again touched, as surely they will be, by the better angels of our nature.

Recruitment Proclamation
by Virginia Governor Letcher
(May 3, 1861)

[RR–I:184]

In Richmond, Governor John Letcher, with the "authority" of the Virginia state convention, called for volunteers to join the seceded state's new army. (This authority was denied by a majority of western Virginians, who themselves "seceded" from their seceded state to become, eventually, West Virginia [See below, page ZZ, June 24, 1861].) Many Virginians, including General Robert E. Lee, resigned from the Federal Army to serve the new army. Fewer but including Winfield Scott, the General in Chief of the Federal Army for the first months of the war, and George H. Thomas, who would become one of the Union's finest generals, did not. (See also Colonel Philip St. George Cooke's response to Letcher's call, page ZZ, below.)

THE SOVEREIGNTY of the Commonwealth of Virginia having been denied, her territorial rights assailed, her soil threatened with invasion by the authorities at Washington, and every artifice employed which could inflame the people of the Northern States and misrepresent our purposes and wishes, it becomes the solemn duty of every citizen of this State to prepare for the impending conflict. These misrepresentations have been carried to such an extent that foreigners and naturalized citizens who, but a few years ago, were denounced by the North and deprived of essential rights, have now been induced to enlist into regiments for the purpose of invading this State, which then vindicated those rights and effectually resisted encroachments which threatened their destruction. Against such a policy and against a force which the Government at Washington, relying upon its numerical strength, is now rapidly concentrating, it becomes the State of Virginia to prepare proper safeguards.

To this end and for these purposes, and with a determination to repel invasion, I, JOHN LETCHER, Governor of the Commonwealth of Virginia, by authority of the Convention, do hereby authorize the commanding-general of the military forces of this State, to call out, and to cause to be mustered into the service of Virginia, from time to time, as the public exigencies may require, such additional number of volunteers as he may deem necessary.

To facilitate this call, the annexed Schedule will indicate the places of rendezvous at which the companies called for will assemble upon receiving orders for service.

[L. S.]   Given under my hand as Governor, and under the seal of the Commonwealth, at Richmond, this 3d day of May, 1861, and in the 85th year of the Commonwealth.

JOHN LETCHER

By the Governor.
GEORGE W. MUNFORD,
    Secretary of the Commonwealth

SCHEDULE

The following places of rendezvous are designated as the point at which companies called from the annexed counties will assemble: Harper's Ferry, Staunton, Alexandria, Warrenton, Culpepper C. H., Gordonsville, Lynchburg, Abingdon, Fredericksburg, King George, Gloucester Point, West Point, Norfolk, Smithfield, Petersburg, Buffalo, Barbourville, Charleston, Parkersburg, Moundsville, Grafton, and Richmond.

Proclamation to the People of Loudon, Fairfax, and Prince William Counties, Virginia by Confederate Brigadier-General G. T. Beauregard

(June 5, 1861)

[RR-I:339] & [OR-SERIES 1, VOL. 2, PT. 1: 907]

Pierre Gustave Toutant Beauregard (1818–1893) had commanded the taking of Fort Sumter, South Carolina, in April, which some saw as the real beginning of the war, and was one of the South's passionately "reckless" spokesmen, accusing the Federal army of having as "their war cry . . . 'Beauty and booty.'"

HEADQUARTERS, DEPT. OF ALEXANDRIA,
Camp Pickens, June 5, 1861

A PROCLAMATION—*To the People of the Counties of Loudon, Fairfax, and Prince William, Virginia.*

A RECKLESS and unprincipled tyrant has invaded your soil. Abraham Lincoln, regardless of all moral, legal, and constitutional restraints, has thrown his Abolition hosts among you, who are murdering and imprisoning your citizens, confiscating and destroying your property, and committing other acts of violence and outrage, too shocking and revolting to humanity to be enumerated.

All rules of civilized warfare are abandoned, and they proclaim by their acts, if not on their banners, that their war-cry is "Beauty and booty."

All that is dear to man, your honor, and that of your wives and daughters —your fortunes and your lives, are involved in this momentous contest.

In the name, therefore, of the constituted authorities of the Confederate States—in the sacred cause of constitutional liberty and self-government, for which we are contending—in behalf of civilization itself, I, G. T.

Beauregard, Brigadier-General of the Confederate States, commanding at Camp Pickens, Manassas Junction, do make this my Proclamation, and invite and enjoin you by every consideration dear to the hearts of freemen and patriots, by the name and memory of your Revolutionary fathers, and by the purity and sanctity of your domestic firesides, to rally to the standard of your State and country; and, by every means in your power, compatible with honorable warfare, to drive back and expel the invaders from your land.

I conjure you to be true and loyal to your country and her legal and constitutional authorities, and especially to be vigilant of the movements and acts of the enemy, so as to enable you to give the earliest authentic information at these headquarters, or to the officers under my command.

I desire to assure you that the utmost protection in my power will be given to you all.

G. T. BEAUREGARD,
Brigadier-General, Commanding

Official—Thomas Jordan,
     Acting Assistant Adj't-General

—Richmond Enquirer

Response to the Virginia Convention's Call for Soldiers by U.S. Army Colonel P. St. G. Cooke

(June 6, 1861)

[RR-II:171–172]

A native of Leesburg, Virginia, Philip St. George Cooke (1809–1895) remained loyal to his country and explained his rationale with spirit and resolve: "At fourteen years of age I was severed from Virginia; the National Government adopted me as its pupil and future defender; it gave me education and a profession, and I then made a solemn oath to bear true allegiance to the United States of America, and to 'serve them honestly and faithfully against all their enemies or opposers whatsoever.' This oath and honor alike forbid me to abandon their standard at the first hour of danger." Cooke's son, however, became a Confederate general and his son-in-law, General J. E. B. Stuart, one of the South's most famous cavalry leaders.

FORT CRITTENDEN,
Utah, June 6, 1861

I HAVE seen the call of the Virginia Convention on all natives of the State in the army and navy, and have been the subject of other more pointed appeals.

The respect which I owe to the opinions of the citizens of my native State demands of me an answer—an exposition of my circumstances and views of duty.

I belong to a district of the State which, I just learn, has voted for Union. At fourteen years of age I was severed from Virginia; the National Government adopted me as its pupil and future defender; it gave me education and a profession, and I then made a solemn oath to bear true allegiance to the United States of America, and to "serve them honestly and faithfully against all their enemies or opposers whatsoever."

23

This oath and honor alike forbid me to abandon their standard at the first hour of danger.

In the national service I have been for thirty-four years a Western man, and if my citizenship be localized, a citizen of Missouri.

My military profession has not prevented attentive observation of political affairs, and I have had of late the vantage ground of a calm position. Thus I have formed strong political opinions, which must have had their weight in deciding my course.

Now, what was the true status of a great sectional struggle when the Virginia Convention resolved upon revolution?

For the first time in our national history her citizens enjoyed a legal right to settle *with their slave property* on every acre of the public domain; and this had just been recognized for the first time by the Republican party in their votes for their territorial acts of Congress. If a barren right, it was too confessedly a mere point of honor. And slavery was recognized by local law, with the acquiescence of that party, in all the territory south of the old Missouri compromise line.

The "Personal Liberty" acts of some Northern States—misrepresented, but really disloyal and irritating—were being reconsidered; some had already been modified or repealed.

The democratic party was gaining strength; was successful in some of the New England States. But for southern defection it had been in control of two of the three great departments of the Government.

The fugitive slave law had just been executed at *Chicago* with unwonted facility by an officer appointed by the new Administration.

But one patent fact remains: The Confederate States had committed an overt act of aggressive *war upon the nation!* they threatened its Capital, and the President had called for militia for public defence.

Years ago public men at the South began to despair of their habitual control in the future of the power of the National Government; they were irritated at this prospect, and unreasonably, for it was to be the legitimate result of our political system, and of sectional institutions. But the politicians of the Cotton States had long familiarized themselves with ultra ambitious schemes; they were committed, especially in South Carolina, beyond any dignity of retraction to vain State rights theories and threats of State action; they embraced wild, dazzling, but unscrupulous and impracticable designs; they resolved to *rule,* if only amid the ruins of their country; they *conspired*; they had influence to sever the great national party; they remorselessly turned their backs on their constant and sorely pressed friends at the North and West; they forced an election by a minority of the people, and then gladly raised the cry of sectional domination, and of imaginary injuries and evils to follow. They *took advantage of their own wrong,* and pronounced a political crime the success of a sectional party, to which they had deliberately contributed.

Then the oligarchy of South Carolina, (a State not very homogeneous, politically or socially, with any other part of the nation,) with contemptuous disregard of the dignity and of the counsels of their neighbors, coolly set themselves to convert a great excitement into temporary madness. They applied the torch to the temple of free Government. South Carolina assumed the bad eminence of leader in revolution and ruin. Thus aided, the arts of demagogues and the violent energies of rebellious spirits elsewhere dragged or dragooned the reluctant *voiceless* inhabitants of six other States into her train. Ever since the leaders have exerted every art to gain over the "Border States," to save themselves from failures; until desperately they lit the torch of war; then Virginia fell into the snare. In a secondary position, she is made a tool—a fender against collision—a battle-ground. When the war tocsin sounded, her Catilines, her mad youths, her city-mobs, drove excitement to frenzy, and a great Union majority in the Convention was overcome. Thus recklessly, for a time, the temperate voice of duty has been drowned, and the good old State may have been plunged into the darkness of moral and physical desolation—the hell of a bitter civil, it may be a servile, war.

I have given the utmost condensation to this sketch of my views and convictions; it is not a time for many words. If I had been on the ground I might have felt tempted to shoulder a musket in defence of the mother of *dead* statesmen, "right or wrong"; but, alas! I might have been first called upon to encounter the associates of childhood in the honest mountains and valleys of her west. What dire complications of crime. To cut this Gordian knot of horrors my sword had instinctively turned against the usurping majesty of cotton.

I owe Virginia little, my country much. She has intrusted me with a distant command, and I shall remain under her flag as long as it waves the sign of the National Constitutional Government.

In these far distant mountains I could only offer patriotic prayers for the result of the vote on the 23d of May. I trust that reason may have then recovered her sway—that the voice of a majority may not have been restrained by bayonets; that sounding above the clamor of anarchy, and still respected, it may have pronounced the loyalty and just attitude of the State.

P. St. George Cooke,
Colonel Second Regiment United States Dragoons

Address Objecting to Secession, to the People of Virginia by the Delegates Assembled in Convention at Wheeling
(June 24, 1861)

[RR–X:210–212]

While the east and south of Virginia supported secession, the counties of western Virginia did not, and Arthur Ingram Boreman, the president of this convention, became, two years later, the new state of West Virginia's first governor. "We call upon the loyal citizens of the commonwealth," wrote the delegates, "to organize and arm for its defense against the conspirators and usurpers at Richmond, and their aiders and abettors."

THE DELEGATES now assembled in convention at Wheeling, deem it proper to address their fellow-citizens throughout the commonwealth, in explanation and vindication of the course they have unanimously felt it incumbent on them to pursue.

It is only necessary to allude briefly to the circumstances which called this convention into existence, to justify, in the fullest manner, any resumption of authority by the people in whose name they act. The General Assembly, which met in extra session at Richmond, in January last, without the excuse of impending danger or other grave necessity, and without constitutional authority, convened a convention, "to adopt such measures as the may deem expedient for the welfare of the commonwealth"; thus tamely relinquishing the very power reposed in themselves by the constitution, and, as the sequel proved, with a corrupt purpose. Elections were held for delegates to the proposed convention, and it being then clearly understood that an active and influential party favored the secession of the commonwealth from the United States, the issue presented everywhere was clearly "Secession" or "No Secession." We need not remind you that by a very large majority of the voters of the commonwealth secession was rejected and repudiated, by the election of delegates professedly opposed to that iniquity, nor that a still larger majority required, that any act of that convention, altering the fundamental law of affecting the relations of the state, should be submitted to the people, and without the approbation of a majority, expressed at the polls, should have no force or effect.

The proceedings of that convention, up to the seventeenth of April last, were evidently intended by those in the secret to persuade the members favorable to the perpetuity of the Union, and the people at large, that it was intended to propose terms on which it could be maintained. On the day named the mask was thrown aside, and the secession ordinance was passed. This was done in secret session, and no immediate promulgation of the fact was made to the people; nor, until since this convention assembled, was the injunction of secrecy so far removed that the vote on the passage of the ordinance was made public. It now appears that more than one third of the whole convention voted against it, and that nine members were absent. Up to this day the debates which preceded the vote are concealed from the people, who are thus denied a knowledge of the causes which, in the opinion of the majority, rendered secession necessary, and justified so gross a disregard of their lately expressed will.

Under the legislative act calling the convention, from which alone that body derived its authority, and under the vote of the people provided for by that act, the secession ordinance had no legal effect until ratified at the polls by a majority of the voters of the commonwealth. The leaders in the secession movement, whose conduct has proved them to be conspirators against the State of Virginia, and the peace and welfare of her people, did not wait until the time fixed for this ratification, to begin their overt acts of treason against the government and people of the United States, as well as the state and people for whom they professed to act. Indeed, two days before the adoption of the ordinance, with the connivance, or, as is alleged, in defiance of a feeble executive, they levied war against both by sending their emissaries to capture the Harper's Ferry armory, and to obstruct the entrance of the harbor on which is situated the Gosport navy yard. This bold assumption of authority was followed by numerous acts of hostility against the United States; by the levy of troops to aid in the capture of the national capital, and the subversion of the national authority, and, to crown the infamy of the conspirators, with whom the executive had now coalesced, by an attempt, without even the pretence of the authority or acquiescence of the people, to transfer their allegiance from the United States to a league of rebellious states, in arms against the former.

In this state of things, the day arrived when the people were to vote for or against the secession ordinance. Threats of personal injury and other intimidations, such as had been uttered upon the floor of the usurping convention against the remaining friends of the Union there, were used by the adherents of the conspirators in every county of the state. Judges charged the grand juries that opposition to disunion would be punished as treason against the commonwealth; and the armed partisans of the conspirators, in various places, arrested, plundered, and exiled peaceable citizens, for no other crime than their adherence to the Union their fathers had constructed, and under which they had been born and lived in prosperity and peace. We are not apprised by any official announcement of the result of the vote taken under such circumstances; but, whatever it may be, we denounce it as unfair and unjust, and as affording no evidence of the will of the people on the subject actually presented for their suffrages, and much less of their consent to be transferred to the self-constituted oligarchy of the south.

In the point of view in which this result, and the transactions which inevitably led to it, should be examined by the people of Virginia, it is unimportant whether secession was of itself desirable or not desirable; because the end cannot justify the means, if the latter are illegal and unholy. In the present case, the great principle which underlies all free government—the principle that the will of the people is the supreme law, or as expressed in the Declaration of Independence, that "governments derive their just powers from the consent of the governed," and in our own Bill of Rights, that "all power is vested in and consequently derived from the people," has not only been violated and set at nought, but has been trampled under foot. In the call of the convention, in the acts of that body, in the circumstances preceding and accompanying the late election, a continued effort has been made, with what success you know, not merely to disregard the will of the people, but to set it at defiance, and to establish the counter principle, that the few should govern the many. The men justly termed conspirators and usurpers because they cannot show your warrant for their acts, were, when this convention met, practically in full possession of every branch of the state government, and still claim the right to exercise their usurped power; and if you submit to their acts of secession and affiliation with usurpers like themselves, you yield to them the right to govern you in perpetuity. Will your bill of rights and constitution afford you any protection against those who have already violated both? Will your connection with a pretended Confederacy, in every state of which the leaders have openly and directly refused to submit their similar acts to the approval or rejection of their people, aid you in the recovery of the fundamental right of which you have been so wantonly robbed?

But is secession right, or is it desirable if it is right? We will not amplify the argument on the first branch of this inquiry. The ratification of the constitution of the United States by our own commonwealth, in express terms, reserves the right to abrogate it to those by whom it was made, the people of the United States; thus repudiating in advance the modern doctrine of separate state secession. This is in strict accordance with the views of our elder statesmen, whose patriotism and ability are held in reverence, not only by us and by our fellow-citizens of the Union, but by good men throughout the world. It is the logic of every honest heart, that a contract, a compact, or call it what you will, can only be set aside by the joint act of those by whom it was made.

But why should secession be desirable? Why should Virginia desire to withdraw from that Union of which she has been for so long an honored member—that Union, the accomplishment of which illumines, with the brightest rays, her own history, and the lives of her most distinguished sons? Shall it be said that what she toiled to achieve in 1787, was destroyed by her own act in 1861? Is there on the page of history the story of a nation that has risen more rapidly to prosperity and power, or more steadily advanced in intellectual and moral culture? There is no such nation, nor is there among the thirty-four states one which has profited more by the association, or one which would suffer more from its dissolution, as is sufficiently indicated by our geographical position.

Impressed with these views, the north-western counties of the state, knowing that a large majority of their people remained, and would remain, faithful to the Union under all circumstances, met in convention at Wheeling on the thirteenth day of May last, to consult upon their condition and to take such steps as it might indicate. It was literally a mass convention, and from the irregular manner of the appointment of its delegates, was not calculated for the despatch of business. As the result of its deliberations, the convention which now addresses you was called, the representation in which is proportioned to that of the General Assembly. The number of counties actually represented is thirty-four, and we have reliable assurance that several which are now with us in spirit, will ere long be present by their regularly appointed delegates. Considering that in so many counties every expression of opinion unfavorable to the conspirators is suppressed, the number already represented is larger than could have been anticipated. Several of the delegates present escaped from their counties at the risk of their lives, while others are still detained at home by force or menaces against them or their families and property. Such is doubtless the case in other counties from which we have no information.

Two courses of action were presented to those who now address you upon their organization, both of which had been debated in the previous convention at this place. The first was the immediate separation of the western or north-western counties from the residue of the state. This was the result rather of a previous and growing belief, now amounting to conviction in the minds of all throughout this section of the state, that diversity, almost opposition, of interests,—different directions of the channels of trade, and the want of legislation adapted to their condition, and indispensable to their moral and material prosperity, rendered the separation desirable under any and all circumstances. But aside from the constitutional requirements which made its accomplishment almost impossible while hostilities continued, the consideration that to separate now, would be to separate from many who, under circumstances even more adverse than those by which they had been themselves surrounded, had maintained their loyalty to the Federal government, caused the abandonment of this course at this time. On the other hand, a sense of duty to those who, like themselves, were constrained to repudiate the action of the Richmond convention and the state authorities, demanded that such a course should be taken as would enable all the loyal citizens of the commonwealth to participate in its advantages, and to enjoy the security it might offer.

Besides submission to palpable usurpation, there was then but one alternative, namely, under the authority of numerous precedents in the history of nations, to assume the conduct of the government, on the ground that those previously intrusted with its administration, by their numerous illegal and unconstitutional acts, in plain derogation of the rights of the people, had, in the language of the Declaration of Independence, "abdicated government, by declaring us out of their protection, and waging war against us"; whereby, in the words of the same instrument, "the legislative powers, incapable of annihilation, have returned to the people for their exercise." This convention, therefore, in humble, but, as they firmly believe, proper imitation of the sages of '76, have, "in the name and on behalf of the good people of Virginia," issued their declaration, "that the preservation of their dearest rights and liberties, and their security in person and property, imperatively demand the reorganization of the government of the commonwealth."

In pursuance of this declaration, we have passed such ordinances as are immediately necessary to reorganize the government, and put it in operation. We have appointed a governor, lieutenant-governor, attorney-general, and executive council, leaving to the General Assembly, which we have directed to be convened, at a very early day, to fill, or to provide for filling, all other offices as soon as in their judgment it can be properly done. The terms of the officers we have appointed are limited to six months, or until the election and qualification of their successors, for which the General Assembly is authorized to provide at the earliest possible period. In all this, our fellow-citizens will clearly perceive that there has been no disposition to assume any power or authority not demanded by the exigencies of their present unhappy condition, or to retain it longer than a regard for their highest interests may require.

In reply to remarks which have been made abroad, we deem it proper to say, that we have not seen occasion to take any steps in reference to the debt of the state. The idea of the repudiation of any part of it which was legally contracted, has not been expressed or entertained by any member of the convention. The only notice the subject has received, has been in connection with the proposed separation of the western counties, and whenever it has been thus named, those desirous of separation have invariably expressed their willingness to assume their equitable portion of the burden. Any promises of payment or projects of arrangement at this time, when the very existence of the commonwealth is threatened, would be worse than idle.

Under all these circumstances, with the firm conviction that the course adopted is the only one by which the state can be retained in the Union, and the liberties and rights of the people secured and perpetuated, we most earnestly call upon our loyal fellow-citizens, in every county of the commonwealth, who are not already represented in the General Assembly and in this convention, to elect members of the legislature, and appoint delegates to this body, at the earliest possible moment. Writs of election will be issued by the executive whenever it appears that they can be executed, and representatives from every county will be most cordially received. No suspension or essential change of any part of the constitution or laws of the commonwealth, unless positively demanded by the exigencies of the times, will be made, until the will of the whole people, or of their authorized representatives, can be freely expressed; and such changes as have been, or may hereafter be, so demanded, will be submitted for ratification at an early day.

We call upon the loyal citizens of the commonwealth to organize and arm for its defence against the conspirators and usurpers at Richmond, and their aiders and abettors. Plans will immediately be devised to give to such organizations the greatest efficiency. The general government will aid and protect us to the utmost of their power, and will most unquestionably recognize the reorganized government as the true and legitimate government of the state. They cannot and will not do otherwise.

The reorganized government appeals to the great body of the people for countenance and support in this hour of great anxiety and trial. They do so confidently, because, while there have been many defections from the great and holy cause of "Liberty and Union" among those to whom you have been accustomed to look for political information and direction, there have been comparatively few among yourselves. In this matter, which appeals to your dearest rights and interests, you have responded spontaneously to the promptings of your honest hearts. Your own experience has taught you the great benefits of the Union, and you recognize the great principle, that a government so beneficial in its operations, so mild in its requirements, so powerful to protect, and so constituted as to diffuse throughout an immense territory the blessings of prosperity and happiness, "should not be changed for light or transient causes." In every county where the free expression of your views has been permitted, your majorities in favor of the maintenance and perpetuity of the Union have far exceeded the calculations of the most sanguine among your friends. Persevere, then, in your most holy war against the corrupt and perjured oligarchy who have usurped your government, and would have sold you to the ambitious despots of an unholy affiliation. In such a cause, we may look for the blessings of that Holy One, who has made it a part of his divine providence that those who, in purity of heart and purpose, strive for the preservation of their dearest rights, their homes and their country, although the struggle may be protracted for long and weary years, shall never strive in vain.

By order of the Convention,

ARTHUR I. BOREMAN,
President

G. L. Cranmer,
Secretary

Letter Regarding the Battle of First Manassas, by Confederate General Thomas J. "Stonewall" Jackson to His Wife

(July 23, 1861)

[TJJ:177–178]

On July 21, the first major battle of the war occurred about twenty-five miles south of Washington, D.C., near Manassas Junction, and the stream called Bull Run, where two Confederate forces led by Generals P. G. T. Beauregard and Joseph Johnston encountered Union forces led by General Irwin McDowell. Washington, D.C., society traveled to the site as if to watch a sporting contest.

Meanwhile, the Confederates broke through the lines and began a rout, however, the spectators fled, blocking the roads for Union retreat. When Confederate General Barnard E. Bee rallied his brigade by pointing out to them the bravery of a fellow brigadier-general: "There is Jackson standing like a stone wall! Let us determine to die here, and we will conquer." Thus, goes the legend, is how "Stonewall" Jackson (1824–1863) earned his nickname. A professor of Natural Philosophy at Virginia Military Institute before the war, in fighting for his native Virginia, Jackson was an intense warrior and became General Robert E. Lee's right-hand man. The historian Hunter Holmes McGuire claims that Jackson said at the conclusion of First Manassas, in the presence of President Davis, "We have whipped them! They ran like dogs! Give me ten thousand men, and I will take Washington tomorrow." Jackson frequently wrote letters to his wife, describing to her what he could not fully describe in official reports to Richmond. He died after receiving a wound at Chancellorsville, a battle in which he helped deliver a resounding defeat to the Union army.

MANASSAS, July 22d

MY PRECIOUS PET,—Yesterday we fought a great battle and gained a great victory, for which all the glory is due to *God alone*. Although under a heavy fire for several continuous hours, I received only one wound, the breaking of the longest finger of my left hand; but the doctor says the finger can be saved. It was broken about midway between the hand and knuckle, the ball passing on the side next the forefinger. Had it struck the centre, I should have lost the finger. My horse was wounded, but not killed. Your coat got an ugly wound near the hip, but my servant, who is very handy, has so far repaired it that it doesn't show very much. My preservation was entirely due, as was the glorious victory, to our God, to whom be all the honor, praise, and glory. The battle was the hardest that I have ever been in, but not near so hot in its fire. I commanded in the centre more particularly, though one of my regiments extended to the right for some distance. There were other commanders on my right and left. Whilst great credit is due to other parts of our gallant army, God made my brigade more instrumental than any other in repulsing the main attack. This is for your information only—say nothing about it. Let others speak praise, not myself.

Address Congratulating the Soldiers of the Army of the West by Union Major-General George B. McClellan
(July 16, 1861)

[MT-I:99]

George B. McClellan (1826–1885), a West Point graduate and veteran of the Mexican War, was immensely popular with his soldiers, and spoke and wrote beautifully and winningly to them. This telegraphed message rather exaggerates the importance or size of the small battle at Rich Mountain, Virginia. By October, however, McClellan, "the young Napoleon," as he was then fancifully dubbed, became the Commander in Chief of the army and the most prominent Union general of the first half of the war.

HEADQUARTERS ARMY OF OCCUPATION, WESTERN VIRGINIA.
Beverly, Va., July 16, 1861

Soldiers of the Army of the West:

I am more than satisfied with you. You have annihilated two armies, commanded by educated and experienced soldiers, entrenched in mountain fastnesses, fortified at their leisure. You have taken five guns, twelve colors, fifteen hundred stand of arms, one thousand prisoners, including more than forty officers. One of the two commanders of the rebels is a prisoner; the other lost his life on the field of battle.

You have killed more than two hundred and fifty of the enemy, who has lost all his baggage and camp equipage. All has been accomplished with the loss of twenty brave men killed and sixty wounded, on your part. You have proved that Union men, fighting for the preservation of our Government, are more than a match for our misguided and erring brethren; more than this, you have shown mercy to the vanquished. You have made long and arduous marches, often with insufficient food, frequently exposed to the inclemency of the weather. I have not hesitated to demand this of you, feeling that I could rely on your endurance, patriotism and courage. In the future, I may have still greater demands to make upon you—still greater sacrifices for you to offer. It shall be my care to provide for you to the extent of my ability; but I know now that by your valor and endurance you will accomplish all that is asked. Soldiers! I have confidence in you, and I trust you have learned to confide in me. Remember that discipline and subordination are qualities of equal value with courage.

I am proud to say you have gained the highest reward that American troops can receive—the thanks of Congress and the applause of your fellow citizens.

GEO. B. MCCLELLAN,
Maj. Gen. U. S. A., Comdg.

Regarding "Contraband," Query by Union General Benjamin Butler to Secretary of War Simon Cameron
(July 30, 1861)

[RR-II:437–438]

For the first year of the war, President Lincoln and Congress did not bend to what seemed inevitable to many who were more aggressive about abolishing slavery. Generals Frémont (see page 43) and Butler saw early opportunities, in their campaigns in slave states, to free slaves by declaring them "contraband." To do so legally was a matter of dispute and not well settled until President Lincoln decided the next year that indeed the purpose of the war, beyond union, was emancipation, the destruction, once and for all, of America's detestable "institution."

Secretary of War Cameron replied on August 8 that Butler had overstepped himself: "You will . . . neither authorize nor permit any interference by the troops under your command with the servants of peaceable citizens in a house or field, nor will you in any manner encourage such citizens to leave the lawful service of their masters, nor will you, except in cases where the public good may seem to require it, prevent the voluntary return of any fugitive to the service from which he may have escaped."

HEADQUARTERS DEPARTMENT OF VIRGINIA,
FORTRESS MONROE, July 30, 1861

Hon. Simon Cameron, Secretary of War:—

SIR: By an order received on the morning of the 26th July from Major-General Dix, by a telegraphic order from Lieut.-General Scott, I was commanded to forward, of the troops of this department, four regiments and a half, including Col. Baker's California regiment, to Washington, via Baltimore. This order reached me at 2 o'clock A.M., by special boat from Baltimore. Believing that it emanated because of some pressing exigency for the defence of Washington, I issued my orders before daybreak for the embarkation of the troops, sending those who were among the very best regiments I had. In the course of the following day they were all embarked for Baltimore, with the exception of some 400, for whom I had not transportation, although I had all the transport force in the hands of the quartermaster here, to aid the Bay line of steamers, which, by the same order from the Lieut.-General, was directed to furnish transportation.

Up to and at the time of the order I had been preparing for an advance movement, by which I hoped to cripple the resources of the enemy at Yorktown, and especially by seizing a large quantity of negroes who were being pressed into their service in building the intrenchments there. I had five days previously been enabled to mount for the first time, the first company of light artillery, which I had been empowered to raise, and they had but a single rifled cannon, an iron six-pounder. Of course, every thing must and did yield to the supposed exigency and the orders. This ordering away the troops from this department, while it weakened the posts at Newport News, necessitated the withdrawal of the troops from Hampton, where I was then throwing up intrenched works to enable me to hold the town with a small force, while I advanced up the York or James River. In the village of Hampton there were a large number of negroes, composed in a great measure of women and children of the men who had fled thither within my lines for protection, who had escaped from maurauding parties of rebels who had been gathering up able-bodied blacks to aid them in constructing their batteries on the James and York Rivers. I had employed the men in Hampton in throwing up intrenchments, and they were working zealously and efficiently at that duty, saving our soldiers from that labor under the gleam of the midday sun. The women were earning substantially their own subsistence in washing, marketing, and taking care of the clothes of the soldiers, and rations were being served out to the men who worked for the support of the children. But by the evacuation of Hampton, rendered necessary by the withdrawal of troops, leaving me scarcely 5,000 men outside the Fort, including the force at Newport News, all these black people were obliged to break up their homes at Hampton, fleeing across the creek within my lines for protection and support. Indeed, it was a most distressing sight to see these poor creatures, who had trusted to the protection of the arms of the United States, and who aided the troops of the United States in their enterprise, to be thus obliged to flee from their homes, and the homes of their masters who had deserted them, and become fugitives from fear of the return of the rebel soldiery, who had threatened to shoot the men who had wrought for us, and to carry off the women who had served us, to a worse than Egyptian bondage. I have, therefore, now within the Peninsula, this side of Hampton Creek, 900 negroes, 300 of whom are able-bodied men, 30 of whom are men substantially past hard labor, 175 women, 225 children under the age of 10 years, and 170 between 10 and 18 years, and many more coming in. The questions which this state of facts presents are very embarrassing.

First, What shall be done with them? and, *Second,* What is their state and condition?

Upon these questions I desire the instructions of the Department.

The first question, however, may perhaps be answered by considering the last. Are these men, women, and children, slaves? Are they free? Is their condition that of men, women, and children, or of property, or is it a mixed relation? What their *status* was under the Constitution and laws, we all know. What has been the effect of rebellion and a state of war upon that *status?* When I adopted the theory of treating the able-bodied negro fit to work in the trenches as property liable to be used in aid of rebellion, and so contraband of war, that condition of things was in so far met, as I then and still believe, on a legal and constitutional basis. But now a new series of questions arises. Passing by women, the children, certainly, cannot be treated on that basis; if property, they must be considered the incumbrance rather than the auxiliary of an army, and, of course, in no possible legal relation could be treated as contraband. Are they property? If they were so, they have been left by their masters and owners, deserted, thrown away, abandoned, like the wrecked vessel upon the ocean. Their former possessors and owners have causelessly, traitorously, rebelliously, and, to carry out the figure, practically abandoned them to be swallowed up by the winter storm of starvation. If property, do they not become the property of the salvors? but we, their salvors, do not need and will not hold such property, and will assume no such ownership: has not, therefore, all proprietary relation ceased? Have they not become, thereupon, men, women, and children? No longer under ownership of any kind, the fearful relics of fugitive masters, have they not by their masters' acts, and the state of war, assumed the condition, which we hold to be the normal one, of those made in God's image. Is not every constitutional, legal, and moral requirement, as well to the runaway master as their relinquished slaves, thus answered? I confess that my own mind is compelled by this reasoning to look upon them as men and women. If not free born, yet free, manumitted, sent forth from the hand that held them never to be reclaimed.

Of course, if this reasoning, thus imperfectly set forth, is correct, my duty, as a humane man, is very plain. I should take the same care of these men, women, and children, houseless, homeless, and unprovided for, as I would of the same number of men, women, and children, who, for their attachment to the Union, had been driven or allowed to flee from the Confederate States. I should have no doubt on this question, had I not seen it stated that an order had been issued by General McDowell in his department, substantially forbidding all fugitive slaves from coming within his lines, or being harbored there. Is that order to be enforced in all military departments? If so, who are to be considered fugitive slaves? Is a slave to be considered fugitive whose master runs away and leaves him? Is it forbidden to the troops to aid or harbor within their lines the negro children who are found therein, or is the soldier, when his march has destroyed their means of subsistence, to allow them to starve because he has driven off the rebel masters? Now, shall the commander of a regiment or battalion sit in judgment upon the question, whether any given black man has fled from his master, or his master fled from him? Indeed, how are the free born to be distinguished? Is one any more or less a fugitive slave because he has labored upon the rebel intrenchments? If he has so labored, if I understand it, he is to be harbored. By the reception of which, are the rebels most to be distressed, by taking those who have wrought all their rebel masters desired, masked their battery or those who have refused to labor and left the battery unmasked?

I have very decided opinions upon the subject of this order. It does not become me to criticize it, and I write in no spirit of criticism, but simply to explain the full difficulties that surround the enforcing it. If the enforcement of that order becomes the policy of the Government, I, as a soldier, shall be bound to enforce it steadfastly, if not cheerfully. But if left to my own discretion, as you may have gathered from my reasoning, I should take a widely different course from that which it indicates.

In a loyal State I would put down a servile insurrection. In a state of rebellion I would confiscate that which was used to oppose my arms, and take all that property, which constituted the wealth of that State, and furnished the means by which the war is prosecuted, beside being the cause of the war; and if, in so doing, it should be objected that human beings were brought to the free enjoyment of life, liberty, and the pursuit of happiness, such objection might not require much consideration.

Pardon me for addressing the Secretary of War directly upon this question, as it involves some political considerations as well as propriety of military action. I am, sir, your obedient servant,

BENJAMIN F. BUTLER

Recruitment Proclamation to the People of Missouri by Confederate Brigadier-General Jeff Thompson of the Missouri State Guards

(August 1, 1861)

Early on in the war, Meriwether Jeff Thompson (1826–1876), a native of Virginia but more recently a mayor of St. Joseph, Missouri, was one of the boldest and most charismatic of the Confederacy's western guerillas, heading a raiding force nicknamed the "Swamp Rats."

HEADQUARTERS MISSOURI STATE GUARD, ⎫
BLOOMFIELD, MO.   ⎭

MISSOURIANS! STRIKE FOR YOUR FIRESIDES AND YOUR HOMES!

To the People of Missouri:

Having been elected to command the gallant sons of the First Military District of Missouri in the second war of independence, I appeal to all whose hearts are with us, immediately to take the field. By a speedy and simultaneous assault on our foes, we can, like a hurricane, scatter them to the winds; while tardy action, like the gentle South wind, will only meet with Northern frosts, and advance and recede, and like the seasons, will be like the history of the war, and will last forever. Come now, strike while the iron is hot! Our enemies are whipped in Virginia. They have been whipped in Missouri. General Hardee advances in the centre, Gen. Pillow on the right, and Gen. McCulloch on the left, with 20,000 brave Southern hearts to our aid. So leave your ploughs in the furrow, and your oxen in the yoke, and rush like a tornado upon our invaders and foes, to sweep them from the face of the earth, or force them from the soil of our State! Brave sons of the Ninth District, come and join us! We have plenty of ammunition, and the cattle on ten thousand hills are ours. We have forty thousand Belgian muskets coming; but bring your guns and muskets with you, if you have them; if not, come without them. We will strike your foes like a Southern thunderbolt, and soon our camp fires will illuminate the Merrimac and Missouri. Come, turn out!

JEFF THOMPSON,
Brig-General Commanding

Regarding Martial Law in Missouri:
Union General J. C. Frémont, President Lincoln, Confederate Brigadier-General Jeff Thompson

Proclamation of Martial Law in Missouri by Union Major-General J. C. Frémont
(August 30, 1861)

[OR: SERIES II, VOL. 1, PT. 1, 221]

Letter from President Lincoln to Major-General Frémont
(September 2, 1861)

[OR: SERIES II, VOL. 1, PT. 1, 766]

Retaliatory Proclamation by Confederate Brigadier-General Jeff Thompson
(September 2, 1861)

[OR: SERIES II, VOL. 1, PART 1, P. 181]

John Charles Frémont (1813–1880), one of California's first leaders, had been the Republican presidential candidate in 1856. Not accustomed to compromise or following orders, Frémont took the law in Missouri into his own hands to free the slaves. President Lincoln, politically wiser and personally cooler, gently pointed out exactly the repercussions to expect from Frémont's "emancipation proclamation" that the guerilla Thompson then promised. From the middle of 1862, Frémont sat out the war.

PROCLAMATION

HEADQUARTERS WESTERN DEPARTMENT,
Saint Louis, August 30, 1861

CIRCUMSTANCES in my judgment are of sufficient urgency to render it necessary that the commanding general of this department should assume the administrative powers of the State. Its disorganized condition,

43

helplessness of civil authority, and the total insecurity of life and devastation of property by bands of murderers and marauders who infest nearly every county in the State and avail themselves of public misfortunes in the vicinity of a hostile force to gratify private and neighborhood vengeance and who find an enemy wherever they find plunder finally demand the severest measures to repress the daily increasing crimes and outrages which are driving off the inhabitants and ruining the State.

In this condition the public safety and success of our arms require unity of purpose without let or hindrance to the prompt administration of affairs. In order therefore to suppress disorders, maintain the public peace and give security to the persons and property of loyal citizens I do hereby extend and declare established martial law throughout the State of Missouri. The lines of the army occupation in this State are for the present declared to extend from Leavenworth by way of posts of Jefferson City, Rolla and Ironton to Cape Girardeau on the Mississippi River. All persons who shall be taken with arms in their hands within these lines shall be tried by court-martial and if found guilty will be shot. Real and personal property of those who shall take up arms against the United States or who shall be directly proven to have taken an active part with their enemies in the field is declared confiscated to public use and their slaves if any they have are hereby declared free men.

All persons who shall be proven to have destroyed after the publication of this order railroad tracks, bridges or telegraph lines shall suffer the extreme penalty of the law. All persons engaged in treasonable correspondence, in giving or procuring aid to the enemy, in fermenting turmoil and disturbing public tranquility by creating or circulating false reports or incendiary documents are warned that they are exposing themselves.

All persons who have been led away from allegiance are required to return to their homes forthwith. Any such absence without sufficient cause will be held to be presumptive evidence against them.

The object of this declaration is to place in the hands of military authorities power to give instantaneous effect to the existing laws and supply such deficiencies as the conditions of the war demand, but it is not intended to suspend the ordinary tribunals of the country where law will be administered by civil officers in the usual manner and with their customary authority while the same can be peaceably administered.

The commanding general will labor vigilantly for the public welfare and by his efforts for their safety hopes to obtain not only acquiescence but active support of the people of the country.

J. C. FRÉMONT,
Major-General, Commanding

WASHINGTON, D. C., September 2, 1861

MAJOR-GENERAL FRÉMONT

MY DEAR SIR: Two points in your proclamation of August 30 give me some anxiety:

First. Should you shoot a man according to the proclamation the Confederates would very certainly shoot our best men in their hands in retaliation; and so man for man indefinitely. It is therefore my order that you allow no man to be shot under the proclamation without first having my approbation or consent.

Second. I think there is great danger that the closing paragraph in relation to the confiscation of property and the liberating slaves of traitorous owners will alarm our Southern Union friends and turn them against us, perhaps ruin our rather fair prospect for Kentucky. Allow me therefore to ask that you will as of your own motion modify that paragraph so as to conform to the first and fourth sections of the act of Congress entitled "An act to confiscate property used for insurrectionary purposes," approved August 6, 1861, and a copy of which act I herewith send you.

This letter is written in a spirit of caution and not of censure. I send it by special messenger in order that it may certainly and speedily reach you.

Yours, very truly,

A. LINCOLN

PROCLAMATION

HDQRS. FIRST MILITARY DIST., MISSOURI STATE GUARD,
Camp Hunter, September 2, 1861

To whom it may concern:

Whereas, Major General John C. Fremont, commanding the minions of Abraham Lincoln in the State of Missouri, has seen fit to declare martial law throughout the whole State and has threatened to shoot any citizen soldier found in arms within certain limits, also to confiscate the property and free the negroes belonging to the members of the Missouri State Guard: therefore, know ye that I, M. Jeff. Thompson, brigadier-general of the First Military District of Missouri, having not only the military authority of brigadier-general but certain police powers granted by Acting Governor Thomas C. Reynolds and confirmed afterward by Governor Jackson do most solemnly promise that for every member of the Missouri State Guard or soldier of our allies the armies of the Confederate States who shall be put to death in pursuance of said order of General Fremont I will hang, draw and quarter a minion of said Abraham Lincoln.

While I am anxious that this unfortunate war shall be conducted if possible upon the most liberal principles of civilized warfare and every order that I have issued has been with that object, yet if this rule is to be adopted (and it must first be done by our enemies) I intend to exceed General Frémont in his excesses and will make all tories that come in my reach rue the day that a different policy was adopted by their leaders. Already mills, barns, warehouses and other private property have been wastefully and wantonly destroyed by the enemy in this district while we have taken nothing except articles strictly contraband or absolutely necessary. Should these things be repeated I will retaliate ten-fold, so help me God.

M. JEFF. THOMPSON,
Brigadier-General, Commanding

The Surrender at Fort Donelson,
Correspondence between Confederate
Brigadier General S. B. Buckner and
Union Brigadier-General U. S. Grant
(February 16, 1862)

[RR–IV:139]

The taking of Fort Donelson by Ulysses S. Grant's troops distinguished Grant (1822–1885) for the first time in his military career. He would become the most important and effective general of the war. His success here and the plain-speaking of his note to Simon Bolivar Buckner (1823–1914), a former colleague, helped make him popular and gave him, for a time, the nickname (playing off his apparent initials) "Unconditional Surrender" Grant. His commander, Major-General Henry Halleck, effused in a message on February 20: "I have received with the highest gratification your reports and letters from Fort Donelson, so gallantly captured under your brilliant leadership. I, in common with the whole country, warmly congratulate you upon this remarkable achievement, which has broken the enemy's center, dispersed the rebels, and given a death-blow to secession. The prisoners by thousands have arrived here, and will be sent off by to-morrow to their respective destinations."

HEADQUARTERS FORT DONELSON,⎱
February 16, 1862 ⎰

SIR: In consideration of all the circumstances governing the present situation of affairs at this station, I propose to the commanding officer of the Federal forces, the appointment of Commissioners to agree upon terms of capitulation of the forces and post under my command, and in that view suggest an armistice until twelve o'clock to-day.

I am, sir, very respectfully, your obedient servant,

S. B. BRUCKNER,
Brigadier-General, C. S. A.

HEADQUARTERS ARMY IN THE FIELD,
Camp near Donelson, Feb. 16

To Gen. S. B. Buckner Confederate Army:

Yours of this date, proposing armistice and appointment of Commissioners to settle terms of capitulation, is just received. No terms, other than an unconditional and immediate surrender can be accepted.

I propose to move immediately upon your works. I am sir, very respectfully, your obedient servant,

U. S. GRANT,
Brig.-Gen. U. S. Commanding

HEADQUARTERS DOVER, TENN.,
February 16, 1862

To Brig.-Gen. U. S. Grant, U.S.A.:

SIR: The distribution of the forces under my command, incident to an unexpected change of commanders and the overwhelming force under your command, compel me, notwithstanding the brilliant success of the confederate arms yesterday, to accept the ungenerous and unchivalrous terms which you propose. I am, sir, your very obedient servant,

S. B. BUCKNER,
Brig.-Gen. C.S.A.

4/16/2008 3:48:08 PM

ATLANTA HISTORY CENTER>MUSEUM SHOP

130 WEST PACES FERRY ROAD NW

ATLANTA, GA 30305-1366

	Rcpt#	8493
4/16/2008	Store:	0010
Assoc: Alice	Cshr:	Alice

ITEM#	QTY	PRICE	EXT PRICE
5720	1	8.95	8.95
FAMOUS DOCUM			

Subtotal:	8.95
8.000 % Tax:	0.72
RECEIPT TOTAL:	9.67

Tend:	20.00
Change:	10.33

Cash: 20.00

Address to the People of Georgia by Howell Cobbs, R. Toombs, M. J. Crawford, Thomas R. R. Cobb

(February 1862)

[RR-IV:192–193]

While short on educational, economic, or judicial equality, the Confederacy boasted an abundant crop of eloquent politicians, few of whom were ever at a loss to condemn the United States for fighting back. All four of the signers of this document were members of the provisional Confederate Congress. Thomas R. R. Cobb (1823–1862), a leader of Georgia's secessionist movement, would serve as a general at Fredericksburg in December 1862, where he was killed. His brother, Howell (1815–1868), a pre-war governor of Georgia and former U.S. Treasury Secretary, also served as a general. Robert Toombs was the Confederacy's first Secretary of State, but resigned to become a general. M. J. Crawford became the leader of a cavalry regiment in the summer of 1862.

(I have dated this address as February as suggested by the "in a few days" in the opening; the new "permanent" Confederate government began February 22, 1862, the anniversary of George Washington's birthday.)

FELLOW-CITIZENS: In a few days the provisional government of the confederate States will live only in history. With it we shall deliver up the trust we have endeavored to use for your benefit to those more directly selected by yourselves. The public record of our acts is familiar to you, and requires no further explanation at our hands. Of those matters which policy has required to be secret it would be improper now to speak. This address therefore will have no personal reference. We are well assured that there exists no necessity for us to arouse your patriotism nor to inspire your confidence. We rejoice with you in the unanimity of our State, in its resolutions and its hopes. And we are proud with you that Georgia has been "illustrated," and we doubt not will be illustrated again by her sons in our holy struggle. The first campaign is over; each party rests in place, while the winter's snow declares an armistice from on high. The results in the field are familiar to you, and we will not recount them. To some important facts we call your attention:

First. The moderation of our own government and the fanatical madness of our enemies have dispersed all differences of opinion among our people, and united them forever in the war of independence. In a few Border States, a waning opposition is giving way before the stern logic of daily developing facts. The world's history does not give a parallel instance of a revolution based upon such unanimity among the people.

Second. Our enemy has exhibited an energy, a perseverance, and an amount of resources which we had hardly expected, and a disregard of constitution and laws which we can hardly credit. The result of both, however, is that power which is the characteristic element of despotism, and renders it as formidable to its enemies as it is destructive to its subjects.

Third. An immense army has been organized for our destruction, which is being disciplined to the unthinking stolidity of regulars. With the exclusive possession of the seas, our enemy is enabled to throw upon the shores of every State the nucleus of an army. And the threat is made, and doubtless the attempt will follow in early spring, to crush us with a giant's grasp by a simultaneous movement along our entire borders.

Fourth. With whatever alacrity our people may rush to arms, and with whatever energy our government may use its resources, we cannot expect to cope with our enemy either in numbers, equipments or munitions of war. To provide against these odds we must look to desperate courage, unflinching daring, and universal self-sacrifice.

Fifth. The prospect of foreign interference is at least a remote one, and should not be relied on.★ If it comes, let it be only auxiliary to our own preparations for freedom. To our God and ourselves alone we should look.

These are stern facts; perhaps some of them are unpalatable. But we are deceived in you if you would have us conceal them in order to deceive you. The only question for us and for you is, as a nation and individually, what have we to do? We answer:

First. As a nation we should be united, forbearing to one another, frowning upon all factious opposition and censorious criticisms, and

---

★The Confederacy unsuccessfully strove to involve Great Britain as an ally.

giving a trustful and generous confidence to those selected as our leaders in the camp and the council-chamber.

Second. We should excite every nerve, and strain every muscle of the body politic, to maintain our financial and military healthfulness, and, by rapid aggressive action, make our enemies feel, at their own firesides, the horrors of a war brought on by themselves.

The most important matter for you, however, is your individual duty. What can you do?

The foot of the oppressor is on the soil of Georgia. He comes with lust in his eye, poverty in his purse, and hell in his heart. He comes a robber and a murderer. How shall you meet him? With the sword at the threshold! With death for him or for yourself! But more than this—let every woman have a torch, every child a firebrand—let the loved homes of youth be made ashes, and the fields of our heritage be made desolate. Let blackness and ruin mark your departing steps if depart you must, and let a desert more terrible than Sahara welcome the vandals. Let every city be levelled by the flames and every village be lost in ashes. Let your faithful slaves share your fortune and your crust. Trust wife and children to the sure refuge and protection of God—preferring even for these loved ones the charnel-house as a home than loathsome vassalage to a nation already sunk below the contempt of the civilized world. This may be your terrible choice, and determine at once and without dissent, as honor and patriotism and duty to God require.

Fellow-Citizens: Lull not yourselves into a fatal security. Be prepared for every contingency. This is our only hope for a sure and honorable peace. If our enemy was to-day convinced that the feast herein indicated would welcome him in every quarter of this confederacy, we know his base character well enough to feel assured he would never come. Let, then, the smoke of your homes, fired by women's hands, tell the approaching foe that over sword and bayonet they will rush only to fire and ruin.

We have faith in God and faith in you. He is blind to every indication of Providence who has not seen an Almighty hand controlling the events of the past year. The wind, the wave, the cloud, the mist, the sunshine, and the storm, have all ministered to our necessities, and frequently succored us in our distresses. We deem it unnecessary to recount the numerous instances which have called forth our gratitude. We would join you in thanksgiving and praise. "If God be for us, who can be against us?"

Nor would we condemn your confident look to our armies, when they can meet a foe not too greatly their superior in numbers. The year past tells a story of heroism and success of which our nation will never be ashamed. These considerations, however, should only stimulate us to greater deeds and nobler efforts. An occasional reverse we must expect—such as has depressed us within the last few days. This is only temporary.

We have no fears of the result—the final issue. You and we may have to sacrifice our lives and fortunes in the holy cause, but our honor will be saved untarnished, and our children's children will rise up to call us "blessed."

> HOWELL COBB,
> R. TOOMBS,
> M. J. CRAWFORD
> THOMAS R. R. COBB

Order Respecting Bell-Metal to the Planters of the Mississippi Valley by Confederate General G. T. Beauregard
(March 8, 1862)

[RR-IV:294]

Anticipating surprise and charges of sacrilege, General Beauregard pleaded for material that, at this stage of the war, was in short supply in the South. The editors of the Norfolk Day-Book, *explained on April 21: "While copper is abundant, the supply of tin is sufficient to convert the copper into bronze. Bells contain so much tin that two thousand four hundred pounds weight of bell-metal, mixed with the proper quantity of copper, will suffice for a field-battery of six pieces. Those who are willing to devote their bells to this patriotic purpose, will receive receipts for them, and the bells will be replaced, if required, at the close of the war, or they will be purchased at fair prices."*

TO THE PLANTERS OF THE MISSISSIPPI VALLEY

HEADQUARTERS ARMY OF THE MISSISSIPPI,
Jackson, Tenn., March 8, 1862

MORE THAN once a people fighting with an enemy less ruthless than yours; for imperilled rights not more dear and sacred than yours; for homes and a land not more worthy of resolute and unconquerable men than yours; and for interests of far less magnitude than you have now at stake, have not hesitated to melt and mould into cannon the precious bells surmounting their houses of God, which had called generations to prayer. The priesthood have ever sanctioned and consecrated the conversion, in the hour of their nation's need, as one holy and acceptable in the sight of God.

We want cannon as greatly as any people who ever, as history tells you, melted their church-bells to supply them; and I, your general, entrusted with the command of the army embodied of your sons, your kinsmen and your neighbors, do now call on you to send your plantation-bells to the nearest railroad dépôt, subject to my order, to be melted into cannon for the defence of your plantations.

Who will not cheerfully and promptly send me his bells under such circumstances?

Be of good cheer; but time is precious.

G. T. BEAUREGARD,
General Commanding

Report on the U.S.S. *Monitor* and *Merrimack* Fight in Hampton Roads, Virginia, by Union Captain G. J. Van Brunt
(March 10, 1862)

[RR-IV:267–268]

The Minnesota's *captain narrates how the* Merrimack *(or* Merrimac, *as Van Brunt spells it) was surprised to find the Union ironclad* Monitor *and how the Confederate vessel finally met its match. "We thought at first it was a raft on which one of the* Minnesota's *boilers was being taken to shore for repairs," recalled a Confederate sailor.*

The Merrimack *had been a Union ship abandoned at the outbreak of the war in Norfolk. It was salvaged and rebuilt by the Confederacy as the world's first ironclad fighting ship. Renamed the* Virginia, *it wreaked havoc on the Union navy and caused some panic in the North until the Union's own ironclad, the* Monitor, *faced off with it in the waters of Hampton Roads.*

REPORT OF CAPTAIN G. J. VAN BRUNT

UNITED STATES STEAMER, *Minnesota,*
March 10, 1862

SIR: On Saturday, the eighth instant, at forty-five minutes after twelve o'clock P.M., three small steamers, in appearance, were discovered rounding Sewall's Point, and as soon as they came into full broadside view, I was convinced that one was the iron-plated steam-battery *Merrimac,* from the large size of her smoke-pipe. They were heading for Newport News, and I, in obedience to a signal from the senior officer present, Capt. John Marston, immediately called all hands, slipped my cables, and got under way for that point, to engage her. While rapidly passing Sewall's Point, the rebels there opened fire upon us from a rifle-battery, one shot from

55

which going through and crippling my mainmast. I returned the fire from my broadside-guns and forecastle-pivot.

We ran without further difficulty within about one and a half miles of Newport News, and there, unfortunately, grounded. The tide was running ebb, and although in the channel there was not sufficient water for this ship, which draws twenty-three feet, I knew the bottom was soft and lumpy, and endeavored to force the ship over, but found it impossible so to do. At this time it was reported to me that the *Merrimac* had passed the frigate *Congress* and ran into the sloop-of-war *Cumberland,* and in fifteen minutes after, I saw the latter going down by the head. The *Merrimac* then hauled off, taking a position, and about half-past two o'clock P.M., engaged the *Congress,* throwing shot and shell into her with terrific effect, while the shot from the *Congress* glanced from her iron-plated sloping sides, without doing any apparent injury. At half-past three o'clock P.M., the *Congress* was compelled to haul down her colors. Of the extent of her loss and injury, you will be informed from the official report of her commander.

At four o'clock P.M., the *Merrimac, Jamestown* and *Patrick Henry,* bore down upon my vessel. Very fortunately, the iron battery drew too much water to come within a mile of us. She took a position on my starboard bow, but did not fire with accuracy, and only one shot passed through the ship's bow. The other two steamers took their position on my port bow and stern, and their fire did most damage in killing and wounding men, inasmuch as they fired with rifled guns; but with the heavy gun that I could bring to bear upon them, I drove them off, one of them apparently in a crippled state. I fired upon the *Merrimac* with my ten-inch pivot-gun, without any apparent effect, and at seven o'clock P.M., she too hauled off, and all three vessels steamed toward Norfolk.

The tremendous firing of my broadside guns had crowded me further upon the mud-bank, into which the ship seemed to have made for herself a cradle. From ten P.M., when the tide commenced to run flood, until four A.M., I had all hands at work, with steamtugs and hawsers, endeavoring to haul the ship off the bank; but without avail, and as the tide had then fallen considerably, I suspended further proceedings at that time.

At two A.M. the iron battery *Monitor,* Com. John L. Worden, which had arrived the previous evening at Hampton Roads, came alongside and reported for duty, and then all on board felt that we had a friend that would stand by us in our hour of trial.

At six A.M. the enemy again appeared, coming down from Craney Island, and I beat to quarters; but they ran past my ship, and were heading for Fortress Monroe, and the retreat was beaten, to allow my men to get something to eat. The *Merrimac* ran down near the Rip Raps, and then turned into the channel through which I had come. Again all hands were called to quarters, and opened upon her with my stern-guns, and made signal to the *Monitor* to attack the enemy. She immediately ran down in my wake, right within range of the *Merrimac,* completely covering my ship, as far as was possible with her diminutive dimensions, and, much to my astonishment, laid herself right alongside of the *Merrimac,* and the contrast was that of a pigmy to a giant. Gun after gun was fired by the *Monitor,* which was returned with whole broadsides by the rebels, with no more effect, apparently, than so many pebble-stones thrown by a child.

After a while they commenced manoeuvering, and we could see the little battery point her bow for the rebel's, with the intention, as I thought, of sending a shot through her bow-porthole; then she would shoot by her, and rake her through her stern. In the mean time the rebels were pouring broadside after broadside, but almost all her shot flew over the little submerged propeller; and when they struck the bomb-proof tower, the shot glanced off without producing any effect, clearly establishing the fact that wooden vessels cannot contend successfully with iron-clad ones, for never before was anything like it dreamed of by the greatest enthusiast in maritime warfare.

The *Merrimac,* finding that she could make nothing of the *Monitor,* turned her attention once more to me in the morning. She had put one eleven-inch shot under my counter, near the water-line, and now, on her second approach, I opened upon her with all my broadside-guns and ten-inch pivot—a broadside which would have blown out of water any timber-built ship in the world. She returned my fire with her rifled bow-gun, with a shell which passed through the chief engineer's state-room, through the engineer's mess-room amidships, and burst in the boatswain's room, tearing four rooms all into one, in its passage exploding two charges of powder, which set the ship on fire, but it was promptly extinguished by a party headed by my first lieutenant. Her second went through the boiler of the tugboat *Dragon,* exploding it, and causing some consternation on board my ship for the moment, until the matter was explained.

This time I had concentrated upon her an incessant fire from my gun-deck, spar-deck, and forecastle pivot-guns, and was informed by my marine officer, who was stationed on the poop, that at least fifty solid shot struck her on her slanting side without producing any apparent effect. By the time she had fired her third shell, the little *Monitor* had come down upon her, placing herself between us, and compelled her to change her position, in doing which she grounded, and again I poured into her all the guns which could be brought to bear upon her. As soon as she got off, she stood down the bay, the little battery chasing her with all speed, when suddenly the *Merrimac* turned around, and ran full speed into her antagonist. For a moment I was anxious, but instantly I saw a shot plunge into the iron roof of the *Merrimac,* which surely must have damaged her, for some time after the rebels concentrated their whole battery upon the tower and pilot-house of the *Monitor,* and soon after the latter stood down for Fortress Monroe, and we thought it probable she had exhausted her supply of ammunition, or sustained some injury. Soon after the *Merrimac* and the two other steamers headed for my ship, and I then felt to the fullest extent my condition. I was hard and immovable aground, and they could take position under my stern and rake me. I had expended most of my solid shot, and my ship was badly crippled, and my officers and men were worn out with fatigue; but even in this extreme dilemma I determined never to give up the ship to the rebels, and after consulting my officers, I ordered every preparation to be made to destroy the ship, after all hope was gone to save her.

On ascending the poop-deck, I observed that the enemy's vessels had changed their course, and were heading for Craney Island; then I determined to lighten the ship by throwing overboard my eight-inch guns, hoisting out provisions, starting water, etc. At two P.M. I proceeded to make another attempt to save the ship, by the use of a number of powerful tugs and the steamer *S. R. Spaulding*—kindly sent to my assistance by Captain Talmadge, Quartermaster at Fortress Monroe—and succeeded in dragging her half a mile distant, and then she was again immovable, the tide having fallen. At two A.M. this morning I succeeded in getting the ship once more afloat, and am now at anchor opposite Fortress Monroe.

It gives me great pleasure to say that, during the whole of these trying scenes, the officers and men conducted themselves with great courage and coolness.

I have the honor to be your very obedient servant,

G. J. VAN BRUNT,
Captain, U. S. N., Commanding Frigate *Minnesota*

Hon. Gideon Welles,
    Secretary of the Navy, Washington, D. C.

Address to the Army of the Potomac by Union Major-General George B. McClellan
(March 14, 1862)

[RR–IV:306–307]

In this inspiring address at the graduation exercise of his army on the eve of the Peninsular Campaign in Virginia, McClellan gave his soldiers an understanding of their purpose and of his confidence in them. However, McClellan's cautious pace and reluctance to attempt to take on the Confederate armies and deliver the "death-blow to the rebellion" (in McClellan's phrase) drove President Lincoln to distraction. McClellan continually overestimated the size of the opposing armies and hence avoided battles: "From first to last, McClellan's military decisions on the Peninsula were based on his belief in a phantom Confederate army," writes historian Stephen Sears.[3]

HEADQUARTERS ARMY OF THE POTOMAC,
Fairfax Court-House, Va., March 14, 1862

Soldiers of the Army of the Potomac:

For a long time I have kept you inactive, but not without a purpose. You were to be disciplined, armed, and instructed; the formidable artillery you now have had to be created; other armies were to move and accomplish certain results. I have held you back that you might give the death-blow to the rebellion that has distracted our once happy country. The patience you have shown, and your confidence in your General, are worth a dozen victories. These preliminary results are now accomplished. I feel that the patient labors of many months have produced their

---

[3] *The Civil War Papers of George B. McClellan.* New York: Ticknor & Fields. 1989. 205.

fruit; the Army of the Potomac is now a real army—magnificent in material, admirable in discipline and instruction, excellently equipped and armed—your commanders are all that I could wish. The moment for action has arrived, and I know that I can trust in you to save our country. As I ride through your ranks, I see in your faces the sure presage of victory; I feel that you will do whatever I ask of you. The period of inaction has passed. I will bring you now face to face with the rebels, and only pray that God may defend the right. In whatever direction you may move, however strange my actions may appear to you, ever bear in mind that my fate is linked with yours, and that all I do is to bring you, where I know you wish to be—on the decisive battle-field. It is my business to place you there. I am to watch over you as a parent over his children; and you know that your General loves you from the depths of his heart. It shall be my care, as it has ever been, to gain success with the least possible loss; but I know that, if it is necessary, you will willingly follow me to our graves, for our righteous cause. God smiles upon us, victory attends us, yet I would not have you think that our aim is to be attained without a manly struggle. I will not disguise it from you; you have brave foes to encounter, foemen well worthy of the steel that you will use so well. I shall demand of you great, heroic exertions, rapid and long marches, desperate combats, privations, perhaps. We will share all these together; and when this sad war is over we will return to our homes, and feel that we can ask no higher honor than the proud consciousness that we belonged to the Army of the Potomac.

GEO. B. MCCLELLAN,
Major-General Commanding

Lecture, "The War and How to End It," by Frederick Douglass at Rochester, New York
(March 25, 1862)

[*Douglass' Monthly,* April 1862]

The abolitionist and ex-slave Frederick Douglass noted in his magazine that this published version of his lecture is "an extract." He wonders, for his predominantly white audience, why do those in the South "hate you." He answers: "The real root of bitterness, that which has generated this intense Southern hate toward the North is Slavery." Though Douglass was disappointed in President Lincoln for some time, he came to be friendly with and to admire "The Great Emancipator."

I STAND HERE to-night to advocate in my humble way, the unrestricted and complete Emancipation of every slave in the United States, whether claimed by loyal or disloyal masters. This is the lesson of the hour.

Through the certain operation of the *changeless laws of the universe,* Emancipation, which has long been a great and solemn national duty, pressing heavily on the national conscience, has at last become a great and all commanding national necessity.

I choose not to insist upon these comprehensive propositions as a colored man to-night nor as one having special reasons for hating slavery, although upon these grounds I might well base a claim to be heard, but my ground is taken as an American citizen, feeling with all others a deep and living interest in the welfare of the whole country.

In the tremendous conflict through which we are passing, all events steadily conspire to make the cause of the slave and the cause of the country identical. He who to-day fights for Emancipation, fights for his country and free Institutions, and he who fights for slavery, fights against his country and in favor of a slaveholding oligarchy.

This was always so, though only abolitionists perceived the fact. The difference between them and others is this: They got an earlier glimpse at the black heart of slavery—than others did. They saw in times of seeming peace, for the peace we have had, was only seeming—what we can only see in times of open war. They saw that a nation like ours, containing two such opposite forces liberty and slavery, could not enjoy permanent peace, and they said so and got mobbed for saying so. But let that pass.

Before I proceed to discuss the subject announced for my lecture this evening, allow me to make a few remarks on the mighty events which have marked and are marking the progress of the war. It requires a large share of wisdom and coolness to properly weigh and measure the great facts which have already passed into history; but it requires a much larger share of these qualities to enable man to discriminate between and to determine the proper relations and bearings of the great living facts transpiring before our eyes.

The obvious reason is this: important events often succeed each other so rapidly, and take the place of each other so quickly, that it becomes almost impossible to give to any one of them that measure of reflection which is necessary to form an intelligent judgement.

We are an intelligent people, apt scholars, but I think that few of us fully appreciate the solemn events that are now passing before our eyes.

It is known that we are at war, at war among ourselves, civil war the worst of all wars, but the real scope and significance of this war is but imperfectly understood by millions of the American people.

The very air is filled with conflicting statements in respect to the cause of this war, and naturally enough, it is also filled with contradictory theories as to the manner of restoring the country to peace.

I shall not stay here to discuss the long train of events, and the certain action of social forces which have finally culminated in this rebellion. The limits of the occasion will not permit any such lengthy discussion. The most that I can do is to point out a few of the leading features of the contest, and enforce the lesson which I think they plainly teach and the path of duty they mark out for our feet.

The first enquiry which concerned the loyal North upon the sudden outburst of this stupendous rebellion naturally related to the strength of the rebels, and the amount of force and skill required for their speedy suppression. Even at this vital point we blundered. We misconceived the real state of the case, and misread the facts then passing before us. We were quite incredulous of the tremendous strength and vigor of the foe against whom we were called upon to battle.

We are a charitable people, and in excess of charity were disposed to put the very best construction upon the strange behavior of our Southern brethren. We admitted that South Carolina might secede. It was like her to do so. She had talked extravagantly about going out of the union, and she must do something extravagant and startling to save a show of consistency. Georgia, too, we thought might possibly go out, but we were quite sure that these twin rebel States would stand alone in their infamy, and that they would soon tire of their isolation, repent of their folly, and come back to the union. Traitors fled the Cabinet, the House and the Senate, and hastened away to fan the flames of treason at home. Still we doubted that any thing very serious would come of it. We treated it as a bubble on the wave, a nine day's wonder. Calm and thoughtful men ourselves, we relied on the sober second thought of others. Even a shot at one of our ships, an insult offered to our flag, caused only a momentary feeling of indignation and resentment, such as a mother might feel toward a naughty child who had thrown away his bread and stamped defiance at her authority. It was not until Beauregard opened his slave-built batteries upon the starving garrison in Charleston harbor that the confiding North, like a sleeping lion, was roused from his lair, and shook his thundering mane in wrath. We were slow to wake, but we did awake. Still we were scarcely conscious of the skill, power and resources of the enemy. We still hoped that wiser and better counsels would ultimately prevail. We could not believe but that a powerful union sentiment still existed at the South, and that a strong reaction would yet take place there in favor of the union. To the very last we continued to believe in the border States. We could not believe that those States would plunge madly into the bloody vortex of rebellion. It required the assaults of a blood thirsty mob spilling the blood of loyal soldiers to convince us of Baltimore treason.

I need not tell you, how in all this study of passing events, we have been grossly mistaken. Every hope based upon the sanity, loyalty, and good disposition of the South has been woefully disappointed. While armies were forming, and the most formidable preparations were making, we continued to dream of peace, and even after the war was fairly begun, we thought to put down the rebellion by a show of force rather than by an exercise of force. We showed our teeth but did not wish to use them. We preferred to fight with dollars rather than daggers. The fewer battles the better was the motto, popular at Washington, and peace in sixty days trembled along the wires. We now see what we could not at first comprehend. We are astonished at the strength and vigor of the foe. Treason had shot its poisonous roots deeper, and has spread them farther than our calculations had allowed for. Now I have a reason for calling attention to this unwillingness on our part to know the worst. It has already caused much trouble, and I have reason to apprehend that it will cause us much more. We need warnings a thousand times repeated. A hint to the wise is enough for the wise, and although we are wise and can take a hint, the trouble is we don't heed it unless it comes in the shape of a rifled cannon ball battering against the walls of our forts, or an iron-clad ram sinking our navy and threatening our whole Atlantic Coast. Let me under score this point of weakness and, as I think, blindness on our part, for it still lingers with us.

Even now, you need not go far to find newspapers clinging still to the delusion that there is a strong union sentiment at the South. While the rebels are waging a barbarous war of unparalleled ferocity, marshalling the savage Indian to the slaughter of your sons, and poisoning the wells in their retreats, we are still speaking of them as our erring brothers, to be won back to the union by fondling, rather than fighting. This has been our great error. We failed to comprehend the vital force of the rebellion. First, because we were dazzled and bewildered by the wild rapidity of the strange events, which burst upon us, and secondly because of our habitual leniency to the South and to slaveholders grimly confronting us at the outset.

I have said that the first question was how to whip the rebels. That was the bitter problem. We were sadly unprepared to fight. Treason had become the warp and woof of the army and navy. Floyd had stolen all the arms, and Cobb had stolen all the money. The nation was at the mercy of the merciless. How to procure arms, and brave men to use them, was naturally first in order. Like the rod of Moses it swallowed all others. It even hushed the voice of abolitionists and wheeled them into line with its imperative demands.

It was the great physical question. Men of muscle understood it as well as men of mind. But now there is another and a mightier question destined to try men's souls more severely than the first.

For not that which is spiritual is first, but that which is natural; after that, that which is spiritual. The physical part of this tremendous conflict is at last in a hopeful way. The great armies of the North are in motion. Baltimore is at the mercy of McHenry, Western Virginia clings to the union, Kentucky is no longer neutral, Missouri has gone to Arkansas. North Carolina is invaded, Florida has followed the fortunes of Bragg, and Tennessee is under Foote.

Brave hearts and strong hands, have met and disposed of the first question. I knew they would from the first. The slaveholding rebels have fought, and have fought well, and will do so again. They are proud, brave and desperate, but proud, brave and desperate as they are, I tell no secret when I say, they can run as well as fight.

General McClellan in his recent address to his army—takes pains to compliment these traitors.* He is "sad" at the thought of striking them.

---

*Douglass refers to the address by McClellan to the Army of the Potomac dated March 14, 1862, but seems to misrepresent the general's words and sentiments.

The traitors themselves show no such weakness. The language of their Generals is altogether of another character. There is no epithet too vile for them, by which to characterize our army. But McClellan, is careful to tell us that the Southern army is composed of foemen worthy of our steel. I do not like this. It looks bad. Instead of being foemen worthy of our steel, they are rebels and traitors worthy of our hemp.

I do not wonder that all the haters of Impartial Liberty at the North are especially devoted to this "sad" reluctant General, who instead of portraying the baseness of the traitors takes pains to compliment them. It is seriously doubted if he will ever try his steel upon them. Thus far he has entirely failed to do any thing of the sort. But, whether McClellan ever overtakes the rebels or not, the Army of the Potomac has moved, and brave men sweep both the Eastern and Western border of the rebellion. So that I look upon the first question, the question as to how to break down the military power of the rebels, as in good hands and the public mind is happily relieved at that point.

But now a higher and more important problem presses for consideration. It is a problem for statesmen rather than Generals. Soldiers can capture a State, but statesmen must govern a State. It is sometimes hard to pull down a house but it is always harder to build one up.

This is the question now to be decided, having broken down the rebel power in the seceded States, how shall we extend the Constitution and the Union over them? We know how to make war, we know how to conquer, but the question is do we know how to make peace? We can whip the South, but can we make the South loyal? Baltimore is in our hands, but her parlors and drawing rooms are full of Traitors. The army is at Nashville, but the people have fled. General Sherman writes loving epistles to erring rebels, but no one will carry them to the rebels, nor will the rebels touch them. The fact is the South hates the North. It hates the Union. The feeling is genuine and all-pervading. Whence comes this hate? This is an imperative inquiry for statesmen who would place the peace of this government on an immovable foundation. You are of the same race, the same language, the same scared historic memories. Why do they hate you? Certainly not because you have been in any manner ungenerous or unjust to them. Why do they hate you? Is it because they are naturally worse than other men? Not at all. I hold that the slaveholder is just as good as his slave system will allow him to be. If I were a slaveholder, and was determined to remain such, I would equal the worst, both in cruelty to the slave and in hatred to the North. I should hate the Declaration of Independence, hate the Constitution, hate the golden rule, hate free schools, free speech, free press, and every other form of freedom. Because in them all, I should see an enemy to my claim of property in man. I should see that the whole North is a point blank and killing condemnation of all my pretensions. The real root of bitterness, that which has generated this intense Southern hate toward the North, is Slavery. Here is the stone of stumbling and the rock of offence. Once I felt it necessary to argue this point. The time for such argument has past. Slavery stands confessed as the grand cause of the war. It has drilled every rebel soldier, loaded, primed, aimed and fired every rebel cannon since the war began. No other interest, commercial, manufacturing or political, could have wrought such a social earthquake amongst us. It has within itself that which begets a character in all around it favorable to its own continuance. It makes slaves of the negroes, vassals of the poor whites and tyrants of the masters. Pride, injustice, ingratitude, lust of dominion, cruelty, scorn, and contempt are the qualities of this rebellion, and slavery breeds them all. The tyrant wants no law above his own will, no associates but men of his own stamp of baseness. He is willing to administer the laws when he can bend them to his will, but he will break them when he can no longer bend them. Where labor is performed under the lash, justice will be administered under the bowie knife. The South is in this respect just what slavery has made her. She has been breeding thieves, rebels and traitors, and this stupendous conflict is the result. She could not do otherwise and cherish slavery in the midst of her.

Now the great question is what shall be the conditions of peace? What shall be done with slavery? We have gradually drifted to this vital question. Slavery is the pivot on which turns all the machinery of this tremendous war, and upon it will depend the character of the future of our peace or want of it.

It is really wonderful how we have been led along towards this grand issue, and how all efforts to evade, postpone, and prevent its coming, have been mocked and defied by the stupendous sweep of events.

It was oracularly given out from Washington many months ago that whether this rebellion should succeed or fail, the status of no man in the country would be changed by the result. You know what that meant. Europe knew what that meant. It was an assurance given to the world in general, and the slaveholding states in particular, that no harm should come to slavery in the prosecution of the war for the Union. It was a last bid for a compromise with the rebels. But despite of diplomatic disclaimers, despite border State influence, despite the earlier proclamation of the President himself, the grand question of Emancipation now compels attention and the most thoughtful consideration of men in high places of the nation.

By the events of this war, Washington has become to the nation what Syracuse was to the State of New York after the rescue of Jerry, the grand centre for abolition meetings. A new Congress has assembled there.

Dr. Cheever, Ralph Waldo Emerson, Gerrit Smith, Wendell Phillips, William Goodell and William Lloyd Garrison may now utter in safety their opinions on slavery in the national capital. Meanwhile Congress has a bill before it for the abolition of slavery in the District of Columbia. Kill slavery at the heart of the nation, and it will certainly die at the extremities. Down with it there, and it is the brick knocked down at the end of the row by which the whole line is prostrate.

More and better, the infernal business of slave-catching by our army in Missouri and on the Potomac is at last peremptorily forbidden under penalty of dismissal from the service. This looks small, but is not so. It is a giant stride toward the grand result.

I thank all the powers of earth and sky that I am permitted to be a witness to this day's events. That slavery could always live and flourish in this country I have always known to be a foul and guilty heresy. That the vile system must eventually go down I have never doubted, even in the darkest days of my life in slavery. But that I should live to see the President of the United States deliberately advocating Emancipation was more than I ever ventured to hope.

It is true that the President lays down his propositions with many qualifications, some of which to my thinking are unnecessary, unjust and wholly unwise. There are spots on the Sun. A blind man can see where the President's heart is. I read the spaces as well as the lines of that message, I see in them a brave man trying against great odds to do right. An honest patriot endeavoring to save his country in its day of peril. It is the first utterance, and first utterances are not according to Carlyle the most articulate and perfect. Time and practice will improve the President as they improve other men. He is tall and strong, but he is not done growing, he grows as the nation grows. He has managed to say one good word, and to say it so distinctly that all the world may hear. He has dared to say that the highest interest of the country will be promoted by the abolition of slavery. And this, bear in mind, is not said in the bitterness of defeat, but when every morning brought news of glorious victories over the slaveholding rebels. The message comes at the call of no desperation. The time selected for sending it to Congress and the nation must be read with the document itself in order to appreciate its true significance.

Right upon the heels of the message comes the appointment of John C. Frémont, a man whose name thrills the young heart of America with every sentiment of honor, patriotism, and bravery. John C. Frémont carries his department in his name. He goes to free the mountains of rebels and traitors and the good wishes to all but traitors will go with him. Here is a new chapter of the war:

Frémont's proclamation was revised and modified by the President*;

---

*See "Martial Law in Missouri," Aug. 30, 1861, above, P. Tk.

Frémont was removed from his post when in the act of striking the foe. Calumny did its worst upon Frémont. But he was brave and calm; with Jessie by his side he could not well be otherwise, and though strong himself without that pride of American women to support him, he must have fallen. I saw them as they passed eastward, after the chief had fallen. One glance at the young general and his noble wife told me that Frémont would rise again. He has risen. The rebels will hear it. His war horse is already pawing on all their mountains! But what shall be the conditions of peace? How shall the Union be reconstructed? To my mind complete Emancipation is the only basis of permanent peace. Any other basis will place us just at the point from which we started. To leave slavery standing in the rebel States is to leave the eggs of treason in the nest from whence we shall have to meet a larger brood of traitors and rebels at another time; it is to transmit to posterity the question that ought to be settled to-day. Leave slavery where it is, and you leave the same generator of hate towards the north which has already cost us rivers of blood and millions of treasure. Leave slavery in the South and it will be as dangerous for a Northern man to travel in the South as for a man to enter a powder magazine with fire. Despots are suspicious, and every slaveholder is an unmitigated despot, a natural foe to every form of freedom. Leave slavery in the South, and you will fill the North with a full fledged breed of servile panderers to slavery baser than all their predecessors.

Leave slavery where it is and you will hereafter, as heretofore, see in politics a divided, fettered North and an united South. You will see the statesmen of the country facing both ways, speaking two languages, assenting to the principles of freedom in the North and bowing to the malign spirit and practices of slavery at the South. You will see all the pro-slavery elements of the country attracted to the South, giving that section ascendancy again in the counsels of the nation and making them masters of the destinies of the Republic. Restore slavery to its old status in the Union and the same elements of demoralization which have plunged this country into this tremendous war will begin again to dig the grave of free institutions.

It is the boast of the South that her institutions are peculiar and homogeneous, and so they are. Her statesmen have had the wit to see that contact with the free North must either make the North like herself, or that she herself must become like the North. They are right. The South must put off the yoke of slavery or the North must prepare her neck for that yoke, provided the union is restored. There is a middle path.—We have pursued that middle path. It is *compromise* and by it we have reached the point of civil war with all its horrid consequences. The question is, shall we start anew in the same old path?

Who wants a repetition of the same event through which we are passing? Who wants to see the nation taxed to keep a standing army in the South to maintain respect for the Federal Government and protect the rights of citizens of the United States? To such a man I say, leave slavery still dominant at the South and you shall have all your wants supplied.

On the other hand abolish slavery and the now disjointed nation like kindred drops would speedily mingle into one. Abolish slavery and the last hindrance to a solid nationality is abolished. Abolish slavery and you give conscience a chance to grow, and you will win the respect and admiration of mankind. Abolish slavery and you put an end to all sectional politics founded upon conflicting sectional interests, and imparting strife and bitterness to all our general elections, and to the debates on the floor of Congress. Abolish slavery and the citizens of each state will be regarded and treated as equal citizens of the United States, and may travel unchallenged and unmolested in all the states of the Union. Abolish slavery and you put an end to sectional religion and morals, and establish free speech and liberty of conscience throughout your common country. Abolish slavery and rational, law-abiding Liberty will fill the whole land with peace, joy, and permanent safety now and forever.

Douglass' Monthly, April, 1862

Official Report of the Battle at Pittsburgh Landing (Shiloh), Tennessee (fought April 6–7, 1862), by Union General U.S. Grant

(April 9, 1862)

[RR-IV:356–357]

On Burying the Dead, Correspondence between Confederate General G.T. Beauregard and Union General U.S. Grant

(April 8–9, 1862)

[RR-IV:357]

Shiloh, fought April 6–7, was a miserably bloody battle for both sides, with both sides claiming victory. "Shiloh was the severest battle fought at the West during the war," Grant reflected years later, "and but few in the East equalled it for hard, determined fighting. I saw an open field, in our possession on the second day, over which the Confederates had made repeated charges the day before, so covered with dead that it would have been possible to walk across the clearing, in any direction, stepping on dead bodies, without a foot touching the ground."

Shiloh helped bring to the fore two generals in the bad graces of the authorities in Washington, D.C., U. S. Grant and W. T. Sherman, who would from here on lead larger and more important Union campaigns. The Confederate Commander of the Army of the Mississippi, Albert Sidney Johnston, was shot and killed on April 6. The first day's battle caught Grant's forces unprepared and off-stride; the second day, however, forced the Confederates to retreat and subsequently pull out of large areas of Tennessee. Thus Shiloh, costly as it was in men, came to be seen as a Union victory.

HEADQUARTERS DIST. WESTERN TENNESSEE,
Pittsburg, April 9, 1862

To Capt. N. H. McLean, A. A. G., Department of Mississippi, St. Louis:

CAPTAIN: It becomes my duty again to report another battle fought between two great armies, one contending for the maintenance of the best government ever devised, and the other for its destruction. It is pleasant to record the success of the army contending for the former principle.

On Sunday morning our pickets were attacked and driven in by the enemy. Immediately the five divisions stationed at this place were drawn up in line of battle to meet them.

The battle soon waxed warm on the left and centre, varying at times to all parts of the line. There was the most continuous firing of musketry and artillery ever heard on this continent, kept up until night-fall.

The enemy having forced the centre line to fall back nearly half-way from their camps to the landing, at a late hour in the afternoon a desperate effort was made by the enemy to turn ou rleft and get posseswsion of the landing, transports, etc.

This point was guarded by the gunboats *Tyler* and *Lexington,* Capts. Gwin and Shirk, commanding, with four twenty-four-pounder Parrott guns, and a battery of rifled guns.

As there is a deep and impassable ravine for artillery or cavalry, and very difficult for infantry at this point, no troops were stationed here except the necessary artillerists and a small infantry force for their support. Just at this moment the advances of Major-Gen. Buell's column and a part of the division of Gen. Nelson arrived, the two generals named both being present. An advance was immediately made upon the point of attack, and the enemy was soon driven back.

In this repulse, much is due to the presence of the gunboats *Tyler* and *Lexington,* and their able commanders, Capts. Gwin and Shirk.

During the night the divisions under Generals Crittenden and McCook arrived.

Gen. Lew. Wallace, at Camp Landing, six miles below, was ordered, at an early hour in the morning, to hold his division in readiness to move in any direction it might be ordered. At eleven o'clock, the order was delivered to move it up to Pittsburgh, but owing to its being led by a circuitous route, did not arrive in time to take part in Sunday's action.

During te night all was quiet, and, feeling that a great moral advantage would be gained by becoming the attacking party, an advance was ordered as soon as day dawned. The result was the gradual repulse of the enemy at all points of the line, from nine until probably five o'clock in the afternoon, when it became evident the enemy was retreating.

Before the close of the action the advance of Gen. T. J. Wood's division arrived in time to take part in the action.

My force was too much fatigued, from two days' hard fighting and exposure in the open air to a drenching rain during the intervening night, to pursue immediately.

Night closed in cloudy and with a heavy rain, making the roads impracticable for artillery by the next mornring.

Gen. Sherman, however, followed the enemy, finding that the main part of the army had retreated in good order.

Hospitals with the enemy's wounded were found all along the road as far as pursuit was made. Dead bodies of the enemy and many graves were also found. I inclose herewith a report of Gen. Sherman, which will explain more fully the result of the pursuit, and of the part taken by each separate command.

I cannot take special notice in this report, but will do so more fully when the reports of the division commanders are handed in.

General Buell, commanding in the field with a distinct army long under his command, and which did such efficient service, commanded by himself in person on the field, will be much better able to notice those of his command who particularly distinguished themselvesw, than I possibly can.

I feel it a duty, however, to a gallant and able officer, Brigadier-Gen. W. T. Sherman, to make special mention. He not only was with his command during the entire two days of the action, but displayed great judgment and skill in the management of his men; although severelky wounded in the hand on the first day, his place was never vacant. He was again wounded and had three horses killed under him. In making this mention of a gallant officer no disparagement is intended to other division commanders or major-generals, Jno. A. McClernand, and Lewis Wallace, and Brigadier-Generals Hurlbut, Prentiss, and W. H. L. Wallace, all of whom maintained their places with credit to themselves and the cause. Gen. Prentiss was taken prisoner on the first day's action, and Gen. W. H. L. Wallace was severely, and probably mortally wounded. His Assistant Adjutant-General, Capt. Wm. McMichael, is missing, and was probably taken prisoner. My personal staff are all deserving of paticular mention, they having been enaged during the entire two days in carrying orders to every part of the field. It consists of Colonel J. D. Webster, Chief of Staff; Lieut.-Col. J. B. McPherson, Chief of Engineers, assisted by Lieuts. W. L. B. Jenney and Wm. Kossac; Capt. J. A. Rawlings, Assistant Adjutant-General; W. S. Hillyer, W. R. Rawley, and C. B. Lagon, Aides-de-Camp; Col G. Pride, Volunteer Aide, and Captain J. P.

Hawkins, Chief Commissary, who accompanied me upon the field. The medical department, under direction of Surgeon Hewitt, Medical Director, showed great energy in providing for the wounded and in getting them from the field regardless of danger.

Col. Webster was placed in special charge of all the artillery, and was constantly upon the field. He displayed, as always heretofore, both skill and bravery. At least in one instance he was the means of placing an entire regiment in position of doing most valuable service, and where it would not have been but for his exertions. Lieut.-Col. McPherson, attached to my staff as Chief of Engineers, deserves more than a passing notice for his activity and courage. All the grounds beyond our camps for miles have been reconnoitered by him, and plans carefully prepared under his supervision give accurate information of the nature of approaches to our lines. During the two days' battle he was constantly in the saddle leading troops as they arrived to points where their services were required. During the engagement he had one horse shot under him.

The country will have to mourn the loss of many brave men who fell at the battle of Pittsburg, or Shiloh, more properly.

The exact loss in killed and wounded will be known in a day or two.

At present I can only give it approximately at one thousand five hundred killed and three thousand five hundred wounded.

The loss of artillery was great, many pieces being disabled by the enemy's shots, and some losing all their horses and many men. There were probably not less than two hundred horses killed.

The loss of the enemy in killed and left upon the field was greater than ours. In the wounded an estimate cannot be made, as many of them must have been sent to Corinth and other points.

The enemy suffered terribly from demoralization and desertion.

A flag of truce was sent in to-day from Gen. Beauregard. I inclose herewith a copy of the correspondence. I am, very respectfully,

Your obedient servant,

U. S. GRANT,
Major-General, Commanding

CORRESPONDENCE BETWEEN
GENERALS BEAUREGARD AND GRANT

HEADQUARTERS DEPARTMENT OF MISSISSIPPI,
Monterey, April 8, 1862

SIR: At the close of the conflict of yesterday my forces being exhausted by the extraordinary length of the time during which they were engaged with yours, on that and the preceding day, and it being apparent that you had received and were still receiving, re-enforcements, I felt it my duty to withdraw my troops from the immediate scene of the conflict. Under these circumstances, in accordance with usages of war, I shall transmit this under a flag of truce, to ask permission to send a mounted party to the battle-field of Shiloh, for the purpose of giving decent interment to my dead. Certain gentlemen wishing to avail themselves of this opportunity to remove the remains of their sons and friends, I must request for them the privilege of accompanying the burial-party; and in this connection I deem it proper to say I am asking what I have extended to your own countrymen under similar circumstances.

Respectfully, General, your obedient servant,

P. G. T. BEAUREGARD,
General Commanding

To Major-General U.S. Grant,
Major-General Commanding U. S. Forces Pittsburgh Landing

HEADQUARTERS ARMY IN FIELD,⎫
Pittsburgh, April 9   ⎭

To General P. G. T. Beauregard, Commanding Confederate Army on Mississippi, Monterey, Tenn.:

Your despatch of yesterday is just received. Owing to the warmth of the weather I deemed it advisable to have all the dead of both parties buried immediately. Heavy details were made for this purpose, and it is now accomplished. There cannot, therefore, be any necessity of admitting within our lines the parties you desired to send on the grounds asked. I shall always be glad to extend any courtesy consistent with duty, and especially so when dictated by humanity.

I am, General, respectfully, your obedient servant,

U.S. GRANT,
Major-General Commanding

Capture of New Orleans, Official Report of Union Commodore David Farragut and Commodore David D. Porter

(April 25, April 29, April 30, 1862)

[RR–IV:510–512]

New Orleans was the largest city in the Confederacy, and of obvious strategic importance, standing as the gateway to the Mississippi River Valley. The Union naval force of twenty-four ships and nineteen mortar boats, led by Admiral David Farragut, captured the city on April 25. General Benjamin Butler, who would become reviled by the South, took charge of the city administration for the U.S. Government on May 1, not tactfully reminding New Orleans' citizens, "Thrice before has the city of New Orleans been rescued from the hands of a foreign government and still more calamitous domestic insurrection by the money and arms of the United States."

U. S. FLAG-SHIP *Hartford,*
At Anchor off City of New Orleans, April 29

Hon. Gideon Welles, Secretary of the Navy:

SIR: I am happy to announce to you that our flag waves over both Forts Jackson and St. Philip, and at New Orleans over the Custom-House.

I am taking every means to secure the occupation by Gen. Butler of all the forts along the coast. Berwick's Bay and Fort Pike have been abandoned; in fact there is a general stampede, and I shall endeavor to follow it up. I am bringing up the troops as fast as possible.

We have destroyed all the forts above the city, four in number, which we understood to be all the impediments between this and Memphis.

I am, very respectfully, your obedient servant,

D. G. FARRAGUT,
Flag-Officer Western Gulf Block'g Squadron

REPORT OF COMMODORE PORTER

United States Steamer *Harriet Lane,*
Mississippi River, April 25, 1862

Sir: I have the honor to inform you that Flag-Officer Farragut, with the fleet, passed Forts Jackson and St. Philip on the morning of the twenty-fourth, and should be in New Orleans by this time, as he can meet with no obstacles such as he has already passed, the way being comparatively open before him.

We commenced the bombardment of Fort Jackson on the eighteenth, and continued it without intermission until the squadron made preparations to move.

The squadron was formed in three lines to pass the forts. Capt. Bailey's division, composed of the following vessels, leading to the attack of Fort St. Philip: *Cayuga, Pensacola, Mississippi, Oneida, Varuna, Katahdin, Kineo, Wissahickon*; Flag-Officer Farragut leading the following, (second line:) *Hartford, Brooklyn, Richmond*; and Commander Bell leading the third division, composed of the following vessels: *Scioto, Iroquois, Pinola, Winona, Itasca,* and *Kennebec.*

The steamers belonging to the mortar flotilla, one of them towing the Portsmouth, were to enfilade the water-battery commanding the approaches. Mortar-steamers *Harriet Lane, Westfield, Owasco, Clifton,* and *Marine*—the *Jackson* towing the *Portsmouth.*

The vessels were rather late in getting under way and into line, and did not get fairly started until half-past three A.M., and the unusual bustle apprised the garrison that something was going on.

In an hour and ten minutes after the vessels had weighed anchor they had passed the forts under a most terrific fire, which they returned with interest.

The mortar-fleet rained down shells on Fort Jackson, to try and keep the men from the guns, whilst the steamers of the mortar-fleet poured in shrapnel upon the water-battery commanding the approach, at a short distance, keeping them comparatively quiet.

When the last vessel of ours could be seen among the fire and smoke to pass the battery, signal was made to the mortars to cease firing, and the flotilla steamers were directed to retire from a contest that would soon become unequal.

It was now daylight, and the fleet having passed along, the forts began to pay their attention to our little squadron of steamers, the *Portsmouth,* which was being towed up, and three of the gunboats which failed to pass through. These latter became entangled in some wrecks and chains placed in the river to obstruct, and which were only partially removed. One of these vessels (the *Winona*) got through as far as Fort St. Philip, but having all the guns bearing on her she sensibly retired. The *Itasca* was fairly riddled, and had a shot through her boiler, and the *Kennebec* escaped unhurt.

I am disposed to think that our squadron received but little damage, considering the unequal contest—one hundred and forty-two guns on board ship opposed to one hundred on shore, placed in a most commanding position. For twenty minutes after the ships passed the forts fired very feebly on the vessels that remained outside; so much so, that the *Portsmouth* was enabled to drop with the current out of gun-shot, though the shot fell pretty freely about her at last. I think the fire from the ships must have been very destructive of life.

The last we saw of our vessels they were standing up the river. Some explosion took place, which made us feel rather uneasy, but which may have been the rebel gunboats. We could see that our squadron had not destroyed all the enemy's vessels at the fort, for three or four of them were moving about in all directions, evidently in a state of excitement.

Before the fleet got out of sight it was reported to me that the celebrated ram *Manassas* was coming out to attack us; and sure enough there she was, apparently steaming along shore, ready to pounce upon the apparently defenceless mortar-vessels. Two of our steamers and some of the mortar-vessels opened fire on her, but I soon discovered that the *Manassas* could harm no one again, and I ordered the vessels to save their shot. She was beginning to emit smoke from her ports or holes, and was discovered to be on fire and sinking. Her pipes were all twisted and riddled with shot, and her hull was also well cut up. She had evidently been used up by the squadron as they passed along. I tried to save her as a curiosity, by getting a hawser around her and securing her to the bank, but just after doing so she faintly exploded. Her only gun went off, and emitting flames through her bow-port, like some huge animal, she gave a plunge and disappeared under the water.

Next came a steamer on fire, which appeared to be a vessel of war belonging to the rebels, and after her two others, all burning and floating down the stream. Fires seemed to be raging all along the "up river," and we supposed that our squadron were burning and destroying the vessels as they passed along. It appears, however, that the *McRae,* one or two river-boats, and their celebrated floating battery, (brought down the night before,) were left unhurt, and were still flying the confederate flag.

The matter of the floating battery becomes a very serious affair, as they are all hard at work at Fort Jackson mounting heavy rifled guns on it, which are no further use to them in the Fort. She mounts sixteen guns, is almost as formidable a vessel as the *Merimac,* perfectly shot-proof, and has four powerful engines in her. I shall at all events take such steps as will prevent her from destroying anything, and we may still hold her in check with the steamers, though they are rather fragile for such a service. This is one of the ill effects of leaving an enemy in the rear. I suppose that the ships fired on her as they passed through, but that her mail resisted the shot. She had steam on this morning, and was moving about quite lively. I tried to put some mortar-shell through her roof, but without effect, as she moved off.

The Forts are now cut off from all communication with New Orleans, as I presume that Flag-Officer Farragut has cut the wires.

I have sent the *Miami* around with Gen. Butler to the back of Fort St. Philip to try and throw in troops at the quarantine, five miles along the Forts, and at the same time open communication that way with the Flag-Officer, and supply him with ammunition.

I am also going to send part of the mortar-fleet to the back of Fort Jackson to cut off the escape of the garrison by that way, and stop supplies. A deserter, who can be relied on, informs us that they have plenty of provisions for two months, plenty of ammunition, and plenty of discomforts. Our shell set the citadel on fire the first afternoon we opened. It burned fiercely for seven hours, but I thought it a fire-raft behind the Fort, as they continually send them down on us, but without any effect.

But few casualties occurred to vessels on this side of the Forts. The *Harriet Lane* lost but one man killed, and one, I fear, mortally wounded. The *Winona* lost three killed and three wounded, and the *Itasca,* with fourteen shot through her, had but few men hurt.

These Forts can hold out still for some time, and I would suggest that the *Monitor* and *Mystic,* if they can be spared, be sent here without a moment's delay, to settle the question.

The mortar-fleet have been very much exposed, and under a heavy fire for six days, during which time they kept the shells going without intermission. One of them, the *Maria I. Carlton,* was sunk by a shot passing down through her magazine, and then through her bottom.

The flotilla lost but one man killed and six wounded. The bearing of the officers and men was worthy of the highest praise. They never once flagged during a period of six days; never had an accident to one of the vessels by firing, and when shell and shot were flying thick above them showed not the least desire to have the vessels moved to a place of safety. The incidents of the bombardment will be mentioned in my detailed report. I merely write this hurried letter to apprize the Department of the state of affairs, and shall send it off at once via Havana.

The sight of this night attack was awfully grand. The river was lit up with rafts filled with pine-knots, and the ships seemed to be fighting literally amidst flames and smoke. Where we were the fire of the enemy was high, and comparatively harmless.

I am in hopes that the ships above fared as well as we did. Though amid such a terrific fire, it was gratifying to see that not a ship wavered, but stood steady on her course; and I am in hopes (and I see no reason to doubt it) that they now have possession of New Orleans.

I am, with great respect, your obedient servant,

DAVID D. PORTER,
Commanding Flotilla

Hon. Gideon Welles,
   Secretary of Navy

Confederate General Order No. 17,
A Call to Destroy Cotton; Secretary of War George W. Randolph and Assistant Adjutant-General J. G. Pickett
(May 3, 1862)

[RR–X:245]

"King Cotton," the South's highly valuable commodity, became more and more valuable as the war proceeded because of the Union naval blockades. Rather than let its cotton be captured by the North, the Confederacy made policies to destroy their stores of cotton whenever it came in danger of being taken.

DESTRUCTION OF COTTON:
OFFICIAL ORDER AND DESPATCH

RICHMOND,
Friday, May 2, 1862

To Major-General M. Lovell:
The following despatch was sent to you on the twenty-fifth of April.

A. T. BLEDSOE,
Assistant Secretary of War

IT has been determined to burn all the cotton and tobacco, whether foreign or our own, to prevent it from falling into the hands of the enemy.

You will therefore destroy it all, if necessary, to prevent them from getting it.

G. W. RANDOLPH
Secretary of War

C. S. OF AMERICA, HEADQUARTERS DEPARTMENT, }
No. 1, Camp Moore, Louisiana, May 3, 1862   }

General Order No. 17.—The enemy, by an overwhelming naval force, having succeeded in passing the defences and gaining possession of the city of New Orleans, are jubilant in the boast, that the struggle which a gallant people are making from a bondage to which death would be preferable, is rapidly closing in disgrace and humiliation to the South. They claim that the great Valley of the West being opened, the remotest commercial interest of the civilized world will have cause to side with them in the iron-handed controversy which they are waging upon us, for the reason that cotton will now flow from every tributary of the Mississippi to seek a market under their protection in the ports of Europe; for without that staple they know full well that a brief period will put an end to their attempt to conquer the South. It is with the people to decide this question for themselves.

If you are resolved to be free, if you are worthy of the heroic blood that has come down to you through hallowed generations, if you have fixed your undimmed eye upon the brightness that spreads out before you and your children, and are determined to shake away forever and ever all political association with the vandal horde that now gather like a pestilence about your fair country; now, my fellow-citizens, is the time to strike! *One sparkling, living touch of fire in manly action for one hour upon each cotton plantation, and the eternal seal of Southern independence is fired and fixed in the great heart of the world.*

It needs no argument to show that, with the destruction of negro property, the cotton and sugar lands of the South would be worthless, and that the mighty effort of this abolition war is for that purpose, is amply proved by a thousand evidences unnecessary to refer to in this order, and which are rapidly culminating in the various schemes of the Federal Congress in reference to the destruction of the slave-holding interest in all the border states.

Your Major-General calls, in this hour of danger, for one heroic effort, and he feels consciously proud that he will not call in vain. *Let not a solitary bale of cotton be left as spoil for the invader, and all will be well.* By order of Major-General Lovell.

J. G. PICKETT,
Assistant Adjutant-General

Official Correspondence from Union Major-General Benjamin Butler and Flag-Officer David Farragut to and from the mayor and military governor of Vicksburg
(May 18, 1862)

[RR-V:426]

The taking of Vicksburg was one of the toughest campaigns of the war, ending only in early July of 1863 when General Grant's troops and Admiral David D. Porter's ships took the city. James L. Autry's reply to the initial Union threat was trumpeted proudly throughout the South. (See details of the siege, page 113, below.)

U. S. S. *Oneida,* NEAR VICKSBURGH,
May 18th, 1862

To the Authorities of Vicksburgh:

The undersigned, with orders from Flag-Officer Farragut and Major-General Butler, respectively, demand, in advance of the approaching fleet, the surrender of Vicksburgh and its defences to the lawful authority of the United States, under which private property and personal rights shall be respected.

Respectfully yours,

S. PHILLIPS LEE, U.S.N.,
Commanding Advance Naval Division

T. WILLIAMS,
Brigadier-General

VICKSBURGH, MISS.,
May 18, 1862

To S. Phillips Lee, Commanding Advance Naval Division:

SIR: As your communication of this date is addressed "To the Authorities of Vicksburgh," and that you may have a full reply to said communication, I have to state that Mississippians don't know and refuse to learn how to surrender to an enemy. If Commodore Farragut or Brig.-Gen. Butler can teach them, let them come and try. As to the defences of Vicksburgh, I respectfully refer you to the reply of Brigadier-General Smith, commanding forces at Vicksburgh, herewith enclosed.

Respectfully,

JAMES L. AUTRY,
Military Governor and Commandant Post

HEADQUARTERS DEFENCES VICKSBURGH, MISS.,
May 18, 1862

S. Phillips Lee, U.S.N., Commanding Advance Naval Division:

SIR: Your communication of this date, addressed "To the Authorities of Vicksburgh," demanding the surrender of the city and its defences, has been received. In regard to the surrender of the defences, I have to reply that having been ordered here to hold these defences, it is my intention to do so as long as it is in my power.

M. L. SMITH,
Brigadier-General Commanding

Report on the Morse Magnetic Telegraph and Balloon Reconnaissance, by Parker Spring, Superintendent of Construction of U.S. Military Telegraph Lines
(June 2, 1862)

[RR–V:535–536]

Observation balloons had been used since the end of the eighteenth century, but this may have been the first time they were war-craft. There are few episodes more wonderful than this balloon reconnaissance, as described by an official of the government's important telegraph team, and its "instant-messaging" during the balloon's ascension.

The telegraph was one of the many technologies that developed during the war and played a vital part in the Union's victory. "Sometimes the lines have been required to take their course through portions of the revolted States, actually in the possession of the enemy, and upon such occasions, the constructing parties have been obliged to perform their labor during the night time only, to avoid detection and capture by the enemy. It would be difficult to enumerate the hazards, vexations and obstacles incident to the construction of military telegraph lines," wrote Colonel Anson Stager, Assistant Quartermaster and Superintendent of the U.S. Military Telegraph, in his report for the fiscal year ending June 30, 1863. "By a close estimate it appears that at least 1,200,000 telegrams have been sent and received over the military lines in operation during the fiscal year . . . at the rate of about 3,300 per diem."

UNITED STATES MILITARY TELEGRAPH, HEADQUARTERS ⎫
Department Potomac, Gaines's Hill, ⎬
Seven Miles from Richmond, June 2, 1862 ⎭

FROM the time the army of the Potomac first left Washington the United States Military Telegraph has never for an hour been allowed to remain in the rear. Before reaching his new headquarters Gen. McClellan almost invariably learns that the wire is on the advance; that an office has already been opened at the point designated before he left his old camp, and that communication to the War Department at Washington is open for him. In several instances when the army had marched fifteen miles in one day, the telegraph had reached the new quarters two hours in advance. When our troops are obliged to remain a few days in one position, wires are immediately run from Gen. McClellan's quarters to the headquarters of all commanders of divisions, thereby placing the entire section of country occupied by our troops under his instant control. Assistance like this is surely valuable to our glorious cause, and, I am happy to say, it is fully appreciated by the General.

Saturday previous to the evacuation of Yorktown, Gen. McClellan ordered me to run a wire into our Battery No. 6, in order to give him telegraphic communication from his headquarters, which were distant about one and a half miles. This battery laid half a mile in front of General Heintzelman, and within half a mile off a long chain of rebel batteries. The office at Battery No. 6 was to be located under ground, in a bomb-proof arrangement, in order to save the precious life of the manipulator, who would be in his hole before daybreak the next morning. I was informed by Gen. Heintzelman's aids that it was a very hazardous experiment; that from the point where the line must cross the fields the rebel officers could be heard distinctly giving command; that the rebel pickets were within two hundred and fifty yards of us, and if we attempted to distribute poles with our wagon we would be fired upon. Of these facts I informed all our men. Regardless of danger, they unanimously voted for the extension. Fortunately that night was dark, and promptly at nine P.M. we were in readiness to commence operations.

After cautioning all hands to work quietly, I detailed the men as follows: Cosgrove, Hoover, Greiner and McGuide to dig holes; Rote, Keiler, Benedict and Jones to distribute poles on their shoulders, who had to carry them a full mile. John Tryer I posted as guard. His duty was to watch the flash of the rebel guns, and notify the men, who were working and could not see, when to fall on the sod, should the rebels hear us and open. Thus far all was quiet in the secesh quarters. Scarcely had our operations commenced when a compliment from Gen. Magruder in the shape of a shell was sent us. Through the timely notice received from our guard, Mr. Tryer, that "he saw a flash, and that something with a fiery tail was coming toward us," we were enabled to drop. It came within fifty yards of us, bursted, but did no damage. After that shot and shell followed in rapid succession, until we completed our task, which, owing to loss of time in dodging, occupied fully five hours. A number of these missiles fell within thirty feet of us, showing conclusively that the rebel pickets had discovered our operations, and were directing the fire of their artillery. We have preserved pieces of a shell that knocked down a pole behind us, which had been erected not five minutes before the shot was fired. The line was run through a soft corn-field, and it was amusing next day, after the evacuation, when we returned to this field, to see the life-like pictures of Tryer, Cosgrove, and several others, nicely portrayed in the mud, and which no artist in the world could excel. They were at once recognized by all hands, and I promised to give you the particulars.

The telegraph has been called upon to perform a still more mysterious wonder. For some time past I have been ordered by Col. Eckert (our superintendent of military telegraphs) to try a telegraphic experiment from a balloon. Saturday morning, when we heard that a great battle must be fought, Professor Lowe notified me that I should extend the wire to his balloon, and we would try it. In one hour we had brought the wire a mile and a half, and I was ready to ascend with the Professor. The battle had commenced. When it had reached its zenith, Professor Lowe and myself, with the telegraph, had reached an altitude of two thousand feet. With the aid of good glasses we were enabled to view the whole affair between these powerful contending armies. As the fight progressed, hasty observations were made by the Professor and given to me verbally, all of which I instantly forwarded to General McClellan and division commanders through the agency of the obedient field instrument which stood by our side in the bottom of the car. Occasionally a masked rebel battery would open upon our brave fellows. In such cases the occupants of the balloon would inform our artillerists of its position, and the next shot or two would, in every case, silence the masked and annoying customers. For hours, and until quite dark, we remained in the air, the telegraph keeping up constant communication with some point. From the balloon to Fortress Monroe, a distance of over a hundred miles, this wire worked beautifully. A number of messages were sent and received between these two points, and had it not been for the tremendous rush of business on the wire, I should have telegraphed you directly from the balloon, while the battle was raging. Sunday morning, at daybreak, we again ascended. Early in the morning the battle was renewed, and with more fierceness than the day before. Incessant firing of musketry and artillery was kept up until noon, when I had the extreme pleasure to announce by telegraph from the balloon, that we could see the enemy retreating rapidly toward Richmond. At this time we could see firing on James River, to the left of Richmond, distance from the balloon, some said, fifteen miles. This fire was of short duration.

The streets of Richmond in the morning presented a deserted appearance, but very few people to be be seen in the streets. During the afternoon and evening of Sunday nothing of interest transpired beyond the removal of the rebel dead and wounded, all of which we could distinctly see from the balloon. Every available machine that had wheels was brought into requisition for this purpose. From the scene of battle into the city of Richmond, the road was literally lined with ambulances, wagons and carts, conveying dead and wounded. About twilight we saw camp-fires innumerable around the city; smoke issued from all their hospitals and barracks, which showed us to a certainty that the main body of their army had fallen back to Richmond. Monday morning we made several ascensions, and found a small force near the last scene of action, and thousands of troops marching out from the city, so you may look momentarily for a report of another severe battle.

I am going to continue my ascensions with Professor Lowe, and should I have an opportunity to give you a telegraphic report from the balloon without a violation of the General's "Order to Correspondents," you shall have it. Our experiments have met the approbation of all officers. Balloon telegraphing is fully established, and I am very happy to inform you that we are the first who have established it successfully. A feeble attempt to telegraph from a balloon was made in Washington last summer, of which I will give you a correct description, and bring good testimony to show it was a complete fizzle. Newspapers were filled with accounts of this *wonderful* experiment. Messages appeared as having been sent to the President and other distinguished individuals. The balloon ascended—so did the telegraph. Not until they had descended as low as the house-tops was the message started. Two thirds of it was sent after the balloon had delivered its passengers safely on *terra firma*. It was such a complete failure that the operator, W. B. Wilson, then at the War Department, who was to receive the despatch, refused to copy it, he having himself seen the balloon landed on the ground, after receiving the first few words. To this Professor Lowe himself will certify.—

Address by the Confederate Colonel of Cavalry John H. Morgan to His Guerrillas after the Defeat of Union General Buell's Cavalry on the Hartsville Road, Tennessee

(August 22, 1862)

[RR-V:587–588]

John Hunt Morgan (1824–1864) was famous for leading raids against Union forces in Tennessee and Kentucky. In this battle with Don Carlos Buell's top cavalry, he effectively cut Buell's communications. "Thus ended an action," Morgan wrote in his official report the same day, "in which my command, not exceeding 700 men . . . succeeded in defeating a brigade of 1,200 chosen cavalry sent by Gen. Buell expressly to take me or drive me out of Tennessee, killing and wounding some 180 and taking 200 prisoners, including the Brigadier-General Commanding and the greater part of the regimental officers." (See the journal of the account of one of Morgan's later raids, page 135, below.)

HEADQUARTERS MORGAN'S BRIGADE, HARTSVILLE,⎫
Tennessee, August 22, 1862　⎭

SOLDIERS: Your gallant bearing during the last two days will not only be inscribed in the history of the country and the annals of this war, but is engraven deeply in my heart.

Your zeal and devotion on the twentieth, at the attack of the trestle-work at Saundersville, and of the Springfield Junction stockade, your heroism during the two hard fights of yesterday, have placed you high on the list of those patriots who are now in arms for our Southern rights.

All communication cut off betwixt Gallatin and Nashville, a body of three hundred infantry totally cut off or taken prisoners, the liberation of those kind friends arrested by our revengeful foes, for no other reason than their compassionate care of our sick and wounded, would have been laurels sufficient for your brows. But, soldiers, the utter annihilation of General Johnson's brigade, composed of twenty-four picked companies of regulars, and sent on purpose to take us, raises your reputation as soldiers, and strikes fear into the craven hearts of your enemies. Gen. Johnson* and his staff, with two hundred men, taken prisoners, sixty-four killed and one hundred wounded, attests the resistance made, and bears testimony to your valor.

But our victories have not been achieved without loss. We have to mourn some brave and dear comrades. Their names will remain in our breasts—their fame outlives them. They died in defence of a good cause; they died, like gallant soldiers, with their front to the foe.

Officers and men, your conduct makes me proud to command you. Fight always as you fought yesterday, and you are invincible.

JOHN H. MORGAN,
Colonel Commanding Cavalry

---

*Union Brigadier-General R. W. Johnson.

Despatches on the Second Battle of Manassas Junction (Bull Run) from Confederate General Robert E. Lee to Confederate President Jefferson Davis
(August 29–Sept. 3, 1862)

[RR–VI:401–402]

The Commander of the Army of Northern Virginia, Lee describes the trouncing of the Union forces at Manassas Junction (August 29–30). Confederate President Jefferson Davis told his congress on September 3: "From these despatches it will be seen that God has again extended his shield over our patriotic army, and has blessed the cause of the Confederacy with a second signal victory on the field already memorable by the gallant achievement of our troops."

Meanwhile, in the Union Army, in response to this defeat, President Lincoln replaced John Pope as commander of the Army of Virginia with his own personal bugbear, George B. McClellan.

HEADQUARTERS MANASSAS JUNCTION,⎱
Nine P.M. Aug. 29, via Rapidan, Aug. 30, 1862 ⎰

To President Davis:

So far this army has steadily advanced and repulsed the frequent attacks of the enemy. The line of the Rappahannock and Warrenton has been relieved. Many prisoners are captured, and I regret, quantities of stores to be destroyed for want of transportation. Anderson not yet up, and I hear nothing of those behind. We have Ewell, Trimble, and Taliaferro wounded—the latter slightly, the others not mortally.

R. E. LEE

HEADQUARTERS ARMY NORTHERN VIRGINIA, }
Grovetown, via Rapidan, Aug. 30—10 P.M. }

To President Davis:

This army achieved to-day, on the plains of Manassas, a signal victory over the combined forces of Generals McClellan and Pope. On the twenty-eighth and twenty-ninth, each wing, under Generals Longstreet and Jackson, repulsed with valor attacks made on them separately. We mourn the loss of our gallant dead in every conflict, yet our gratitude to Almighty God for his mercies rises higher each day. To him and the valor of our troops a nation's gratitude is due.

R. E. LEE

HEADQUARTERS ARMY NORTHERN VIRGINIA, }
Chantilly, Sept. 3, 1862 }

His Excellency, Jefferson Davis, President Confederate States of America:
MR. PRESIDENT: My letter of the thirtieth ult. will have informed your Excellency of the progress of this army to that date. General Longstreet's division having arrived the day previous, was formed in order of battle on the right of Gen. Jackson, who had been engaged with the enemy since morning, resisting an attack commenced on the twenty-eighth. The enemy, on the latter day, was vigorously repulsed, leaving his numerous dead and wounded on the field. His attack on the morning of the twenty-ninth was feeble, but became warmer in the afternoon, when he was again repulsed by both wings of the army. His loss on this day, as stated in his published report, herewith inclosed, amounted to eight thousand killed and wounded.

The enemy being reënforced, renewed the attack on the afternoon of the thirtieth, when a general advance of both wings of the army was ordered, and, after a fierce combat, which raged until after nine o'clock, he was completely defeated and driven beyond Bull Run. The darkness of the night, his destruction of the stone bridge after crossing, and the uncertainty of the fords, stopped the pursuit.

The next morning the enemy was discovered in the strong position at Centreville, and the army was put in motion toward the Little River turnpike, to turn his right. Upon reaching Ox Hill, on the first of September, he was again discovered in our front on the heights of Germantown, and about five P.M. made a spirited attack upon the front and right of our columns, with a view of apparently covering the withdrawal of his trains on the Centreville road, and masking his retreat. Our position was maintained with but slight loss on both sides. Major-General Kearny★ was left by the enemy dead on the field. During the night the enemy fell back to Fairfax Court-House, and abandoned his position at Centreville. Yesterday, about noon, he evacuated Fairfax Court-House, taking the roads, as reported to me, to Alexandria and Washington.

I have, as yet, been unable to get official reports of our loss or captured in these various engagements. Many gallant officers have been killed or wounded. Of the general officers, Ewell, Trimble, Taliaferro, Fields, Jenkins, and Mahone, have been reported wounded; Colonels Means, Marshall, Baylor, Neff, and Gadberry killed. About seven thousand prisoners have already been paroled; about the same number of small arms collected from the field, and thirty pieces of cannon captured, besides a number of wagons, ambulances, etc. A large number of arms still remain on the ground. For want of transportation valuable stores had to be destroyed as captured, while the enemy, at their various dépôts, are reported to have burned many millions of property in their retreat. Nothing could surpass the gallantry and endurance of the troops, who have cheerfully borne every danger and hardship, both on the battle-field and march.

I have the honor to be, very respectfully, your obedient servant,

R. E. LEE,
General

★Major-General Philip Kearny rode his horse into a cornfield where Confederate soldiers were hiding; they shot and killed him.

Proclamation to the People of Maryland by Confederate General Robert E. Lee
(September 8, 1862)

[OR: SERIES 1, VOL. 19, PT. 2: 601–602]

After the victory at Manassas Junction (Second Bull Run), General Robert E. Lee headed north into Maryland, where he hoped the Army of Northern Virginia might divert Union forces from other Confederate army sites. He expected political support from the border state and that his weary army might find food.

HEADQUARTERS ARMY OF NORTHERN VIRGINIA,—⎫
Near Fredericktown, Md., September 8, 1862 ⎭

To the People of Maryland:

It is right that you should know the purpose that brought the army under my command within the limits of your State, so far as that purpose concerns yourselves. The people of the Confederate States have long watched with the deepest sympathy the wrongs and outrages that have been inflicted upon the citizens of a commonwealth allied to the States of the South by the strongest social, political, and commercial ties. They have seen with profound indignation their sister State deprived of every right and reduced to the condition of a conquered province. Under the pretense of supporting the Constitution, but in violation of its most valuable provisions, our citizens have been arrested and imprisoned upon no charge and contrary to all forms of law. The faithful and manly protest against this outrage made by the venerable and illustrious Marylander, to whom in better days no citizen appealed for right in vain, was treated with scorn and contempt; the government of your chief city has been usurped by armed strangers; your legislature has been dissolved by the unlawful arrest of its members; freedom of the press and of speech has been suppressed; words have been declared offenses by an arbitrary decree of the Federal Executive, and citizens ordered to be tried by a military commission for what they may dare to speak. Believing that the people of Maryland possessed a spirit too lofty to submit to such a government, the people of the South have long wished to aid you in throwing off this foreign yoke, to enable you again to enjoy the inalienable rights of freemen, and restore independence and sovereignty to your State. In obedience to this wish, our army has come among you, and is prepared to assist you with the power of its arms in regaining the rights of which you have been despoiled.

This, citizens of Maryland, is our mission, so far as you are concerned. No constraint upon your free will is intended; no intimidation will be allowed within the limit of this army, at least. Marylanders shall once more enjoy their ancient freedom of thought and speech. We know no enemies among you, and will protect all, of every opinion. It is for you to decide your destiny freely and without constraint. This army will respect your choice, whatever it may be; and while the Southern people will rejoice to welcome you to your natural position among them, they will only welcome you when you come of your own free will.

R. E. Lee,
General, Commanding

Despatch on the Battle of Antietam by Union General Joseph Hooker
(September 17, 1862)

[RR-V:454]

The Union survived the important battle of Antietam (or Sharpsburg) in Maryland, sending Confederate General Robert E. Lee's army into retreat in Virginia. During the day's battle, nearly five thousand men were killed. "Fighting Joe" Hooker (1814–1879) observed, "The carnage has been awful," and he himself was wounded.

CENTREVILLE, MD.,
Wednesday, Sept. 17

A GREAT battle has been fought and we are victorious. I had the honor to open it yesterday afternoon, and it continued until ten o'clock this morning, when I was wounded, and compelled to quit the field.

The battle was fought with great violence on both sides. The carnage has been awful.

I only regret that I was not permitted to take part in the operations until they were concluded, for I had counted on either capturing their army or driving them into the Potomac.

My wound has been painful, but it is not one that will be likely to lay me up. I was shot through the foot.

J. HOOKER,
Brigadier-General

Measure by the Mississippi House of Representatives Sustaining Confederate President Davis on Retaliation for Lincoln's Emancipation Proclamation
(October 11, 1862)

[RR-VI:185–186]

When President Lincoln presented his preliminary Emancipation Proclamation on September 22, many in the South felt further justified in their decision to secede. After all, slavery, the "institution" by which the South chose to define itself, was under attack, just as plantation owners had feared it would be. In retaliation for Lincoln's "barbarous conduct," Mississippi vowed to support Davis in any action he took.

RICHMOND,
October 11, 1862

THE following preamble and resolutions, submitted to the House of Representatives by Mr. Barksdale, of Mississippi, were adopted on the eleventh instant, by a vote of thirty-five yeas to twenty-two nays.

Three propositions were before the House—one of Mr. Russell, from the Judiciary Committee; another from Mr. Foote, from the Committee on Foreign Affairs; and a third by Mr. Barksdale, in behalf of a minority of the last-named Committee.

The measure which was adopted recites the atrocities of the Lincoln Government—declares that justice and humanity alike demand that they should be met by retaliatory measures, and that the President will be sustained by the legislative department of the Government in whatever course he may deem it proper to pursue. There was no division of sentiment in the House upon the question or policy of retaliation, and the difference existed only as to the manner:

Whereas, the Northern States, now represented by the Federal Government of the late Union, commenced the present war of invasion to enforce an unfounded and tyrannical claim of dominion over sovereign States which had withdrawn from the Union; and, pretending that these States are in rebellion, have sought to deny to them, from the beginning of the war, the rights accorded to belligerents by the usages of nations; and, after prosecuting this war, without success, more than a year since this government was recognized by European nations as a belligerent power, have continued, under the same pretext, to inflict upon the good people of these States inhuman injuries in contemptuous disregard of the usages of civilized warfare, exacting from them treasonable oaths and service, and, upon refusal, subjecting unarmed citizens, women and children to banishment, imprisonment, and death; wantonly burning their dwelling houses, ravaging the land, murdering men for pretended or trivial offences; making rapine of private property a systematic object of the war; organizing the abduction of slaves by armies and agents of Government; endeavoring to foment servile insurrection by tampering with slaves, by proclaiming schemes for emancipating them, by passing laws to equalize the races; by protecting slaves in resisting their masters, and by preparing armed bands of negroes to fight in the presence of negro slaves for the subjugation of the white race; permitting outrages on women to be committed by a licentious soldiery, encouraged, in a memorable instance, by the order of a major-general and the acquiescence of his government; attempting, until restrained by a threat of retaliation, to murder privateersmen for engaging in a mode of warfare expressly sanctioned by the Constitution of the United States and the Confederate States, and by the laws of nations; refusing, with double inhumanity, to exchange prisoners, until constrained by the long duration and adverse fortune of the war; attempting to ruin our cities by filling up the entrances to their harbors with stone and diverting the ancient channels of great rivers; cutting off our supplies of medicines, needed as well for suffering women, children, and captive enemies, as for the sick of our armies, and perpetrating other atrocities, which would be disgraceful to savages. And, whereas, the said Government of the United States, in the same spirit of barbarous ferocity, has recently enacted a law entitled, "An Act to suppress insurrection, to punish treason and rebellion, to seize and confiscate the property of rebels, and for other purposes"; and has announced by a proclamation issued by Abraham Lincoln, the President thereof, that, in pursuance of said law, on the first day of January, 1863, all persons held as slaves within any State or designated part of a State, the people whereof shall be in rebellion against the United States, shall be thenceforward and forever free; and has thereby made manifest that the vast war of invasion which it wages with such lawless cruelty is conducted with a view, by judicial murders, banishments, and otherwise, to exterminate the loyal population of these States; to transfer their property to their enemies; to emancipate their slaves; to destroy their labor system; to subvert their institutions, human and divine, upon which it is founded, employing slaves and other negroes for these purposes, with an atrocious design of adding servile insurrection and the massacre of families to the calamities of war; and, whereas, since the passage of said act executive and military orders have evinced a determined purpose of the enemy to carry out this policy of rapine and extermination with brutal and surprising severity; and whereas, justice and humanity require the government of the confederate States to endeavor to punish and repress the atrocious practices and designs of the enemy by inflicting severe retribution; therefore,

Resolved, by the Congress of the confederate States, that the President will be sustained in resorting to such measures of retaliation as in his judgment may be demanded by the above-recited lawless and barbarous conduct and designs of the enemy.

Letter after Antietam from President Lincoln to Major-General George B. McClellan
(October 13, 1862)

[ALLT:282–285]

After the President's initial admiration for him and support for his advancement as the leader of the army in 1861, McClellan never followed through in the manner in which Lincoln expected or desired, and McClellan never respected the President's intelligence or political views. With the Confederate retreat after Antietam, Lincoln took advantage of the good news of this "victory" to announce on September 22 his preliminary Emancipation Proclamation, which policy McClellan disliked. While Lincoln cajoled him on military matters, the proud and touchy McClellan resented any second-guessing, polite and discreet as it was. Secretary of War Edwin Stanton remarked of McClellan: "If he had a million men he would swear the enemy has two millions, and then he would sit down in the mud and yell for three."

EXECUTIVE MANSION
Washington, D.C., October 13, 1862

Major-General McClellan:

My dear Sir: You remember my speaking to you of what I called your overcautiousness. Are you not overcautious when you assume that you cannot do what the enemy is constantly doing? Should you not claim to be at least his equal in prowess, and act upon the claim? As I understand, you telegraphed General Halleck that you cannot subsist your army at Winchester unless the railroad from Harper's Ferry to that point be put in working order. But the enemy does now subsist his army at Winchester, at a distance nearly twice as great from railroad transportation as you would have to do without the railroad last named. He now wagons from Culpeper Court-House, which is just about twice as far as you would have to do from Harper's Ferry. He is certainly not more than half as well provided with wagons as you are. I certainly should be pleased for you to have the advantage of the railroad from Harper's Ferry to Winchester, but it wastes all the remainder of autumn to give it to you, and in fact ignores the question of time, which cannot and must not be ignored. Again, one of the standard maxims of war, as you know, is to "operate upon the enemy's communications as much as possible without exposing your own." You seem to act as if this applies against you, but cannot apply in your favor. Change positions with the enemy, and think you not he would break your communications with Richmond within the next twenty-four hours? You dread his going into Pennsylvania, but if he does so in full force, he gives up his communications to you absolutely, and you have nothing to do but to follow and ruin him. If he does so with less than full force, fall upon and beat what is left behind all the easier. Exclusive of the water-line, you are now nearer Richmond than the enemy is by the route that you can and he must take. Why can you not reach there before him, unless you admit that he is more than your equal on a march? His route is the arc of a circle, while yours is the chord. The roads are as good on yours as on his. You know I desired, but did not order, you to cross the Potomac below, instead of above, the Shenandoah and Blue Ridge. My idea was that this would at once menace the enemy's communications, which I would seize if he would permit.

If he should move northward, I would follow him closely, holding his communications. If he should prevent our seizing his communications and move toward Richmond, I would press closely to him, fight him if a favorable opportunity should present, and at least try to beat him to Richmond on the inside track. I say "try"; if we never try, we shall never succeed. If he makes a stand at Winchester, moving neither north nor south, I would fight him there, on the idea that if we cannot beat him when he bears the wastage of coming to us, we never can when we bear the wastage of going to him. This proposition is a simple truth, and is too important to be lost sight of for a moment. In coming to us he tenders us an advantage which we should not waive. We should not so operate as to merely drive him away. As we must beat him somewhere or fail finally, we can do it, if at all, easier near to us than far away. If we cannot beat the enemy where he now is, we never can, he again being within the intrenchments of Richmond.

Recurring to the idea of going to Richmond on the inside track, the facility of supplying from the side away from the enemy is remarkable, as it were, by the different spokes of a wheel extending from the hub toward the rim, and this whether you move directly by the chord or on the inside arc, hugging the Blue Ridge more closely. The chord-line, as you see, carries you by Aldie, Hay Market, and Fredericksburg; and you see how turnpikes, railroads, and finally the Potomac, by Aquia Creek, meet you at all points from Washington; the same, only the lines length-ened a little, if you press closer to the Blue Ridge part of the way.

The gaps through the Blue Ridge I understand to be about the fol-lowing distances from Harper's Ferry, to wit: Vestal's, 5 miles; Gregory's, 13; Snicker's, 18; Ashby's, 28; Manassas, 38; Chester, 45; and Thornton's, 53. I should think it preferable to take the route nearest the enemy, dis-abling him to make an important move without your knowledge, and compelling him to keep his forces together for dread of you. The gaps would enable you to attack if you should wish. For a great part of the way you would be practically between the enemy and both Washington and Richmond, enabling us to spare you the greatest number of troops from here. When at length running for Richmond ahead of him enables him to move this way, if he does so, turn and attack him in the rear. But I think he should be engaged long before such point is reached. It is all easy if our troops march as well as the enemy, and it is unmanly to say they cannot do it. This letter is in no sense an order.

Yours truly,
A. LINCOLN

Appeal to the People for the Wants of the Army, by North Carolina Governor Vance
(October 15, 1862)

[RR–VI:23–24]

The war impoverished the South, and while the noncombatants, primarily women, children, the elderly, and millions of slaves stayed home to farm or work, the Confederate soldiers faced harsh winters and meager rations, which, coupled with illness and the brutalities of war, caused widespread desertions from the ranks. The governors of the Confederate states regularly called on their citizens for contributions of money and supplies. Virginia Governor Letcher, for example, proclaimed on November 13, "Who can contemplate the prospect for the soldiers in the future, as winter advances, while the slaves on our farms and in our streets are comfortably clad, without emotions calculated to open his purse and heart to remedy the evil?" In 1863, Governor Zebulon Vance would complain not about "speculators" buying up necessities or slaves using them, but about Confederate guerrillas stealing them: "If God Almighty had yet in store another plague worse than all the others which he intended to have let loose on the Egyptians in case Pharaoh still hardened his heart, I am sure it must have been a regiment or so of half-armed, half-disciplined Confederate Cavalry."

AFTER the most strenuous exertions on the part of its officers, the State finds it impossible to clothe and shoe our soldiers without again appealing to that overflowing fountain of generosity—the private contributions of our people. The rigors of winter are approaching, our soldiers are already suffering, and must suffer more if our sympathies are not practical and active. The quartermaster's department is laboring faithfully to provide for them; but owing to speculation and extortion, will fall short. The deficiency must be supplied by the people. We shall have an active winter campaign, and how can our troops, if ragged, cold, and barefoot, contend with the splendidly equipped columns of the enemy?

The articles most needed, and which the State finds it most difficult to supply, are shoes, socks, and blankets, though drawers, shirts, and pants would be gladly received. If every farmer who has hides tanning would agree to spare one pair of shoes, and if every mother in North Carolina would knit one strong pair of either thick cotton or woollen socks for the army, they would be abundantly supplied. A great lot of blankets also might yet be spared from private use, and thousands could be made from the carpets upon our parlor-floors. With good warm houses and cotton bed-clothing, we can certainly get through the winter much better than the soldiers can, with all the blankets we can give them.

The colonels of militia regiments throughout the State are hereby appointed agents for the purchase and collection of all such articles as can be spared by our people, who, through their respective captains, are ordered immediately to canvass every county and visit every citizen in their beats for this purpose. A liberal price will be paid for every thing where the owner feels that he or she is not able to donate it, and active agents will immediately forward them to our suffering regiments. Expenses will be allowed the officers engaged in this duty, and transportation furnished the colonels or their agents to bring the articles to Raleigh.

And now, my countrymen and women, if you have any thing to spare for the soldier, in his name I appeal to you for it. Do not let the speculator have it, though he offer you enormous prices; spurn him from your door, and say to him that our brave defenders have need for it, and shall have it without passing through his greedy fingers. Do not place yourselves among the extortioners—they are the vilest and most cowardly of all our country's enemies; and when this war is ended, and people come to view the matter in its proper light, you will find that the most detested tories are more respected than they. When they tempt you with higher prices than the State offers, just think for a moment of the soldier, and what he is doing for you. Remember, when you sit down by the bright and glowing fire, that the soldier is sitting upon the cold earth; that in the wind which is whistling so fearfully over your roof, only making you feel the more comfortable because it harms you not, he is shivering in darkness on the dangerous outpost, or shuddering through the dreary hours of his watch. Remember that when you come forth in the morning well fed and warmly clad, leading your families toward the spot where the blessed music of the Sabbath bells tells you of the peaceful worship of the God of peace, the soldier is going forth at the same moment, perhaps, half fed, after a night of shivering and suffering, to where the roar of artillery and shout of battle announce that he is to die that your peace and safety may be preserved. Oh! remember these things, generous and patriotic people of North Carolina, and give freely of your perishable goods to those who are giving all that mortal man can give for your safety and your rights.

A. B. VANCE
Raleigh, October 15, 1862

Farewell Address to the Army of the Potomac, by Union General George B. McClellan
(November 7, 1862)

[RR-VI:179]

"I said I would remove him if he let Lee's army get away from him,"
President Lincoln said to General Francis Blair of McClellan, "and I must
do so. He has got the 'slows,' Mr. Blair." After being relieved of his command
for a second time, McClellan offered dignified and encouraging words to his
men. Shut out of military influence on the war, however, McClellan went into
politics and became Lincoln's major challenger for the presidency in 1864.

HEADQUARTERS ARMY OF THE POTOMAC,
Camp near Rectortown, November 7, 1862

Officers and Soldiers of the Army of the Potomac:
An order of the President devolves upon Major-General Burnside the
command of this army. In parting from you I cannot express the love and
gratitude I bear you. As an army you have grown up under my care. In
you I have never found doubt or coldness. The battles you have fought
under my command will proudly live in our nation's history. The glory
you have achieved, our mutual perils and fatigues, the graves of our comrades fallen in battle and by disease, the broken forms of those whom
wounds and sickness have disabled—the strongest associations which can
exist among men—unite us still by an indissoluble tie. We shall ever be
comrades in supporting the constitution of our country and the nationality of its people.

GEO. B. MCCLELLAN,
Major-General U.S.A.

Report on an Inspection of the Union Army's Horses by John S. Rarey to Commander in Chief of the Union Army, Major-General H. W. Halleck
(December 19, 1862)

[RR-VI:275–276]

An estimated 1,000,000 horses died in the Civil War; 3,000 would be killed in action during the three days of battle at Gettysburg.

Washington, D.C., December 19, 1862

GENERAL: Pursuant to your orders, I visited the army of the Potomac, on the twelfth instant, to inspect the horses and mules in the cavalry, artillery and teams of the army.

The movement of troops on that day, and the engagement at Fredericksburgh that followed during the six days that I remained with the army, gave me but little opportunity to see the management of the horse department in detail, though I had the opportunity to see them on duty.

Having gone there very unfavorably impressed with accounts drawn from the dark side of the picture by those taking the rejected and disabled horses of the army as their stand-point, I found these animals in better condition than I had expected. The mule teams, with some exceptions, were in good condition, and I doubt if ever an army under similar circumstances was better provided for in this respect.

The cavalry horses suffer most, and many of them were scarcely fit for service. The duties that they have to perform—excursions that sometimes require from twenty-four to thirty-six hours without food or rest—the heavy weight they have to carry, and the unskillful manner in which they are ridden, makes it almost impossible to be otherwise, except they were treated with the greatest care. The artillery horses suffer much, but are a grade better than the cavalry.

The greatest abuse and destruction of the horses in the army is, I believe, in the want of skill, judgment, and care of the individual man to his individual horse. A more diligent looking after of this detail by the officers in charge would be highly beneficial; the good effect of which has been seen, in some instances, where diligence has been exercised with judgment by officers attending to this important but much neglected duty.

The manner in which food is given, where only a sufficiency is allowed, is highly important, as much is wasted and trampled under foot.

I believe that for cavalry service on a winter campaign, a saddle-blanket to cover the back and loins of the horse, to be left on when the saddle is removed, would be of great service. The Arabs, who live more with the horse than any other people, and who are older in horsemanship than any other nation in the world, never remove the saddle from the horse's back when on a long journey. Their saddles have always blankets attached that cover the back and loins of the horse. They argue that the vital part, when heated by riding, should never be made to feel the effects of cold.

As one who loves the horse, who appreciates his intelligence and keen sensibilities, and can anticipate his wants, I do most deeply deplore the dejection of spirit, suffering and loss of life consequent upon the exigencies of war; but while war rages this law must continue.

In an army of fifty thousand horses, subjected to the service and exposure of the army, there must necessarily be a large percentage of disabled and diseased horses constantly accumulating. It is ever so with the soldiers of the army, who are gifted with intelligence and reason, and whose first law of nature is self-preservation, and for the comfort and welfare of whom the greatest energies of the people and the officers of the army are exerted.

How can it be otherwise with the horse? He is not invincible to exposure, which he can scarcely bear as well as man, and with whom he must suffer alike, if not more, in time of war.

I am happy to see the extensive hospitals lately erected in this city to restore disabled horses. I believe they are conducted on the best and most economical principle, and will, I have no doubt, be the means of restoring thousands of horses to the army, that will be better on their second service than they were on their first.

Hoping that the Government will, as an act of humanity, as well as economy, use every effort in its power for the protection of this noble animal, I remain, General, very truly, your obedient servant,

JOHN S. RAREY

To MAJOR-GENERAL HALLECK,
    Commander-in-Chief United States Army, Washington, D.C.

Final Emancipation Proclamation by President Lincoln

(Jan. 1, 1863)

[RR-VI:207–208]

On January 12, Confederate President Jefferson Davis responded to his rival president's proclamation in a message to his congress: "The people of this Confederacy . . . cannot fail to receive this proclamation as the fullest vindication of their own sagacity in foreseeing the uses to which the dominant party in the United States intended from the beginning to apply their power; nor can they cease to remember with devout thankfulness that it is to their own vigilance in resisting the first stealthy progress of approaching despotism that they owe their escape from consequences now apparent to the most skeptical."

William W. Brown, an author and former slave, wrote at the time, "'What shall be done with the slaves if they are freed?'You had better ask, 'What shall we do with the slaveholders if the slaves are freed?' The slave has shown himself better fitted to take care of himself than the slaveholder."

While the Emancipation Proclamation freed the slaves in Confederate states and areas, it did not free them elsewhere. That comprehensiveness would have to wait until the Thirteenth Amendment to the Constitution, not ratified until the end of 1865. (See page 201, below.)

THE EMANCIPATION PROCLAMATION BY THE PRESIDENT OF THE UNITED STATES OF AMERICA

WHEREAS, on the twenty-second day of September, in the year of our Lord one thousand eight hundred and sixty-two, a proclamation was issued by the President of the United States containing among other things the following, to wit:

"That on the first day of January, in the year of our Lord one thousand eight hundred and sixty-three, all persons held as slaves within any State, or designated part of a State, the people whereof shall then be in rebellion against the United States, shall be then, thenceforth and forever free; and the Executive Government of the United States, including the military and naval authorities thereof, will recognize and maintain the freedom of such persons, and will do no act or acts to repress such persons, or any of them, in any efforts they may make for their actual freedom.

"That the Executive will, on the first day of January aforesaid, by proclamation, designate the States and parts of States, if any, in which the people therein respectively shall then be in rebellion against the United States, and the fact that any State, or the people thereof, shall on that day be in good faith represented in the Congress of the United States by members chosen thereto, at elections wherein a majority of the qualified voters of such State, shall have participated, shall, in the absence of strong countervailing testimony, be deemed conclusive evidence that such State and the people thereof are not then in rebellion against the United States."

Now, therefore, I, Abraham Lincoln, President of the United States, by virtue of the power in me vested as Commander-in-chief of the Army and Navy of the United States in time of actual armed rebellion against the authority and Government of the United States, and as a fit and necessary war measure for suppressing said rebellion, do, on this first day of January, in the year of our Lord one thousand eight hundred and sixty-three, and in accordance with my purpose so to do, publicly proclaimed for the full period of one hundred days from the day of the first above-mentioned order and designate, as the States and parts of States wherein the people thereof respectively are this day in rebellion against the United States, the following, to wit: Arkansas, Texas, Louisiana, except the parishes of St. Bernard, Plaquemines, Jefferson, St. John, St. Charles, St. James, Ascension, Assumption, Terre Bonne, Lafourche, St. Mary, St. Martin, and Orleans, including the City of New Orleans. Mississippi, Alabama, Florida, Georgia, South-Carolina, North-Carolina, and Virginia, except the forty-eight counties designated as West Virginia, and also the counties of Berkeley, Accomac, Northampton, Elizabeth City, York, Princess Ann, and Norfolk, including the cities of Norfolk and Portsmouth, and which excepted parts are, for the present, left precisely as if this proclamation were not issued.

And by virtue of the power and for the purpose aforesaid, I do order and declare that all persons held as slaves within said designated States and parts of States are, and henceforward shall be free; and that the Executive Government of the United States, including the Military and Naval authorities thereof, will recognize and maintain the freedom of said persons.

And I hereby enjoin upon the people so declared to be free, to abstain from all violence, unless in necessary self-defence, and I recommend to them that in all cases, when allowed, they labor faithfully for reasonable wages.

And I further declare and make known that such persons of suitable condition will be received into the armed service of the United States to garrison forts, positions, stations, and other places, and to man vessels of all sorts in said service.

And upon this act, sincerely believed to be an act of justice, warranted by the Constitution, upon military necessity, I invoke the considerate judgment of mankind and the gracious favor of Almighty God.

In witness whereof, I have hereunto set my hand and caused the seal of the United States to be affixed.

[L. S.]   Done at the City of Washington, this first day of January, in the year of our Lord one thousand eight hundred and sixty-three, and of the Independence of the United States of America the eighty-seventh.

ABRAHAM LINCOLN

BY THE PRESIDENT—WILLIAM H. SEWARD,
Secretary of State

Report on the *Alabama's* Destruction of the U.S.S. *Hatteras,* by Confederate Captain Raphael Semmes
(January 11, 1863)

[RR–X: 225–226]

"It was a grand, though fearful sight, to see the guns belching forth, in the darkness of the night, sheets of living flame, the deadly missiles striking the enemy with a force that we could feel," recalled a Confederate officer on the Alabama. *The* Alabama, *built in England, in 1862, and transferred in late August to a Confederate crew in the Azores, became, as intended, the bane of United States shipping. "We then commenced our cruise of twenty-two months, during which she more successfully accomplished the work for which she was constructed than any single ship of any nation in any age," recalled the* Alabama's *Executive Officer, Lieutenant John Macintosh Kell. The Union had no idea such a Confederate ship was in the Gulf.*

C. S. STEAMER *Alabama,* BAHIA,
MAY 17, 1863

I ARRIVED at Galveston (under sail) on the eleventh of January, and just before nightfall made the enemy's fleet lying off the bar, consisting of five ships of war. One of the steamers was soon after perceived to get under way, and steer in our direction. I ordered steam to be got up, but set sail on the ship as a decoy, that I might entice the enemy's ship sufficiently far from the fleet to offer her battle. I wore ship and stood away from the bar, permitting the enemy to approach me by slow degrees. When the enemy had approached sufficiently near, I took in all sail, and wearing short around, ran up within hail. It was now dark, it being about seven o'clock.

The enemy hailed, "What ship is that?" We responded, "Her Majesty's steamer *Petrel.*" The reply was, "I will send a boat on board." We now hailed in turn, to know who the enemy was, and when we had received the reply that he was the "United States steamer *Hatteras,*" we again hailed him, and informed him that we were the Confederate steamer *Alabama*; and at the same time I directed the First Lieutenant to open fire upon him. Our fire was promptly returned, and a brisk action ensued, which lasted, however, only thirteen minutes, as at the end of that time the enemy fired off gun and showed a light; and upon being hailed by us to know if he had surrendered, he replied that he had, and that he was in a sinking condition. I immediately despatched boats to his assistance, and had just time to remove the crew when the ship went down.

The casualties were slight on both sides, although the action was fought at a distance of from one hundred and fifty to four hundred yards. Our shot all told on his hull about the water line, and hence the small number of killed and wounded on the part of the enemy—two of the former and three of the latter. We had none killed and only one wounded. The *Hatteras* mounted eight guns, and had a crew of eighteen officers and one hundred and eight men. The *Alabama* also mounted eight guns, (with a small captured piece, a twenty-four pounder, too light to be of any service,) and had a crew of one hundred and ten men, exclusive of officers. Four of the *Hatteras'* guns were thirty-two pounders—the same calibre as our broadside guns, but our pivot guns were heavier than hers, this being the only disparity between the two ships.

We received a few shot holes from the enemy, doing no material damage. The enemy's steamer steamed out in pursuit of us soon after the action commenced, but missed us in the darkness of the night. Being embarrassed with a large number of prisoners, I steamed directly for Jamaica, where I arrived on the twentieth of January. Here I landed my prisoners, repaired damages, coaled ship, and on the twenty-fifth of January I proceeded to sea again. On the twenty-eighth of January I touched at the city of St. Domingo, in the island of the same name, and landed the crews of two of the enemy's ships which I had burned. I sailed again on the same day, and made my way to ——, thence to the island of ——, and thence to this place, where I arrived yesterday—burning, bonding, and destroying enemy's ships, as per list enclosed. I have the honor to be,

Very respectfully, your obedient servant,

R. SEMMES,
Commander

HON. S. R. MALLORY,
    Secretary of the Navy

Vicksburg Siege Diary of a Confederate Soldier, John W. Sattenwhite
(May 18–July 4, 1863)

[RR-VII:170–173]

Vicksburg, Mississippi, on the bluffs of the Mississippi River, was a target of the Union from the spring of 1862, when Admiral Farragut demanded its surrender, until its capitulation on July 4, 1863. Major-General U.S. Grant, the head of the Army of the Tennessee from the fall of 1862, tried many unsuccessful approaches before hitting on a combined operation with Admiral Porter's ships and various diversionary tactics that allowed Grant's forces to land on the eastern side of the Mississippi below Vicksburg on April 30, 1863. Many of the citizens of Vicksburg who remained in the fortified town lived in caves "honeycombed" into the hillsides. John W. Sattenwhite served with Company A of the Sixth Missouri Volunteers.

MAY 18, 1863.—This beautiful morning finds us among the hills of Vicksburgh surrounded by breastworks. About six o'clock this evening we took our position in the outside intrenchments to meet the enemy. We skirmished with them until dark. During the night we moved our position and fell back to the next, second line of works.

May 19.—This morning the fight commenced with vigor, heavy fighting all day. The enemy attempted to charge, but were repulsed with heavy loss; we captured five stands of colors. We are held in reserve, moving from one position to another. We lay all night on the extreme left. Went to the support of some Tennessee troops. We had several wounded to-day.

May 20.—Our regiment moved this morning and took position as reserve on the left of the centre. The enemy attempted to turn our right, but were gallantly repulsed by our boys.

May 21.—The firing commenced this morning at daylight. Heavy firing all day. Several wounded in our regiment to-day. A heavy shower of rain fell this evening.

May 22.—About twelve o'clock to-day the heaviest firing of artillery and musketry ever heard by our troops; the earth trembled and the air was filled with missiles of death. The enemy were repulsed. The firing continued all day. We changed our position. We were called upon to go to the assistance of the Louisiana troops, which we did under a heavy fire. We took our position to the left of Fort Beauregard.

May 23.—The firing was confined principally to heavy skirmishing. They have gained some very advantageous positions for artillery. Our confidence is still growing stronger each hour. General Green's brigade crossed the works last night, charged the advance of the enemy, captured some prisoners and arms, together with a great many ditching-tools. (Gallant conduct.)

May 24.—Skirmishing very heavy. The enemy made no attempt to charge, but were discovered to be undermining our works for the purpose of blowing them up. They were driven off, however, by hand-grenades thrown by our boys. They were very destructive.

May 25.—Heavy skirmishing all day with artillery and small arms continued until about four o'clock, when the enemy sent in a flag of truce, asking for permission to bury their dead. Hostilities ceased for the night. The mortar-boats were also engaged in shelling the city and camps. We hear that Johnston has defeated General McClernand's Federal command. Small loss on our lines to-day.

May 26.—The enemy made no attempt to charge our works. Firing heavy from the line of skirmishing. Our brigade was moved this evening tot he extreme right fronting the river, where several mortars are engaged in shelling. As we came through the city the shells flew thick and fast. One hundred and twelve prisoners, captured by our forces, came in to-day. No firing in front of us. Day very warm. We have no shelter from the sun. We have been on half-rations of coarse corn-bread and poor beef for ten days.

May 27.—This morning a portion of our brigade was ordered into the ditches on the right fronting the river; about twelve o'clock the lower fleet came up and opened fire upon us without any injury. The gunboat *Cincinnati,* from the upper fleet, attempted to run by our batteries, but failed, and was sent to the bottom. Afterward the lower fleet moved back down the river; we were then ordered out of the ditches. About four o'clock we took up the line of march, moved to the centre, and took our position in the ditches at Fort Beauregard, to the left of the Jackson road, where we were exposed to a very heavy artillery fire, the first that we have been in in the ditches.

May 28.—The enemy has made no attempt to charge our works, but we are under a heavy fire of artillery, and a strong line of skirmishers still lying in the ditches. One man mortally wounded in our regiment. The mortar-boats have been very diligent to-day.

May 29.—The enemy opened the whole line of artillery at half-past seven o'clock; continued one and a half hours with great vigor, after which every thing was quiet until half-past five in the evening, when the artillery again opened, and continued their fire for one hour. The entire earth seemed to yield to their thundering. You might have seen rebels hugging the ground as close as moles. The fleet was also engaged in front of the city. All quiet now, except an occasional Minie ball, which makes not a very pleasant noise.

May 30.—This morning our company was ordered to take position in the front ditches, immediately in range of eight pieces of artillery, which opened upon us; the firing continued until near dark, the fiercest I ever heard. Shell flew in every direction, exploding immediately over the ditch to the right and left, tearing away the banks in many places, and completely covering us with dust. We lost four killed and three wounded in our regiment. None of our company hurt, fortunately.

May 31.—This morning, about three o'clock, the enemy commenced a very heavy cannonading; the heavens were perfectly checkered with the fuses in the shells; it lasted about one hour and a half. The remainder of the day was unusually quiet. We hear that General Johnston is at Jackson with a heavy force. Two men killed in our regiment to-day.

Monday, June 1.—Early in the day firing light; about half-past six in the evening eight or ten heavy guns opened upon us, which shook the earth and were very frightful; but our brave boys never flinched. Every man was at his post ready for any emergency. Three killed and two wounded in our regiment. We are now eating bean-bread, and half-rations at that. The mortar-boats are engaged in shelling the city.

June 2.—The firing in the early part of the day was moderate; at half-past six o'clock in the evening a most terrific bombardment commenced. Not less than fifteen pieces of artillery were playing upon us. Our regiment was very fortunate—not a man hurt. Rebels hugged the ground very close. The mortar-boats were busy the whole time shelling the city. Half-rations of pea-bread and poor beef constitute our living— hard fare. Our regiment was relieved to-night by the Thirty-eighth Mississippi; we moved to the right of the Jackson road; kept as reserve; good night's rest.

June 3.—We are laying to the right of the Jackson road. Heavy firing all day. We lost to-day Lieut. Yancey, of company K. Our rations are changed; we now get one half rations bread, rice and corn-meal mixed. We hear again that Johnston is advancing in force. It's our only hope.

June 4.—The firing is more moderate to-day. The fleet has kept up a pretty continued fire all day; the firing upon the ditches has been confined to skirmishers. The loss of our brigade since the eighteenth of May in killed and wounded is two hundred and seventy-five. We are still in reserve.

June 5.—The weather is very warm. The bombardment with artillery is heavy; both land and water-batteries are engaged; the mortar-boats are reported to have been moved from the front of the city. Rumor says that Price occupies Helena, but not credited.

June 6.—Day warm; firing moderate all day; the enemy can be seen moving to the left. We hear that Loring engaged them at Black River.

June 7.—Very warm; we hear the engagement of the upper fleet; supposed to be at Milliken's Bend. The mortar-boats are at work; the artillery kept up a fire the entire night.

June 8.—The mortar-boats have been engaged all day; the land firing was unusually moderate; occasionally a shell would make us hunt our holes. Secesh lay very close to the ground.

June 9.—The firing heavier than usual. The *grapevine* brings us the news that two divisions of Bragg's army have arrived at Memphis. The mortar-boats were very quiet during the day, but kept up a heavy fire during the entire night.

Appendix—The report of the orderly sergeant of this company (company A, Sixth Missouri) shows a loss of sixty-eight men killed, wounded, and missing; six commissioned officers killed and wounded.

June 10.—Heavy rain fell to-day; it had no effect upon the firing; it continued heavy. A wetter, dirtier, muddier lot of rebels were never seen; but we kept our powder dry. Our beef gave out to-day. We are now drawing one quarter of a pound of bacon to the man.

June 11.—The morning cloudy, but cleared about noon. About four o'clock we were ordered to arms; we moved up about six hundred yards, and took our position in rear of the Twenty-seventh Louisiana regiment, to the right of the Jackson road, where we laid under a heavy fire of artillery all night; it was though the enemy were preparing to make an assault at that point.

June 12.—We occupied the position we took on yesterday evening until nine o'clock this morning, when all fear subsided, and we returned to our old position. Day pleasant. About four o'clock this evening our mortar opened, which has just been put into position; it attracted the entire line of the enemy's guns; they all opened upon her, and the firing was, for about two hours, very heavy.

June 13.—The morning beautiful. I have just finished my breakfast of half rations coarse cornbread and a slice of raw bacon, with a cup of bean coffee. Regiment moved this morning, and relieved Green's brigade in the ditches. No loss in regiment to-day.

June 14.—Day very warm; the firing to-day heavier than usual, both front and rear. We hear that Johnston is crossing Black River, and Loring is at Hawkins's Ferry. Our regiment in the ditches.

June 15.—Day pleasant; slight fall of rain in the morning; the firing very heavy. Sergeant Ed. Payne of our company had two fingers shot off the right hand. One man killed, five wounded in our regiment. Three of our companies were compelled to leave the ditches, in consequence of an enfilading fire. I visited the hospitals in town to-day. Had a very interesting chit-chat with the Yankees to-night.

June 16.—Our regiment remained in the ditches until dark, when General Green relived us. The firing to-day was very heavy; loss to-day, one killed. We lay in the hollow in the rear of the ditches we had just left, all night.

June 17.—We moved this morning, and took our position in the hollow as reserves, in rear of the Third Louisiana, and to the left of the Jackson road, to reënforce, if necessary, what is called Fort Beauregard, which point the enemy are undermining. We made ourselves safe by digging holes in the ground for protection. We hear that three divisions of the Federal army have been defeated at McMinnville. The day pleasant.

June 18.—Firing very heavily all day. We lost three men wounded, S. N. Petcher, of our company, among them. Our rations changed: one quarter of a pound of flour, one quarter of a pound of bacon to the man, quite light. No news from the rear.

June 19.—C. R. Marion, of our company, was killed this morning, while sharp-shooting. A Minie ball penetrated his right eye; came out at the top of the head. A braver man never fell. The firing was heavy all day. We still hear of Johnston's advance. Very still to-night; an occasional shot is all that is heard.

June 20.—The firing commenced this morning with great vigor, continued heavy for eight hours, when it was reduced to the scale of moderation. About four o'clock we were called into line, moved up to the parapet; a false alarm; we returned to our holes after about two hours, which we spent in waiting for Yanks, but they failed to come. Captain Norwood slightly wounded; Dugan killed in camp at the time.

June 21.—The firing more moderate than usual. It is reported that a great many of the enemy's guns have been removed. No loss in our regiment to-day.

June 22.—Firing moderate; weather fine. James Dye went to hospital sick; three wounded in the regiment. We continue to get news of Johnston's approach.

June 23.—Firing not heavy, but very steady. A very refreshing rain fell during the night. Two wounded in regiment. The firing was very heavy on the right during the night. Captain Sawe wounded to-day in camp. The mortar-boats have been very quiet for several days.

June 24.—Firing heavy, front and rear. We hear Lee has gained another victory in Virginia, and threatens Maryland and Pennsylvania. The enemy are advancing rapidly on our works; we are looking for a blow-up every hour.

June 25.—And one mingled with many distressing events. All was quiet until about four o'clock P.M., when the train which was prepared by the enemy to blow up our works was fired. The explosion was terrific. They then attempted to mount our works, but were kept back. The firing was confined mostly to small arms, which was very heavy. Continued all night; we were up with arms in hand and without sleep all night. Colonel Erwin killed; also Lieutenant W. S. Lipscomb, Viers, J. M. Good, Alf. Eaton, D. S. Lipscomb, and George N. Ferrel, wounded. Jack Satterwhite, slightly. The hand-grenades thrown by the enemy were very destructive. Twenty-four killed and wounded in our regiment.

June 26.—The firing continued heavy all day; the enemy have made no further attempt to mount our works; the throwing of hand-grenades was indulged in by both parties. The Fifth Missouri came to our assistance last night. Day very warm; the enemy can be seen working in front of us; we have repaired that portion of the works blown up by the enemy; all right again. The fleet engaged our batteries to-day, with what effect we have not learned; firing very heavy. We had a good night's rest.

June 27.—Firing moderate to-day. We were relieved at twelve o'clock, for six hours only, by the Fifth Missouri; at six o'clock in the evening we returned to the ditches; were relieved at twelve o'clock at night. Elisha Viers, of our company, died to-day, from wounds received on the twenty-fifth. Lee's victory confirmed. Five killed and three wounded in regiment to-day. David Sigman, of our company, killed; James Parker wounded.

June 28.—Returned to the ditches; relieved by the Fifth Missouri; forty-two killed and wounded since the twenty-fifth; no loss to-day; weather pleasant; no news from the outside. The enemy are working vigorously; we throw a great many hand-grenades among them.

June 29.—Firing very moderate; we are digging to meet the under-mining foe. The Second, Fifth, and Sixth Missouri are guarding the threatened point. We relieve each other every six hours. Weather pleasant; no loss to-day.

June 30.—Firing moderate; we threw among them to-day, a keg containing one hundred pounds of powder, with a fuse in it—we are not apprised of the damage it done. Our muster-rolls were ordered to be made out to-day; no loss.

July 1.—This day is long to be remembered. The firing in the morning was light. Our regiment went into the ditches at twelve o'clock;

about three o'clock the mine which had been prepared by the enemy under our works was fired; great was the explosion. Lieutenants Crenshaw and Roseberry were buried alive, together with several others. Lieutenant Burr, Geo. Ferrell, Ed. Eaton, and Dunlap of our company wounded. Lieutenant Brather of company B lost his leg. Day very warm. The enemy made no attempt to charge.

July 2.—Firing moderate. The troops are becoming very much disheartened. All seem to be of the opinion that we will be compelled to surrender.

July 3.—This evening about three o'clock, our authorities sent out a flag of truce, to make arrangements to surrender the place. The firing ceased—every thing as still as death. We all knew that the fatal hour had arrived; the preliminaries were not agreed upon, and the flag returned, firing commencing again.

July 4.—To-day the place and its contents was surrendered to the Federal authority—a sore stroke to the Confederacy. The enemy came into town in small numbers, about twelve o'clock. They put their fireworks into operation after dark, by the way of celebrating the Fourth, but were very civil, and treated us with a great deal of kindness. The army will all be paroled and move out. Officers will retain and carry out their side-arms.

Official Correspondence Ending the Siege of Vicksburg between Union General U.S. Grant and Confederate Lieutenant-General J.C. Pemberton
(July 3–4, 1863)

[RR-VII:151–152]

Parole Form for the Confederate Officers and Soldiers of Vicksburg
(July 1863)

[RR-VII:163]

Confederate President Jefferson Davis considered Vicksburg "the nailhead that held the South's two halves together." With the Union in control now of the Mississippi and the Confederacy's simultaneous loss at Gettysburg, many in the North and South believed that the outcome of the war was inevitable.

OFFICIAL CORRESPONDENCE

HEADQUARTERS, VICKSBURGH,
July 3, 1863

Major-Gen. Grant, Commanding U. S. Forces:

GENERAL: I have the honor to propose to you an armistice for — hours, with a view to arranging terms for the capitulation of Vicksburgh. To this end, if agreeable to you, I will appoint three commissioners to meet a like number to be named by yourself at such place and hour to-day as you may find convenient. I make this proposition to save the further effusion of blood, which must otherwise be shed to a frightful extent, feeling myself fully able to maintain my position for a yet indefinite period. This communication will be handed you under a flag of truce by Major-General James Bowen.

Very respectfully, your obedient servant,

J. C. PEMBERTON

To this General Grant replied as follows:

HEADQUARTERS, DEPARTMENT OF TENNESSEE,
In the Field, near Vicksburgh, July 3, 1863

Lieut.-General J. C. Pemberton, Commanding "Confederate" Forces, etc.:

GENERAL: Your note of this date, just received, proposes an armistice of several hours, for the purpose of arranging terms of capitulation through commissioners to be appointed, etc. The effusion of blood you propose stopping by this course, can be ended at any time you may choose, by an unconditional surrender of the city and garrison. Men who have shown so much endurance and courage as those now in Vicksburgh, will always challenge the respect of an adversary, and I can assure you, will be treated with all the respect due them as prisoners of war. I do not favor the proposition of appointing commissioners to arrange terms of capitulation, because I have no other terms than those indicated above.

I am, General, very respectfully,
Your obedient servant,

U. S. GRANT,
Major-General

HEADQUARTERS, DEPARTMENT OF TENNESSEE,
Near Vicksburgh, July 3, 1863

Lieut.-General J. C. Pemberton, Commanding Confederate Forces, Vicksburgh, Miss.:

GENERAL: In conformity with the agreement of this afternoon, I will submit the following propositions for the surrender of the city of Vicksburgh, public stores, etc. On your accepting the terms proposed, I will march in one division as a guard, and take possession at eight A.M. to-morrow. As soon as paroles can be made out and signed by the officers and men, you will be allowed to march out of our lines, the officers taking with them their regimental clothing, and staff, field and cavalry officers one horse each. The rank and file will be allowed all their clothing, but no other property. If these conditions are accepted, any amount of rations you may deem necessary can be taken from the stores you now have, and also the necessary cooking utensils for preparing them, and thirty wagons also, counting two two-horse or mule teams as one. You will be allowed to transport such articles as cannot be carried along. The same conditions will be allowed to all sick and wounded officers and privates, as fast as they become able to travel. The paroles for these latter must be signed, however, whilst officers are present authorized to sign the roll of prisoners.

I am, General, very respectfully,
Your obedient servant,

U. S. GRANT,
Major-General

HEADQUARTERS, VICKSBURGH,
July 3, 1863

Major-Gen. Grant, Commanding U. S. Forces:

GENERAL: I have the honor to acknowledge the receipt of your communication of this date, proposing terms for the surrender of this garrison and post. In the main your items are accepted; but in justice both to the honor and spirit of my troops, manifested in the defence of Vicksburgh, I have the honor to submit the following amendments, which, if acceded to by you, will perfect the agreement between us at ten o'clock to-morrow. I propose to evacuate the works in and around Vicksburgh, and to surrender the city and garrison under my command, by marching out with my colors and arms and stacking them in front of my present lines, after which you will take possession; officers to retain their side-arms and personal property, and the rights and property of citizens to be respected.

I am, General, yours, very respectfully,

J. C. PEMBERTON,
Lieutenant-General

To this General Grant immediately replied as follows:

HEADQUARTERS DEPARTMENT OF TENNESSEE,
Before Vicksburgh, July 4, 1863

Lieut.-General Pemberton, Commanding Forces in Vicksburgh:

GENERAL: I have the honor to acknowledge your communication of the third of July. The amendments proposed by you cannot be acceded to in full. It will be necessary to furnish every officer and man with a parole signed by himself, which, with the completion of the rolls of prisoners, will necessarily take some time. Again, I can make no stipulation with regard to the treatment of citizens and their private property. While I do not propose to cause any of them any undue annoyance or loss, I cannot consent to leave myself under restraint by stipulations. The property which officers can be allowed to take with them will be as stated in the proposition of last evening—that is, that officers will be allowed their private baggage and side-arms, and mounted officers one horse each. If you mean by your proposition for each brigade to march to the front of the lines now occupied by it, and stack their arms at ten o'clock A.M., and then return to inside and remain as prisoners until properly paroled, I will make no objections to it. Should no modification be made of your acceptance of my terms by nine o'clock A.M., I shall regard them as having been rejected, and act accordingly. Should these terms be accepted, white flags shall be displayed along your lines to prevent such of my troops as may not have been notified from firing upon your men.

I am, General, very respectfully,

Your obedient servant,

U. S. GRANT,
Major-General U. S. A.

HEADQUARTERS, VICKSBURGH,
July 4, 1863

Major-General U. S. Grant, Commanding U. S. Forces:

GENERAL: I have the honor to acknowledge the receipt of your communication of this date, and in reply to say that the terms proposed by you are accepted.

Very respectfully, your obedient servant,

J. C. PEMBERTON,
Lieutenant-General

The following is the form of parole administered to the prisoners:

VICKSBURGH, MISSISSIPPI,
July —, 1863

To All Whom it May Concern, Know Ye That: I, A—— B——, of company —, regiment —— volunteers, C. S. A., being a prisoner of war in the hands of the United States forces, in virtue of the capitulation of the city of Vicksburgh and its garrison, by Lieutenant-General John C. Pemberton, C. S. A., commanding, on the fourth day of July, 1863, do, in pursuance of the terms of said capitulation, give this my solemn parole under oath:

That I will not take up arms again against the United States, nor serve in any military, police, or constabulary force in any fort, garrison, or field-work held by the confederate States of America, against the United States of America; nor as guard of prisons, depots, or stores, nor discharge any duty usually performed by soldiers against the United States of America, until duly exchanged by the proper authorities.

Sworn to and subscribed before me, at Vicksburgh, on the — day of July, 1863.

———————— and Paroling Officer

Address to the Soldiers of the Army of Northern Virginia on the Advance into Pennsylvania by Confederate General R. E. Lee

(June 27, 1863)

[RR–VII:323]

While U.S. Grant was taking Vicksburg, the most famous battle of the war was occurring the first three days of July near the town of Gettysburg in southern Pennsylvania. On advancing into Pennsylvania, Confederate General Robert E. Lee (whose right-hand man Stonewall Jackson had died after being shot at Chancellorsville) did not expect to conquer the North but to win a dramatic victory on Union ground that would convince the northern public that the war would not be worthwhile to continue, and, perhaps, thereby allow the Confederacy to gain recognition as an independent nation. There was also hope that the invasion of Pennsylvania, with Washington, D.C., not far east, would draw northward some of the overwhelming Union forces around Vicksburg and Chattanooga.

HEADQUARTERS ARMY OF NORTHERN VIRGINIA,
Chambersburgh, Pa., June 27

THE Commanding General has observed with marked satisfaction the conduct of the troops on the march, and confidently anticipates results commensurate with the high spirit they have manifested. No troops could have displayed greater fortitude or better performed the arduous marches of the past ten days. Their conduct in other respects has, with few exceptions, been in keeping with their character as soldiers, and entitles them to approbation and praise.

There have, however, been instances of forgetfulness on the part of some that they have in keeping the yet unsullied reputation of the army, and that the duties exacted of us by civilization and Christianity are not less obligatory in the country of the enemy than in our own. The

Commanding General considers that no greater disgrace could befall the army, and through it our whole people, than the perpetration of the barbarous outrages upon the innocent and defenceless, and the wanton destruction of private property, that have marked the course of the enemy in our own country. Such proceedings not only disgrace the perpetrators and all connected with them, but are subversive of the discipline and efficiency of the army, and destructive of the ends of our present movement. It must be remembered that we make war only upon armed men, and that we cannot take vengeance for the wrongs our people have suffered without lowering ourselves in the eyes of all whose abhorrence has been excited by the atrocities of our enemy, and offending against Him to whom vengeance belongeth, without whose favor and support our efforts must all prove in vain.

The Commanding General therefore earnestly exhorts the troops to abstain with most scrupulous care from unnecessary or wanton injury to private property; and he enjoins upon all officers to arrest and bring to summary punishment all who shall in any way offend against the orders on this subject.

R. E. LEE,
General

Address on Taking Command of the Army of the Potomac by Union General George Meade (General Order No. 66)
(June 28, 1863)

[RR–VII:135]

President Lincoln had lost confidence in Major-General Joseph Hooker as commander of the Army of the Potomac. Earlier in the month, as Lee's army threateningly advanced after Chancellorsville, Lincoln wrote to Hooker: "If the head of Lee's army is at Martinsburg, and the tail of it on the plank road between Fredericksburg and Chancellorsville, the animal must be very slim somewhere. Could you not break it now?" Hooker could not, and so the president replaced him with Major-General George G. Meade (1815–1872). Robert E. Lee, who knew Meade from before the war, remarked prophetically, "General Meade will commit no blunder on my front, and if I make one he will make haste to take advantage of it."

June 28, 1863

By direction of the President of the United States, I hereby assume command of the army of the Potomac. As a soldier, in obeying this order, an order totally unexpected and unsolicited, I have no promises or pledges to make. The country looks to this army to relieve it from the devastation and disgrace of a hostile invasion. Whatever fatigues and sacrifices we may be called upon to undergo, let us have in view constantly the magnitude of the interests involved, and let each man determine to do his duty, leaving to an all-controlling Providence the decision of the contest. It is with just diffidence that I relieve in the command of this army an eminent and accomplished soldier, whose name must ever appear conspicuous in the history of its achievements; but I rely upon the hearty support of my companions in arms to assist me in the discharge of the duties of the important trust which has been confided to me.

GEORGE G. MEADE,
Major-General Commanding

Account of the Battle of Gettysburg by Union Sergeant John W. Plummer of Company D, First Minnesota
(July 1–4, 1863)

[RR–X:178–181]

There are thousands of accounts of the Battle of Gettysburg in letters, diaries, and memoirs by participants on both sides. This, written in its immediate aftermath, as a letter to Plummer's brother, is particularly fine. The bloodiest battle of the Civil War saw more than 50,000 casualties, with nearly 7,000 killed.

One of the Confederates' most costly maneuvers was Pickett's Charge, for which Robert E. Lee took full blame, and about which General George Pickett exclaimed in a letter to his fiancée, "Well, it is all over now. The awful rain of shot and shell was a sob—a gasp. I can still hear them cheering as I gave the order, 'Forward!' The thrill of their joyous voices as they called out, 'We'll follow you, Marse George, we'll follow you!' Oh, how faithfully they followed me on—on—to their death, and I led them on— on—on—Oh, God!"

After the three days of battle, Lee commanded a retreat, and, with Meade refusing or unable to pursue him, the Army of Northern Virginia, escaped. (See below, page 140, for Lee's regrets over his command at Gettysburg.) President Lincoln, frustrated again by the lack of persistence of his leading general, remarked to his secretary, "We had them in our grasp. We had only to stretch forth our hands and they were ours. And nothing I could say or do could make the army move."

JOHN W. PLUMMER'S ACCOUNT

ON the first of July, 1863, we started from Uniontown, Md., early in the morning, for Pennsylvania, via Tenalytown. We arrived after very slow marching at Tenalytown about noon, which is about seven miles from W——n, and thirteen from Gettysburg, and halted in a woods, cooked our dinners, and were given to understand that we were to remain dur-

ing the rest of the day at least. So on the thought of that, one of my comrades and I went off and found a creek, and washed our shirts and socks,
having had no opportunity of performing this needful operation of late;
but we had scarcely got back when the order came to march, and we had
the alternative of carrying our wet shirts or throwing them away, and
trust to Providence to get some more; but we decided to carry them,
heavy though they were. Hot was the day, and tired were we, with the
prospect of a long and rapid march before we halted again. We spread
them out on our knapsacks, so that in travelling along they were drying
and continually lessening our load. When about three miles from
Tenalytown, we began to hear the first rumors and reports we had heard
of a battle then progressing at Gettysburg, and also plainly see the two
lines of smoke of the two contending parties' fire. That accounted for
our sudden orders to march. Rumors came thicker as we neared the
field, from citizens, cavalrymen, and orderlies; but, as usual on such occasions, so contradictory we could make nothing definite or reliable out of
them, though the weight of them seemed to satisfy us that at the close of
the battle our forces were worsted, and had to fall back some distance,
though we did not get near enough to the field that night to see many
wounded men or skedaddlers, if there were many of the latter class.

We halted about three miles from Gettysburg about nine o'clock that
night, and had orders to build breastworks of the fence rails; but as we
were pretty tired, and couldn't really see the necessity of work that far
from the field, we boys did not build any, but lay down to sleep, which,
as it afterwards proved, was just as well, as no fighting was done there.
The country, after we crossed the Pennsylvania line, seemed very much
like some of the poorer parts of Virginia, and the people like the
Virginians, for they seemed perfectly indifferent to our army passing
through, and the great conflict which was raging and still to rage so near
their homes, and on the result of which depended the fate of the whole
country. One group in particular, we saw, were, we believed, truly loyal,
as one of them, a very intelligent looking woman, said to us while passing, with *much feeling, "It gives us so much pleasure to see our good Union soldiers coming!"* Many a fervent "God bless you!" and "Good for you!"
were uttered by the tired and weary soldiers, and many, too, forgot their
weariness and their loads, feeling that for such they could fight and
endure any hardship without grumbling. One of our boys, poor fellow!
he is now dead, (Russ Allen,) said, "Boys, who wouldn't fight for such as
these?" Just that little expression, and the way it was expressed, seemed
to put new life into all of us, and we resolved, if possible, to give them
yet more pleasure by driving the invaders from their soil.

The next morning we were called up about daylight, and before we had time to get coffee, had to march for the battle-field, where we arrived soon. Troops were moving around in every direction, getting in position for the coming battle. Our corps was marched to the centre; but before being placed in position on the line we were to occupy, we were closed in column to hear an order and an appeal to the troops by General Gibbons, our division commander. It was good, and we all felt better after hearing it. It told of the great issue at stake in the coming contest— appealing to all to do their duty and win the gratitude and esteem of our friends and of the nation, and ordered that every one found skulking away in time of action should suffer death. I have always thought it would do good to make these addresses to troops before going into action, to rouse their enthusiasm and make them fight much better. Napoleon used to, and the Southerners do; but it is practised but little in our army. One thing our armies lack is enthusiasm; and no efforts are made to create it, when, in many cases, it would accomplish more than real bravery or bull-dog courage; so I think, at least. Well, our corps and batteries got into position about nine o'clock, and occasionally a shot was fired from our guns, and some sharp skirmishing was carried on in front of our lines. Our brigade was not in front; so we went to making coffee and cooking, and filling up the inner man, preparatory to the coming struggle.

About two o'clock the rebels opened on us from some of their bat- teries, and the way the ambulances, hospital men, stragglers, and darkies did skedaddle for the rear, was amusing to those old fellows who had got used, somewhat, to such things as shells. Several men of the brigade were wounded, and one shell killed a sergeant of Company I, named Woodworth, and wounded three others. After lying there about two hours, or till four o'clock, we were ordered to get our things on and be ready to move, as the Third corps on our left was going in, and we might be needed to help them. The artillery and musketry then commenced firing on the left, and continued with but little change for two hours, when our men began to give way slowly. We were at once ordered up to the left to support our batteries, and check the rebels' advance. We were marched up there about a quarter of a mile, and ordered to lie down in front of the batteries, as the shot and shell were coming over pretty plentifully. From there we could look all over the field, see our lines, the rebel lines, and their batteries very plainly. As I saw our men fall back, rally, and fall back again, skedaddlers rushing to the rear in squads, I never felt so bad in my life. I thought sure the day was gone for us, and felt that I would prefer to die there, rather than live and suffer the disgrace and humiliation a defeat of our army there would entail on us; and if ever I offered a sincere prayer in my life, it was then, that we might be saved from defeat. We all felt bad, but resolved, when our chance came, to do our best to retrieve the fortunes of the day, hardly expecting to come out of the conflict unharmed.

Our turn soon came. We were ordered forward against the enemy, who were then within musket range of us; and if any ever were willing and anxious to go forward into what we all could see was a deadly place, our boys were. We had who open fields to advance over, while the rebels were coming down over another open field, and the Third corps falling back before. We went forward on a run, and with a yell, till about half way across the second field, when we were ordered, for some unaccountable reason to us, to halt, and the bullets were coming like hailstones, and whittling our boys like grain before the sickle. "Why don't they let us charge?" cried all of us. "Why do they stop us here to be murdered?" Every one seemed anxious to go forward, and some run way out ahead and beckoned for us to come on. We have always believed that a determined charge would break any line, and that more would be accomplished and less life lost, than by lying down and firing two or three hours. We felt that we could check and force them to retreat, and we wanted to go against them with a vengeance and get over the deadly ground as soon as possible. We were halted again when across the second field; and though by this time few were left, we were just as anxious to go forward. We were almost together, and the rebels had nearly flanked the right of the regiment. But what surprised me most was to see some of the rebels, not fifty yards from us, standing out openly and loading and firing as deliberately as though they were in no danger whatever. Ah! there is no mistake but what some of those rebels are just as brave as it is possible for human beings to be. I expected they wold turn and run when they saw us coming so determinedly, and I believe they would, had we gone right on. We had fired but a few shots before we were ordered to fall back. 'Twas some time before we could hear the order, and when we did the right of the regiment was half way back. We dreaded to go back for the danger of it, more than staying there; and we felt, though obeying orders, that we were being disgraced to fall back when we knew we could hold our own. We fell back, and it was then I had the first feeling of fear during the fight. I felt almost sure I would be hit, and I saw many wounded going back.

When we got back to the colors, where we rallied, scarce twenty-five men were to be found. Most who went in were killed, wounded, or helping off the wounded. The enemy advanced no farther, and soon some of our boys who did not fall back when ordered, came in bringing in prisoners, and they said when we fell back the rebels were making for the rear as fast as possible. It was now about dark. Another line came up of the First corps, and went in where we came out, found no enemy, advanced their pickets over the battle-field to enable us to get off our wounded, which they at once commenced to do. We were ordered to join the brigade again, on the right; and Lieutenant Heffelfinger took a couple of the boys and went and had all our wounded carried to the hospital that night. As we were going to the right to join the brigade, musketry was heard very plain, seemingly scarce half a mild off, and completely in our rear; in fact, some of the bullets whistled over our heads. Now we were sure that the battle was gone up for us, for the fighting continued fierce, and seemed growing nearer all the time. We made up our minds that we were whipped, and expected before morning to see the whole army routed, and flying for Baltimore. The prospect was gloomy and discouraging in the extreme to us, but, thank God, that time we were deceived, and our affairs and position were much better than the most sanguine of us could believe possible. The firing soon ceased on the right and what seemed our rear; the troops were got in their places, and put in position for the contest, whenever it should open again. Our brigade was placed almost in the same position we had previous to the charge in the afternoon, viz.: the left centre of the army, and the left of the Second division. We then lay down to get some sleep, with our equipment on and guns by our sides; and I here say I never slept better and had more pleasant dreams in my life than I had on the battle-field of Gettysburg, with dead men and horses lying all around me; but the excitement and exhaustion had been so great that a man could sleep in any condition, and under any circumstances.

We got up about daylight, expected and awaited an attack from the enemy at any moment, but till afternoon all was quiet, except occasionally a shot from their or our batteries. Most of us got some coffee during the forenoon, by going one or two at a time back to the rear, where they were allowed fires and cooking, which of course greatly refreshed us. A man's appetite generally, during a battle, is not very voracious. About half past twelve o'clock, as we had gathered around one of our Lieutenants to hear the yesterday's Baltimore Clipper read, bang! comes one of their shells over us, striking about twenty yards from us. That stopped the reading; each man took his place, lay down, and for the next two hours hugged the ground just about as close as human beings are generally in the habit of doing. The first gun was the signal for a hundred more to open, at less than half a mile distance, while till then their existence was perfectly unknown to us. Such an artillery fire has never been witnessed in this war. The air seemed to be filled with the hissing, screaming, bursting missiles, and all of them really seemed to be directed at us. They knew our exact position, for before we lay down they could with the naked eye plainly see us, and where our lines were, and tried to explode their shells directly over us; but fortunately most of them just went far enough to clear us, while many struck in front of us and bounded over us. We lay behind a slight rise of ground, just enough, by lying close, to hide us from the view of the rebels. A good many shell and pieces struck mighty close to us, and among us, but strange to say, none of us were injured, while the troops that lay behind us had many killed and wounded. Our batteries replied, but for the first time in our experience, they were powerless to silence the rebels, and in fact, many of our guns were silenced. So many of their horses and men were killed that they could not work their guns, and drew them off the field. Caisson after caisson blew up, and still the rebels' fire was fierce and rapid as ever.

I kept thinking, surely they cannot fire much longer; their guns will get so hot they will have to stop, and they cannot afford, so far from their base, to waste so much ammunition. It was awful hot where we lay, with the sun shining down on us, and we so close to the ground that not a breath of air could reach us. We kept wishing and hoping they would dry up, as much to get out of the heat as the danger, for the latter we thought little of, after they had fired a while; but Lee had an object to attain by throwing away so much ammunition. He calculated by concentrating his fire on our centre that he could use up our batteries, drive away and demoralize our infantry lines, for owing to the shape of our lines, a shell coming from the rebels, if it failed to do any damage to the front lines, could scarcely fail to go into the reserves that lay back of us; and in fact many more were killed in the rear than in the front, though their fire was directed at the front line and batteries nearly altogether. Had he succeeded in doing what he expected, and got the position we occupied, we were defeated, and so badly that I much doubt our ability to stop their progress towards Baltimore, or anywhere they chose to go. But Mr. Lee got fooled for once, and threw away a mighty sight of good ammunition, and derived little benefit from it.

Well, after firing about two hours and a half, they slackened up, and soon the order came, "Be ready, for they are running," (their infantry). We had expected it, and it was not many seconds before every man had on his armor, and was anxiously awaiting the coming of the foe. They had to advance more than half a mile across open fields. They came out of the woods in three lines, and advanced in good order till they got more than half way to us, and in good range of our muskets, which of course we used, as did the battery pour grape and canister, when they closed in to their left, and massed together for a charge, on the part of the line held by the Second Philadelphia brigade of our division. As they closed together, we (our brigade) marched by flank to confound them, firing at them continually, pouring most of our shot into their flank, where every shot must tell. The Second brigade gave way before the rebels got to them, and commenced to fall back. Our brigade was hurried up, and the Third were brought up to the rescue, and with the Second, which soon rallied again, we charged the rebels just as they had planted one of their colors on one of our guns. A Vermont brigade was sent out to flank them, which they did handsomely. The rebels, now seeing the position they had got in, threw away their guns and gave themselves up by hundreds, and thus ended the great assault of Lee on the third. Not enough went back of Pickett's division to make a good line of skirmishers. Another line came out on the left shortly afterwards, but they were repulsed as completely as the first, and with the exception of a little artillery firing, was the last of the fighting at Gettysburg.

During the assault the rebels poured into us lots of shell and grape from their batteries, but we scarce paid any attention to it, having all we could attend to in the infantry. Our boys felt bully during all the fight of the third, and no one thought of running or of the danger, except the Second brigade; and some of these regiments, Baxter Zouaves, for instance, never were known to stand fire. We took revenge for what they had done to our poor fellows the day before, and we never had had such a chance before. Most of us fired over twenty rounds, and at close range enough to do splendid execution; and if we didn't kill some Secesh in that battle we never did, and I fear never will during the war.

During the fight of the third, it might be said, almost, that every man fought on his own hook, for our division had been so used up the day before, that few officers were left. Generals Hancock and Gibbon were wounded early. Each man acted as though he felt what was at stake in the contest, and did all in their power to drive the enemy, without regard to officers, or whether there were any or not. Regiments all mixed up together, and in the last charge nearly all the flags of the division were together in a corner where the rebels got a hold. The flags of the rebel division were about the same, and when the assault was fully repulsed, they laid them on the ground in front of us, for anybody to get who chose, and, as might be expected, the brave men of the Second brigade were on hand to pick them up when there was no danger, and claim all the honor. They are welcome, though, to all they can get, for among those who knew them and saw them in the fight, they will have to show something besides flags to establish their bravery on that field. The sights on the field were horrible, by far the worst of any field we have seen; but I have not the time or disposition to describe them. Never before were our batteries so used up. Some of them had not men and horses enough for two guns, and the four batteries of our corps had to be consolidated into two before leaving the field.

The morning of the fourth we drew rations, and plenty of them; and right there, where we had fought the day before, we cooked and ate a hearty breakfast, for by this time we were pretty hungry, and many of us out of grub. That day and the forenoon of the next, our men were busy burying the dead. About noon of the fifth we left the field to follow the rebels, who were now known to be making for the Potomac as fast as possible.

I have here tried to give you a slight sketch of the part we took in the great battle. It is very imperfect, and many things are left out I should like to have put in; but I think I have taken up space enough any way; so for the rest, if God spares my life, and my memory serves me, you must wait till about nine months from now, and I will try, if agreeable, to favor you. So, for the present, good by.

JOHN W. PLUMMER

Journal on Confederate Calvary Brigadier-General John Morgan's Raid through Kentucky by Lieutenant-Colonel R. A. Alston
(July 1–8, 1863)

[RR-VII:358–360]

Alston was on the great cavalry raider General John Morgan's staff, a South Carolinian, and an editor of the Vidette *newspaper (Hartsville, Tennessee). Later paroled, Alston was back in the South by January 1864. Morgan, who was captured in Ohio on July 26, escaped from prison in November, and resumed his raiding until he was killed by Union forces in Tennessee on September 4, 1864.*

THE following is the journal of Lieutenant-Colonel Alston, Morgan's Chief of Staff, who was captured by the national pickets on the fifth of July. The journal is complete from the morning of the first to noon of the eighth, at which time he was sent to Camp Chase, Ohio.

July 1st, 1863.—On the banks of the Cumberland. The river very high. No boats. General M. obliged to build a number of boats, which he accomplished with very little delay, and commenced crossing at sundown.

July 2d.—Bucksville. He had great difficulty in making the horses swim, but by united and systematic exertion succeeded in getting the entire command of —— regiments over by ten A.M., though the command was very much scattered. At eleven o'clock, scouts came into Bucksville and reported the enemy advancing, and within four miles of the town. It was supposed to be only a scouting party, and a portion of Dick Morgan's command was sent out to make a reconnoissance. The report of the scouts of the enemy advancing proved to be correct, and a message was received from Colonel Ward that he was attacked. Colonel Grigsby was sent to reënforce him, and succeeded in driving the Yankees back in great confusion upon their reënforcements. My regiment lost two mortally wounded and two others slightly. Five of the Yankees were known to be killed and a number wounded, with about fifteen prisoners. No tidings heard of the Second brigade until dark, when they arrived and reported that Colonel Johnson, commanding, had experienced great difficulty in crossing, and that in addition to the precipitous banks and absence of all boats or other means of transportation, the enemy were hovering on the river and harassing him as far as they could. He was, however, quite successful in driving them back. Yesterday a young man, calling himself Charles Rogers, dressed in full confederate uniform, came into our lines and expressed a desire to join our command. I suspicioned him, and, after a few questions, I was convinced that he was a spy. I threatened to shoot him, when he confessed that he had been lying, and that his name was Simon Blitz—in fact he convicted himself of being a spy. I hated to shoot him, although he deserved it.

July 3d.—My regiment behaved very gallantly in yesterday's fight with the enemy frequently having hand-to-hand encounters. To-day (third) we experienced the same difficulty in getting the artillery on, and had to press a number of oxen for the purpose. After two halts for the column to close up, our advance proceeded to Columbia. They were met by detachments from three regiments (Forty-fifth Ohio, Second Ohio, and First Kentucky) said to be under command of Colonel Wolford. A brief engagement followed, in which we drove the enemy in great haste through the town, capturing six prisoners, killing two, among them Captain Carter, and wounding three. Our loss was two killed and two wounded, among them Captain Cassel, a most dashing and daring officer, wounded in the thigh. Our men behaved badly at Columbia, breaking open a store and plundering it. I ordered the men to return the goods, and made all the reparation in my power. These outrages are very disgraceful, and are usually perpetrated by men accompanying the army simply for plunder. They are not worth a ——, and are a disgrace to both armies. Passed through Columbia, and camped six miles from Green River Bridge.

July 4th.—New-Market, Ky. A day of gloom, deep gloom, to our entire command. How many who rose this morning full of enthusiasm and hope now "sleep the sleep that knows no waking." The sun rose bright and beautiful, the air was cool and balmy, all nature wore the appearance of peace and harmony. While riding along, affected by the stillness of all around, Captain Magennis, the Adjutant-General, rode up and remarked how dreadful to reflect that we were marching on to engage in deadly strife, and how many poor fellows would pass into eternity before the setting of yonder sun. I have no doubt the poor fellow was moved to these reflections by one of those unaccountable presentiments which are so often the harbingers of evil. (Before dark he was a corpse.) About sunrise we drove in the enemy's pickets and were soon near their fortifications, which had been erected to prevent our crossing. General Morgan sent in a flag of truce and demanded the surrender, but the Colonel quietly remarked: "If it was any other day he might consider the demand, but the Fourth of July was a bad day to talk about surrender, and he must therefore decline." This Colonel is a gallant man, and the entire arrangement of his defence entitles him to the highest credit for military skill. We would mark such a man in our army for promotion.

We attacked the place with two regiments, sending the remainder of our force across at another ford. The place was judiciously chosen and skillfully defended, and the result was that we were repulsed with severe loss—about twenty-five killed and twenty wounded. Among the killed, as usual, were our best men and officers, including Colonel Chenault, Major Brent, Captain Tribble, Lieutenants Cowan, Ferguson, and another lieutenant whose name I do not remember. Our march thus far has been very fatiguing—bad roads, little rest or sleep, little to eat, and a fight every day. Yet our men are cheerful, even buoyant, and to see them pressing along barefooted, hurrahing and singing, would cause one to appreciate what those who are fighting in a just and holy cause will endure. About three o'clock, as I rode on about forty yards in advance, I heard the General exclaim something in a very excited tone, which I could not understand, and heard at the same time the report of a pistol. I turned, and, great God! to my horror I saw Captain Magennis falling from his horse, with the blood gushing out of his mouth and breast. His only remark was: "Let me down easy." In another moment his spirit had fled. He was killed by Captain Murphy because Magennis, by the direction of General Morgan, had ordered Murphy to restore a watch taken from a prisoner. Thus was the poor fellow's language of the morning dreadfully realized. I was terribly affected. I had seen blood flow freely on many a battle-field—my friends had been killed in the morning—but this caused a deeper impression and shock than any occurrence I ever witnessed. Truly this has been a sad day. General Morgan looks haggard and weary, but he never despairs. May to-morrow dawn more bright than to-day closes.

July 5th.—Another day of gloom, fatigue, and death. Moved on Lebanon at sunrise—placed our men in line. Sent around Colonel J—— with his brigade to the Danville road to cut off reënforcements, which we knew were expected from Danville. I went in with a flag of truce. It was fired on five times. Officer apologized, saying he thought it was a man with a white coat on. Very dangerous mistake, at least for me. Demanded unconditional surrender. Told Colonel Hanson we had his reënforcements cut off, and resistance was useless. He refused to surrender, and I then ordered him to send out the noncombatants, as we would be compelled to shell the town. He posted his regiment in the dépôt and in various houses, by which he was enabled to make a desperate resistance. After a fight of seven hours, General Morgan, finding the town could be taken in no other way, ordered a charge to be made. This ought to have been done at first, but General Morgan said, when it was urged on him, that he wished to avoid the destruction of private property as much as possible, and he would only permit it as a last and final resort. Colonel Hanson still held out in hopes of receiving reënforcements, and only surrendered after we had fired the buildings in which he was posted. His force consisted of the Twentieth Kentucky, about three hundred and seventy men, and twenty or twenty-five stragglers from other commands.

By this surrender we obtained a sufficient quantity of guns to arm all our men who were without them; also a quantity of ammunition, of which we stood sorely in need. At the order to charge, Duke's regiment rushed forward, and poor Tommy Morgan, who was always in the lead, ran forward and cheered the men with all the enthusiasm of his bright nature. Almost at the first volley he fell back, pierced through the heart. His only words were: "Brother Cally, they have killed me." Noble youth! how deeply lamented by all who knew you! This was a crushing blow to General Morgan, as his affection for his brother exceeded the love of Jonathan to David. It caused a terrible excitement, and the men were in a state of frenzy. It required the utmost energy and promptitude on the part of the officers to prevent a scene of slaughter, which all would deeply have lamented. Our men behaved badly here, breaking open stores and plundering indiscriminately. All that officers could do was done to prevent, but in vain. These occurrences are very disgraceful, and I am truly glad that they form exceptions to the general conduct.

While I was paroling the prisoners, a courier arrived, informing me that the enemy were approaching with two regiments of cavalry and a battery of artillery, and that skirmishing was then going on with our pickets. I was therefore obliged to order the prisoners to Springfield on the double-quick. Soon after we left Lebanon, the hardest rain I ever experienced commenced to fall, and continued till nine o'clock. Arrived at Springfield at dark, when I halted the prisoners in order to parole those who were not paroled at Lebanon, and formally dismissed them. This detained me at Springfield two hours after the command had passed. Wet and chilly, worn out, horse tired and hungry. Stopped to feed her. Falling asleep, was aroused by one of the men. Started on to the command. When I reached the point on the Bardstown road where I had expected the Second brigade to encamp, was halted by a party of cavalry. Supposing them to be our own pickets, I rode up promptly to correct them for standing in full view of any one approaching, when lo!

to my mortification, I found myself a prisoner. My God! how I hated it, no one can understand. The first thought, after my wife and children, was my fine mare, Fannie Johnson, named after a pretty little cousin, of Richmond, Va. I said: "Poor Fannie, who will treat you as kindly as I have?" I turned her over to the captain and begged him to take good care of her, which he promised to do.

July 6th.—Travelled all day. Treated very kindly by Captain Smith. Sick, worn out, completely wearied out. Spirits cheerful. Met Captain Walcott on the road from Springfield. He got Captain Smith to parole me. Captain Smith anxious to do so, as he had more prisoners than he could well take care of. Accompanied Captain Walcott to Danville. Staid all night there.

July 7th.—Arrived at Nicholasville. Ordered before the Provost-Marshal. Sent on to Lexington. Arrived in the afternoon, and immediately ordered to prison. Visited by some sweet, pretty, and kind ladies. God bless them! I know he will.

July 8th.—Great rejoicing in Lexington over the fall of Vicksburgh. (I do not believe it.) It is a great disaster, one among the very worst that could befall us. But even if it is so, and even should Lee's army be destroyed and every town in the South burned, the rebellion would be unsubdued. There are a hundred thousand men in the South who feel as I do, that they would rather an earthquake should swallow the whole country than yield to our oppressors—men who will retire to the mountains and live on acorns, and crawl on their bellies to shoot an invader wherever they can see one.

Offer of Resignation by Confederate General R. E. Lee (August 8, 1863) to Confederate President Jefferson Davis; Reply by President Davis (August 11, 1863)

[OR: SERIES 1, VOL. LI, PART 2:752–3; VOL. XXIX, PART 2:639–640]

Disheartened by his poor health, discouraged by his sense that perhaps he had missed military opportunities that his more vigorous self would not have missed, General Robert E. Lee, commander of the Army of Northern Virginia, offered his resignation to President Davis only a month after his army's narrow escape from Gettysburg into Virginia. Davis, in a rare moment of sympathy and warmth, reassured Lee that there was no better man to lead the Confederates' largest, most vital army.

CAMP ORANGE,
August 8, 1863

HIS EXCELLENCY JEFFERSON DAVIS,
President of the Confederate States:

MR. PRESIDENT: Your letters of July 28 and August 2 have been received, and I have waited for a leisure hour to reply, but I fear that will never come. I am extremely obliged to you for the attention given to the wants of this army, and the efforts made to supply them. Our absentees are returning, and I hope the earnest and beautiful appeal made to the country in your proclamation may stir up the virtue of the whole people, and that they may see their duty and perform it. Nothing is wanted but that their fortitude should equal their bravery to insure the success of our cause. We must expect reverses, even defeats. They are sent to teach us wisdom and prudence, to call forth greater energies, and to prevent our falling into greater disasters. Our people have only to be true and united, to bear manfully the misfortunes incident to war, and all will come right in the end.

I know how prone we are to censure and how ready to blame others for the non-fulfillment of our expectations. This is unbecoming in a generous people, and I grieve to see its expression. The general remedy for the want of success in a military commander is his removal. This is natural, and, in many instances, proper. For, no matter what may be the ability of the officer, if he loses the confidence of his troops disaster must sooner or later ensue.

I have been prompted by these reflections more than once since my return from Pennsylvania to propose to Your Excellency the propriety of selecting another commander for this army. I have seen and heard of expression of discontent in the public journals at the result of the expedition. I do not know how far this feeling extends in the army. My brother officers have been too kind to report it, and so far the troops have been too generous to exhibit it. It is fair, however, to suppose that it does exist, and success is so necessary to us that nothing should be risked to secure it. I therefore, in all sincerity, request Your Excellency to take measures to supply my place. I do this with the more earnestness because no one is more aware than myself of my inability for the duties of my position. I cannot even accomplish what I myself desire. How can I fulfill the expectations of others? In addition I sensibly feel the growing failure of my bodily strength. I have not yet recovered from the attack I experienced the past spring. I am becoming more and more incapable of exertion, and am thus prevented from making the personal examinations and giving the personal supervision to the operations in the field which I feel to be necessary. I am so dull that in making use of the eyes of others I am frequently misled. Everything, therefore, points to the advantages to be derived from a new commander, and I the more anxiously urge the matter upon Your Excellency from my belief that a younger and abler man than myself can readily be attained. I know that he will have as gallant and brave an army as ever existed to second his efforts, and it would be the happiest day of my life to see at its head a worthy leader—one that would accomplish more than I could perform and all that I have wished. I hope Your Excellency will attribute my request to the true reason, the desire to serve my country, and to do all in my power to insure the success of her righteous cause.

I have no complaints to make of any one but myself. I have received noting but kindness from those above me, and the most considerate attention from my comrades and companions in arms. To Your Excellency I am specially indebted for uniform kindness and consideration. You have done everything in your power to aid me in the work committed to my charge, without omitting anything to promote the general welfare. I pray that your efforts may at length be crowned with success, and that you may long live to enjoy the thanks of a grateful people.

With sentiments of great esteem, I am, very respectfully and truly, yours,

R. E. LEE
General

RICHMOND, VA.,
August 11, 1863

GENERAL R. E. LEE,
  Commanding Army of Northern Virginia:

YOURS of 8th instant has been received. I am glad that you concur so entirely with me as to the want of our country in this trying hour, and am happy to add that after the first depression consequent upon our disaster in the west, indications have appeared that our people will exhibit that fortitude which we agree in believing is alone needful to secure ultimate success.

It well became Sidney Johnston, when overwhelmed by a senseless clamor, to admit the rule that success is the test of merit; and yet there has been nothing which I have found to require a greater effort of patience than to bear the criticisms of the ignorant, who pronounce everything a failure which does not equal their expectations or desires, and can see no good result which is not in the line of their own imaginings. I admit the propriety of your conclusions, that an officer who loses the confidence of his troops should have his position changed, whatever may be his ability, but when I read the sentence I was not at all prepared for the application you were about to make. Expressions of discontent in the public journals furnish but little evidence of the sentiment of an army. I wish it were otherwise, even though all the abuse of myself should be accepted as the results of honest observation. I say I wish I could feel that the public journals were not generally partisan nor venal.

Were you capable of stooping to it, you could easily surround yourself with those who would fill the press with your laudations, and seek to exalt you for what you had not done, rather than detract from the achievements which will make you and your army the subject of history and object of the world's admiration for generations to come.

I am truly sorry to know that you still feel the effects of the illness you suffered last spring, and can readily understand the embarrassments you experience in using the eyes of others, having been so much accustomed to make your own reconnaissances. Practice will, however, do much to relieve that embarrassment, and the minute knowledge of the country which you have acquired will render you less dependent for topographical information.

But suppose, my dear friend, that I were to admit, with all their implications, the points which you present, where am I to find that new commander who is to possess the greater ability which you believe to be required? I do not doubt the readiness with which you would give way to one who could accomplish all that you have wished, and you will do me the justice to believe that if Providence should kindly offer such a person for our use, I would not hesitate to avail of his services.

My sight is not sufficiently penetrating to discover such hidden merit, if it exists, and I have but used to you the language of sober earnestness when I have impressed upon you the propriety of avoiding all unnecessary exposure to danger, because I felt our country could not bear to lose you. To ask me to substitute you by some one in my judgment more fit to command, or who would possess more of the confidence of the army, or of the reflecting men of the country, is to demand an impossibility.

It only remains for me to hope that you will take all possible care of yourself, that your health and strength may be entirely restored, and that the Lord will preserve you for the important duties devolved upon you in the struggle of our suffering country for the independence which we have engaged in war to maintain.

As ever, very respectfully and truly, yours,

JEFFERSON DAVIS

President Lincoln's letter to Representative Conkling of Illinois on the Public Dissatisfaction with His Presidency
(August 16, 1863)

[RR-VII:459–461]

Never more efficiently did President Lincoln explain and defend his Emancipation Proclamation than to Representative James C. Conkling of Illinois, who, in inviting the President to Illinois to speak, criticized Lincoln's most important policies.

EXECUTIVE MANSION, WASHINGTON,
August 26, 1863

Hon. James C. Conkling:

MY DEAR SIR: Your letter inviting me to attend a mass meeting of unconditional Union men, to be held at the capital of Illinois on the third of September, has been received. It would be very agreeable to me thus to meet my old friends at my own home, but I cannot just now be absent from this city so long as a visit there would require.

The meeting is to be composed of all those who maintain unconditional devotion to the Union; and I am sure that my old political friends will thank me for tendering, as I do, the nation's gratitude to those other noble men whom no partisan malice or partisan hope can make false to the nation's life.

There are those who are dissatisfied with me. To such I would say, you desire peace, and you blame me that we do not have it. But how can we obtain it? There are but three conceivable ways. First, to suppress the rebellion by force of arms. This I am trying to do. Are you for it? If you are so, we are agreeg. If you are not for it, a second way is to give up the Union. I am against this. If you are you should say so plainly. If you are not for force, nor yet for dissolution, there only remains some imaginary compromise.

I do not believe that any compromise embracing the maintenance of the Union is now possible. All that I learn leads to a directly opposite belief. The strength of the rebellion is its military, its army. That army dominates all the country and all the people within its range.

Any officer of terms made by any man or men within that range in opposition to that army, is simply nothing for the present; because such man or men have no power whatever to enforce their side of a compromise, if one were made with them.

To illustrate: Suppose refugees from the South and peace men of the North get together in convention and frame and proclaim a compromise embracing a restoration of the Union. In what way can that compromise be used to keep General Lee's army out of Pennsylvania?

General Meade's army can keep Lee's army out of Pennyslvania; and I think can ultimately drive it out of existence. But no paper compromise to which the cotnrollers of General Lee's army are not agreed can at all affect that army. In an effort at such compromise we would waste time, which the enemy would improve to our disadvantage, and that would be all.

A compromise, to be effect, must be made either with those who control the rebel army, or with the people first liberated from the domination of that army by the success of our army. Now, allow me to assure you that no word or intimation from the rebel army, or from any of the men controlling it, in relation to any peace compromise, has ever come to my knowledge or belief. All charges or intimations to the contrary are deceptive and groundless. And I promise you that if any such proposition shall hereafter come it shall not be rejected and kept secret from you. I freely acknowledge myself to be the servant of the people, according to the bond of service, the United States Constitution; and that, as such, I am responsible to them.

But to be plain. You are dissatisfied with me about the negro. Quite likely there is a difference of opinion between you and myself upon that subject. I certainly wish that all men could be free, while you, I suppose, do not. Yet I have neither adopted nor proposed any measure which is not consistent with even your views, provided that you are for the Union.

I suggested compensated emancipation, to which you replied that you wished not to be taxed to buy negroes. But I had not asked you to be taxed to buy negroes, except in such way as to save you from greater taxation to save the Union exclusively by other means.

You dislike the Emancipation Proclamation, and perhaps would have it retracted. You say it is unconstituional. I think differently. I think the Constitution invests its Commander-in-Chief with the law of war in

time of war. The most that can be said, if so much, is that slaves are property. Is there, has there ever been, any question that by the law of war,
property, both of enemies and friends, may be taken when needed?

And is it not needed whenever taking it helps us or hurts the enemy?

Armies, the world over, destroy enemy's property when they cannot
use it; and even destroy their own to keep it from the enemy. Civilized
belligerents do all in their power to help themselves and hurt the enemy,
except a few things regarded as barbarous or cruel. Among the exceptions are the massacre of vanquished foes and non-combatants, male and
female.

But the Proclamation, as law, is valid or is not valid. If it is valid, it cannot be retracted, any more than the dead can be brought to life. Some of
you profess to think its retraction would operate favorably for the Union.
Why better after the retraction than before the issue?

There was more than a year and a half of trial to suppress the rebellion before the Proclamation issued, the last one hundred days of which
passed under an explicit notice that it was coming, unless averted by
those in revolt returning to their allegiance. The war has certainly progressed as favorably for us, since the issue of Proclamation as before.

I know, as fully as one can know the opinions of others, that some of
the commanders of our armies in the field, who have given us our most
important victories, believe the emancipation policy and the aid of colored troops constitute the heaviest blow yet dealt to the rebellion, and
that at least one of these important successes could not have been
achieved when it was, but for the aid of black soldiers.

Among the commanders holding these views are some who have
never had any affinity with what is called Abolitionist, or with the
"Republican party politics"; but who held them purely as military opinions. I submit these opinions as being entitled to some weight against the
objections often urged, that emancipation and arming the blacks are
unwise as military measures, and were not adopted as such in good faith.

You say you will not fight to free negroes. Some of them seem willing to fight for you. But no matter. Fight you, then, exclusively to serve
the Union. I issued the Proclamation on purpose to aid you in saving the
Union.

Whenever you shall have conquered all resistence to the Union, if I
shall urge you to continue fighting, it will be an apt time then for you to
declare you will not fight to free negroes.

I thought that in your struggle for the Union, to whatever extent the
negroes should cease helping the enemy, to that extent it weakened the
enemy in his resistence to you. Do you think differently? I thought that
whatever negroes can be got to do as soldiers leaves just so much less for
white soldiers to do in saving the Union? Does it appear otherwise to

you? But negroes, like other people, act upon motives. Why should they do any thing for us if we will do nothing for them? If they stake their lives for us they must be prompted by the strongest motive, even the promise of freedom. And the promise, being made, must be kept.

The signs look better. The Father of Waters again goes unvexed to the sea. Thanks to the great North-West for it. Nor yet wholly to them. Three hundred miles up, they met New-England, Empire, Keystone, and Jersey, hewing their way right and left. The sunny South too, in more colors than one, also lent a hand. On the spot their part of the history was jotted down in black and white. The job was a great national one, and let none be banned who bore an honorable part in it. And while those who have cleared the great river may well be proud, even that is not all. It is hard to say that any thing has been more bravely and better done than at Antietam, Murfreesboro, Gettysburg, and on many fields of lesser note.

Nor must Uncle Sam's web-feet be forgotten. At all the waters' margins they have been present, not only on the deep sea, the broad bay, and the rapid river, but also up the narrow, muddy bayou, and wherever the ground was a little damp, they have been and made their tracks.

Thanks to all. For the great Republic—for the principle it lives by and keeps alive for man's vast future—thanks to all.

Peace does not appear so distant as it did. I hope it will come soon, and come to stay; and so come as to be worth the keeping in all future time. It will then have been proved that, among freemen, there can be no successful appeal from the ballot to the bullet, and that they who take such appeal are sure to lose their case, and pay the cost.

And then, there will be some black men who can remember that, with silent tongue, and clenched teeth, and steady eye, and well-poised bayonet, they have helped mankind on to this great consummation, while, I fear there will be some white men unable to forget that, with malignant heart and deceitful speech, they have striven to hinder it.

Still, let us not be over-sanguine of a speedy final triumph. Let us be quite sober. Let us diligently apply the means, never doubting that a just God, in his own good time, will give us the rightful result.

Yours very truly

A. LINCOLN

Statement by the Attaché of the Provost Marshall Office, William Kempf, on the Massacre of Union Sympathizers in Lawrence, Kansas
(August 21, 1863)

[RR-VII:399–401]

William C. Quantrill (1837–1865), a "bushwacker," was given a captaincy in 1862 by the Confederate Army for his guerrilla raids in Missouri and Kansas. In Lawrence, he and his men murdered civilian men, women, and children sympathetic to the Union and executed free blacks. In the spring of the final year of the war, he was killed by Union troops.

YESTERDAY, the twenty-first of August, about half-past four o'clock, the citizens of Lawrence were surprised to hear a body of cavalry ride rapidly toward the Kansas River. As soon as the first of these men reached the river by Massachusetts Street and the streets east and west of it, they raised a shout, which was repeated down the streets as far as it was possible to hear. The citizens, startled by the noise, rushed into the streets to ascertain the cause. Many of the citizens were then shot down. With the quickness of lightning, the news spread over town that the accursed Quantrill, with his bushwhackers, was in town. The surprise was so complete that it was utterly impossible for the citizens to undertake any thing whatever for their defence. The few who heroically run out with their guns were quickly murdered, as were, in fact, all who showed themselves during the first half-hour. The hills above and the woods below the town were well guarded by guerrillas, so that it was impossible for persons living on the outskirts of town to make their escape. Every thing was done by command, or well understood beforehand by these murderers. After they had spread over town, they commenced to plunder in the most deliberate manner conceivable. Every store was broken open by a few men, guarded against surprise from the inside. The first thing they looked after was the safe; then every thing else of value. Every safe was bursted open when they could not get the key; but they were so well informed about every thing, that they sent, in several instances, to the private residences of persons, demanding the keys for the safes in the stores. Well-informed citizens think they took three hundred thousand dollars in cash along with them. It would seem they took more. They had been in town some time before they commenced burning the buildings.

The inmates of the Eldridge House were roused by somebody violently beating the gong. Most of them soon assembled in the hall, and it was found that not an arm was in the house. Captain Banks told them the best thing they could do was to surrender, and this being agreed upon, Captain Banks took a white sheet, and waved it from the balcony. This was greeted by a universal shout from the guerrillas. The commander of the bushwhackers around the house asked Banks: "Do you surrender this house?" "We do, and hope that you will treat our women and children with decency." To this the rebels agreed, and Banks asked for Colonel Quantrill. Quantrill was sent for, and soon came. He asked Banks whether he was a Federal officer, and being answered in the affirmative, assured Banks that they would all be treated as prisoners, and should not be molested. They were all searched, and every thing valuable taken away from them—even the finger-rings of men and women. The whole house was then ransacked, and every thing of value taken out by the guerrillas. The prisoners were marched over to the Whitney House, and there guarded.

By this time most of the plunder had been secured on horses driven together from all parts of the town. The safes had all been broken, some blown up by powder, others deliberately chiselled open. They picked out the horses, only retaining the best, and driving the poorer ones off.

At about seven o'clock they set fire to the court-house. We heard several explosions, which at a distance would have been taken for cannon-shots. We heard some persons riding down the street, commanding their friends to burn the stores; and we soon heard the crackling of the fire, and saw most of the buildings east and west of us wrapped in flames. To the south we could not see from the houses we were in.

During all this time citizens were being murdered everywhere. Germans and negroes, when caught, were shot immediately. Many persons were shot down after they had been taken prisoners, and had been assured that they would not be hurt if they would surrender. Messrs. Trask and Baker, and two other citizens, were so taken, and while being marched toward the river as prisoners, after being assured that they would not be harmed, some guerrillas asked their names. Mr. Trask gave the names, when they were immediately fired upon, and all four killed on the spot, except Mr. Baker, who is not expected to live, however. Mr. Dix had been taken prisoner and his house set on fire, when one of the fiends told him, if he would give them his money, he would not be killed; otherwise he would. Mr. Dix went into the burning house, and got a thousand dollars, and handed it over. He was told to march toward the river, and had not proceeded twenty steps when he was shot dead from behind. Mr. Hampson, clerk of the Provost-Marshal, had a revolver, and tried to defend the few things he had saved from the Johnson House. His wife interfered, and they told him if he would surrender he should be treated as a prisoner, and be safe from harm. He surrendered, and was immediately shot from behind, the ball entering near the spine, and coming out below the kidneys in front. The wound is not considered fatal.

In one instance, the wife and a daughter of a man threw themselves over his body, begging for his life; but one of the murderers deliberately thrust his revolver down between the two women, and killed the man.

Before ten o'clock the body of the guerrillas left with their plunder, leaving a guard over the prisoners in town, and a few stragglers. The few persons wounded were wounded at this time by the passing fiends. In the earlier part of the day most persons were fired at from very near, and killed instantly.

One of the first persons out was Colonel Deitzler. Mr. Williamson and myself helped him carry off the dead. The sight that met us when coming out, I cannot describe. I have read of outrages committed in the so-called dark ages, and horrible as they appeared to me, they sank into insignificance in comparison with what I was then compelled to witness. Well-known citizens were lying in front of the spot where their stores or residences had been, completely roasted. The bodies were crisp and nearly black. We thought, at first, that they were all negroes, till we recognized some of them. In handling the dead bodies, pieces of roasted flesh would remain in our hands. Soon our strength failed us in this horrible and sickening work. Many could not help crying like children. Women and little children were all over town, hunting for their husbands and fathers, and sad indeed was the scene when they did finally find them among the corpses laid out for recognition. I cannot describe the horrors; language fails me, and the recollection of the scenes I witnessed makes me sick when I am compelled to repeat them.

The town is a complete ruin. The whole of the business part, and all good private residences are burned down. Every thing of value was taken along by the fiends. No store is left, and it is necessary that the good people of Leavenworth send provisions immediately. Persons who were rich yesterday are now utterly destitute.

One of the first places surrounded was the Eldridge House. It seems the guerrillas demanded a surrender before firing into it. After a short consultation the occupants concluded to surrender, and a white flag (sheet) appeared from the balcony, which was greeted with cheers. Quantrill was sent for, and made his appearance. On being asked what were his intentions, he replied, "Plunder"; he finally agreed that they should be protected, and gave them an escort to a place of safety. The last-named place not being found safe on account of indiscriminate shooting by the men, Quantrill allowed them to go to the Whitney House, kept by Mr. Stone. Quantrill said Mr. Stone once saved his life, and he was not the man to forget past favors. As soon as the Eldridge was surrendered, the house was searched. The inmates of the rooms were aroused from their beds, and their money, jewelry, and other valuables demanded of them. Some gentlemen from Ohio who occupied one room were not as expeditious as the guerrillas thought, and they commenced firing through the door. One ball took effect in the calf of the leg of one of them. This same man was again shot through the shoulder, but is now doing well at the Merchants', in this city. Soon after, the building was destroyed; whether it was fired or caught from the adjoining buildings, we have not heard. It is supposed that a gentleman who has been connected with L. Levenson & Co., who had a store underneath, was burned.

After the second move, the Eldridge House party, which numbered about sixty, were safely, as they supposed, located in the Whitney House. Quantrill had chosen this place for his headquarters, and swore he would shoot any of his men who attempted to molest any of them. Many people, knowing this, slipped in and were saved. One brute came in upon his horse while the party were going from one place to the other, and was told by one of Quantrill's head men, named Porter, that he would kill him if he did not dry up. Every thing went on very well while Quantrill was there; he promised that he would be the last man to leave the town, and none of his men should return. He took a lunch, and finally ordered the command to move out of the city, which they did. After mounting his horse, he lifted his hat to the ladies, and bowing politely, said: "Ladies, I now bid you good morning. I hope when we meet again, it will be under more favorable circumstances." Putting spurs to his horse, he was soon out of sight. He was dressed in a dark-colored shirt, blue blouse, and had on a black hat. After Quantrill left, four of his men came back and said they were determined to kill some one out of the crowd—didn't much care who; that they had been promised the privilege of killing all they pleased, and through some reason, Quantrill had been humbugged. One of the party said that he had a sister killed in the prison at Kansas City, and another said that he had a sister shot by Union men; the third said he wanted to kill Miss Lydia Stone, the landlord's daughter; the fourth was a sober man, and seemed anxious to help save the lives of those in the house. It seems that one of the party had forcibly taken possession of a gold ring from Miss Stone, and she informed Quantrill of the fact, who told the fellow if he did not hand it over he would shoot him. But Miss Stone escaped. They wanted also to kill Mr. R. S. Stevens and another man, but they made their escape through a back-door to the bank of the river, where they could be protected by the few soldiers across the river. The men prowled through the house, but did not find what they wanted. Finally they ordered all in the house to form a line outside. This was done. One gentleman answered, Central Ohio. The fellow said that was as bad as Kansas, and shot him, but the wound did not prove fatal. Others were shot. Mr. Stone remonstrated with them, when one of them shot him through the head, killing him almost instantly. The party then left. It is reported that three of them were killed before getting out of town.

The banks were robbed, as well as the safes of the stores and offices. One man gave up all he had, and was then shot down. It is supposed they carried away in greenbacks some ten thousand dollars. The other property—except horses—they took away, was not much. The loss is estimated at between one and two millions.

Among the houses saved was that of ex-Governor Robinson, which, fortunately, is situated on the bank of the river. The guerrillas came and ordered the family (Mr. Robinson not being at home) to take out what they wanted, as they were going to burn it. They then left for town. When they returned, they were greeted with a volley from a small party of the Twelfth Kansas, on the opposite side, and three killed. Thinking the game would not pay, the scamps left.

General Lane had a miraculous escape. He heard the firing, and saw Willis's stable burning, and made tracks through a large corn-field near his house. Inquiries were made by the gang for Lane's house, and a Mr. Spicer was detailed by them to show his house. Placing a pistol to his head they compelled him to pilot them to Lane's house. They could not catch the General, but burnt his house. The General soon after made his appearance, and is now after the murderers.

Eighteen soldiers out of twenty-two, of the Kansas Fourteenth, at their recruiting rendezvous, near Lawrence, were shot; also a number of negroes of the Second colored regiment, were killed.

There were many heroic deeds performed by the ladies. In many instances they placed themselves between their husbands and fathers and danger when the drunken fiends held cocked pistols at them. One lady we hear spoken of and deserves particular mention; her name is Miss Lydia Stone, daughter of the landlord of the Whitney House. She moved round through the crowd doing all she could to alleviate the suffering. The dead body of one person was on fire, and she at once procured water and put it out. When the scoundrels came back a second time, saying they would kill some one, she replied, that: "They might as well kill me as any b██████Heroic deeds were performed by other ladies whose names have escaped us.

One of the most cowardly acts was the shooting at men, women, and children as they passed down under the bank toward the river.

There is no doubt but that Quantrill had spies at Lawrence. One man at the Eldridge House acted as a guide, and pointed out prominent men and things.

One fellow got Captain Banks's uniform and made quite a display with it.

A riding party of two ladies and gentlemen were met just outside the city, and compelled to go back. Quantrill invited the ladies to ride beside him into town, and they did so.

General Collamore was suffocated to death by damps in his well. When he first discovered the guerrillas in town, he went into the well, and his hired man, named Keith, covered it up. After the trouble was over, the man went to the well and found the General at the bottom. He went down after him, and unfortunately met the same fate. A neighbor, named Lowe, passing along, went down to rescue both of them, and was also suffocated.

It was peculiarly noticeable that the fury of the incarnate fiends was particularly directed against the Germans and the few unfortunate negroes who were in the doomed city.

Union War Department General Orders Number 329, on the Enlistment of Colored Troops
(October 13, 1863)

[RR-VIII:145]

There were officially no black soldiers fighting for the Union until the Final Emancipation Proclamation. To encourage more slave-owners in the border states to enlist and thereby emancipate their slaves, the War Department offered three hundred dollars per soldier.

WAR DEPARTMENT, ADJUTANT-GENERAL'S OFFICE,
Washington, D. C., October 13, 1863

WHEREAS, the exigencies of the war require that colored troops be enlisted in the States of Maryland, Missouri, and Tennessee, it is

ORDERED BY THE PRESIDENT, That the Chief of the Bureau for the Organization of Colored Troops shall establish recruiting stations at convenient places within said States, and give public notice thereof, and be governed by the following regulations:

First. None but able-bodied persons shall be enlisted.

Second. The State and county in which the enlistments are made shall be credited with the recruits enlisted.

Third. All persons enlisted into the military service shall for ever thereafter be FREE.

Fourth. Free persons, and slaves with the written consent of their owners, and slaves belonging to those who have been engaged in or given aid or comfort to the rebellion, may now be enlisted—the owners who have not been engaged in or given aid to the rebellion being entitled to compensation as hereinafter provided.

Fifth. If within thirty days from the date of opening enlistments, notice thereof and of the recruiting stations being published, a sufficient number of the description of persons aforesaid to meet the exigencies of the service should not be enlisted, then enlistments may be made of slaves without requiring consent of their owners, but they may receive compensation as herein provided for owners offering their slaves for enlistment.

Sixth. Any citizen of said States, who shall offer his or her slave for enlistment into the military service, shall, if such slave be accepted, receive from the recruiting officer a certificate thereof, and become entitled to compensation for the service of said slave, not exceeding the sum of three hundred dollars, upon filing a valid deed of manumission and of release, and making satisfactory proof of title. And the recruiting officer shall furnish to any claimant of descriptive list of any person enlisted and claimed under oath to be his or her slave, and allow any one claiming under oath that his or her slave has been enlisted without his or her consent, the privilege of inspecting the enlisted man for the purpose of identification.

Seventh. A board of three persons shall be appointed by the President, to whom the rolls and recruiting lists shall be furnished for public information, and, on demand exhibited to any person, claiming that his or her slave has been enlisted against his or her will.

Eighth. If a person shall, within ten days after the filing of said rolls, make a claim for the service of any person so enlisted, the board shall proceed to examine the proof of title, and, if valid, shall award just compensation, not exceeding three hundred dollars for each slave enlisted belonging to the claimant, and upon the claimant filing a valid deed of manumission and release of service, the board shall give the claimant a certificate of the sum awarded, which, on presentation, shall be paid by the chief of the Bureau.

Ninth. All enlistments of colored troops in the State of Maryland, otherwise than in accordance with these regulations, are forbidden.

Tenth. No person who is or has been engaged in the rebellion against the Government of the United States, or who in any way has or shall give aid or comfort to the enemies of the Government, shall be permitted to present any claim or receive any compensation for the labor or service of any slave, and all claimants shall file with their claims an oath of allegiance to the United States. By order of the President.

E. D. Townsend,
Assistant Adjutant-General

This order was extended, on October twenty-sixth, to Delaware, at the personal request of Governor Cannon.

Address Delivered at the Dedication of the Cemetery at Gettysburg, by President Abraham Lincoln
(November 19, 1863)

[ALGS]

Massachusetts orator Edward Everett, wrote Lincoln on November 20 to say, "I should be glad if I could flatter myself that I came as near the central idea of the occasion in two hours as you did in two minutes." Lincoln replied: "In our respective parts yesterday, you could not have been excused to make a short address, nor I a long one. I am pleased to know that, in your judgment, the little I did say was not entirely a failure."[4] The Gettysburg Address has become, after only the Declaration of Independence, the most famous speech in American history.

FOUR SCORE and seven years ago our fathers brought forth on this continent, a new nation, conceived in Liberty, and dedicated to the proposition that all men are created equal.

Now we are engaged in a great civil war, testing whether that nation, or any nation so conceived and so dedicated, can long endure. We are met on a great battle-field of that war. We have come to dedicate a portion of that field, as a final resting place for those who here gave their lives that that nation might live. It is altogether fitting and proper that we should do this.

But, in a larger sense, we can not dedicate—we can not consecrate—we can not hallow—this ground. The brave men, living and dead, who

---

[4] "Lincoln spoke only 105 or 110 words a minute, in part because he paused often for emphasis," writes Ronald C. White, Jr., in *Lincoln's Greatest Speech* (New York: Simon and Schuster. 2002. 165).

struggled here, have consecrated it, far above our poor power to add or detract. The world will little note, nor long remember what we say here, but it can never forget what they did here. It is for us the living, rather, to be dedicated here to the unfinished work which they who fought here have thus far so nobly advanced. It is rather for us to be here dedicated to the great task remaining before us—that from these honored dead we take increased devotion to that cause for which they gave the last full measure of devotion—that we here highly resolve that these dead shall not have died in vain—that this nation, under God, shall have a new birth of freedom—and that government of the people, by the people, for the people, shall not perish from the earth.

ABRAHAM LINCOLN
November 19, 1863

Letter on the Treatment of "Secesh"
by Union Major-General W. T. Sherman
to Major R. M. Sawyer
(January 31, 1864)

[RR-VIII:351–353]

In this ruthlessly argued letter, which William Tecumseh Sherman meant for the benefit of local Southerners rather than for his associate, Sherman explains the few rules of war. Though fond of the South, where he had served as Superintendent of the Louisiana State Military Academy, he always had detested secessionist ideas. In December 1860, after South Carolina's declaration of sovereignty, Sherman declared to a secession-minded friend, "You are rushing into war with one of the most powerful, ingeniously mechanical and determined people on earth—right at your doors." And now, a few years later, arguing for the South's complete surrender, he reminds his intended readers that "Satan, and the rebellious saints of heaven, were allowed a continuance of existence in hell merely to swell their just punishment. To such as would rebel against a government so mild and just as ours was in peace, a punishment equal would not be unjust." And so Sherman delivered the punishment over the next year to Georgia and the Carolinas as the commander of the Military Division of the Mississippi.

HEADQUARTERS DEPARTMENT OF THE TENNESSEE,⎫
Vicksburgh, January 31, 1864 ⎭

Major R. M. Sawyer, A. A. General, Army of the Tennessee, Huntsville:

DEAR SAWYER: In my former letter I have answered all your questions save one, and that relates to the treatment of inhabitants, known or suspected to be hostile, or "secesh." This is in truth the most difficult business of our army, as it advances and occupies the Southern country. It is almost impossible to lay down rules, and I invariably leave this whole

subject to the local commanders, but am willing to give them the benefit of my acquired knowledge and experience.

In Europe, whence we derive our principles of war, as developed by
their histories, wars are between kings or rulers, through hired armies,
and not between peoples. These remain, as it were, neutral, and sell their
produce to whatever army is in possession.

Napoleon, when at war with Prussia, Austria, and Russia, bought forage and provisions of the inhabitants, and consequently had an interest to
protect farms and factories which ministered to his wants. In like manner, the allied armies in France could buy of the French inhabitants
whatever they needed, the produce of the soil or manufactures of the
country. Therefore, the rule was and is, that wars are confined to the
armies, and should not visit the homes of families or private interests.

But, in other examples, a different rule obtained the sanction of historical authority. I will only instance that, when, in the reign of William
and Mary, the English army occupied Ireland, then in a state of revolt,
the inhabitants were actually driven into foreign lands, and were actually
dispossessed of their property, and a new population introduced. To this
day, a large part of the north of Ireland is held by the descendants of the
Scotch emigrants, sent there by William's order and an act of Parliament.

The war which prevails in our land is essentially a war of races. The
Southern people entered into a clear compact of government, but still
maintained a species of separate interests, history, and prejudices. These
latter became stronger and stronger, till they have led to a war which has
developed fruits of the bitterest kind.

We of the North are, beyond all question, right in our lawful cause,
but we are not bound to ignore the fact, that the people of the South
have prejudices which form part of their nature, and which they cannot
throw off without an effort of reason or the slower process of natural
change. Now, the question arises, Should we treat as absolute enemies all
in the South who differ from us in opinion or prejudice, kill or banish
them; or, should we give them time to think, and gradually change their
conduct so as to conform to the new order of things, which is slowly and
gradually creeping into their country?

When men take arms to resist our rightful authority, we are compelled
to use force, because all reason and argument cease when arms are
resorted to. When the provisions, forage, horses, mules, wagons, etc., are
used by our enemy, it is clearly our duty and right to take them, because
otherwise they might be used against us.

In like manner, all houses left vacant by an inimical people are clearly
our right, or such as are needed as storehouses, hospitals, and quarters.
But a question arises as to dwellings used by women, children, and non-
combatants. So long as non-combatants remain in their houses and keep

to their accustomed business, their opinions and prejudices can in no wise influence the war, and, therefore, should not be noticed. But if any one comes out into the public streets and creates disorder, he or she should be punished, restrained, or banished either to the rear or front, as the officer in command adjudges. If the people, or any of them, keep up a correspondence with parties in hostility they are spies, and can be punished with death or minor punishment.

These are well-established principles of war, and the people of the South, having appealed to war, are barred from appealing to our Constitution, which they have practically and publicly defied. They have appealed to war, and must abide its rules and laws. The United States, as a belligerent party claiming right in the soil as the ultimate sovereign, have a right to change the population, and it may be and is both politic and just, we should do so in certain districts. When the inhabitants persist too long in hostility, it may be both politic and right we should banish them and appropriate their lands to a more loyal and useful population. No man will deny that the United States would be benefited by dispossessing a single prejudiced, hard-headed, and disloyal planter, and substitute in his place a dozen or more patient, industrious, good families, even if they be of foreign birth. I think it does good to present this view of the case to many Southern gentlemen, who grew rich and wealthy, not by virtue alone of their industry and skill, but by reason of the protection and impetus to prosperity given by our hitherto moderate and magnanimous Government. It is all idle nonsense for these Southern planters to say that they made the South, that they own it, and that they can do as they please—even to break up our Government, and to shut up the natural avenues of trade, intercourse, and commerce.

We know, and they know, if they are intelligent beings, that, as compared with the whole world, they are but as five millions are to one thousand millions—that they did not create the land—that their only title to its use and usufruct is the deed of the United States, and if they appeal to war, they hold their all by a very insecure tenure.

For my part, I believe that this war is the result of false political doctrine, for which we are all as a people responsible, namely, that any and every people have a right to self-government; and I would give all a chance to reflect, and when in error to recant. I know, slave-owners finding themselves in possession of a species of property in opposition to the growing sentiment of the whole civilized world, conceived their property in danger, and foolishly appealed to war; and by skilful political handling, involved with themselves the whole South on the doctrines of error and prejudice. I believe that some of the rich and slaveholding are prejudiced to an extent that nothing but death and ruin will extinguish, but hope that as the poorer and industrial classes of the South realize their relative weakness, and their dependence upon the fruits of the earth and good-will of their fellow-men, they will not only discover the error of their ways, and repent of their hasty action, but bless those who persistently maintained a constitutional government, strong enough to sustain itself, protect its citizens, and promise peaceful homes to millions yet unborn.

In this belief, whilst I assert for our Government the highest military prerogatives, I am willing to bear in patience that political nonsense of slave rights, State rights, freedom of conscience, freedom of press, and such other trash, as have deluded the Southern people into war, anarchy, bloodshed, and the foulest crimes that have disgraced any time or any people.

I would advise the commanding officers at Huntsville, and such other towns as are occupied by our troops, to assemble the inhabitants and explain to them these plain, self-evident propositions, and tell them that it is for them *now* to say, whether they and their children shall inherit the beautiful land which, by the accident of nature, has fallen to their share. The Government of the United States has in North-Alabama any and all rights which they choose to enforce in war, to take their lives, their homes, their lands, their every thing, because they cannot deny that war does exist there, and war is simply power unrestrained by constitution or compact. If they want eternal war, well and good—we will accept the issue and disposesses them, and put our friends in possession. I know thousands and millions of good people who, at simple notice, would come to North-Alabama and accept the elegant houses and plantations now there. If the people of Huntsville think differently, let them persist in war three years longer, and then they will not be consulted. Three years ago, by a little reflection and patience, they could have had a hundred years of peace and prosperity, but they preferred war; very well, last year they could have saved their slaves, but now it is too late—all the powers of earth cannot restore to them their slaves any more than their dead grandfathers. Next year their lands will be taken; for in war we can take them, and *rightfully*, too; and in another year they may beg in vain for their lives. A people who will persevere in war beyond a certain limit, ought to know the consequences. Many, many people, with less pertinacity than the South, have been wiped out of national existence.

My own belief is, that even now the non-slaveholding classes of the South are alienating from their associates in war. Already I hear crimination. Those who have property left, should take warning in time.

Since I have come down here, I have seen many Southern planters who now hire their negroes, and acknowledge that they knew not the earthquake they were to make by appealing to secession. They thought that the politicians had prepared the way, and that they could part in peace. They now see that we are bound together as one nation, by indissoluble ties, and that any interest or any people that set themselves up in antagonism to the nation, must perish.

While I would not remit one jot or tittle of our nation's rights, in peace or war, I do make allowances for past political errors and false prejudices. Our national Congress and Supreme Courts are the proper arenas in which to discuss conflicting opinions, and not the battle-field.

You may not hear from me again; and if you think it will do any good, call some of the people together, and explain these my views. You may even read to them this letter, and let them use it, so as to prepare them for my coming.

To those who submit to the rightful law and authority, all gentleness and forebearance; but to the petulant and persistent secessionist, why, death is mercy, and the quicker he or she is disposed of, the better. Satan, and the rebellious saints of heaven, were allowed a continuance of existence in hell merely to swell their just punishment. To such as would rebel against a government so mild and just as ours was in peace, a punishment equal would not be unjust.

We are progressing well in this quarter. Though I have not changed my opinion that we may soon assume the existence of our national Government, yet years will pass before ruffianism, murder, and robbery will cease to afflict this region of our country.

Truly your friend,

W. T. SHERMAN,
Major-General Commanding

Witness Testimony on the Fort Pillow Massacre (April 12, 1864), before the Joint Commission on the Conduct and Expenditures of the War
(April 18–22, 1864)

[38TH CONGRESS, 1ST SESSION,
REPORT NO. 65: 17–19; 21–22; 104–105]

Fort Pillow, Tennessee, on the Mississippi River, was manned by five hundred and eighty Union troops; two hundred and ninety-two were in "Colored" artillery regiments. Confederate President Jefferson Davis saw the Union's use of freed blacks and former slaves as illegal, unethical, and unfair, and implemented or approved policies whereby his armies would treat black soldiers and white officers of black troops not as prisoners of war (a bad enough fate!) but as insurrectionists—and thus deserving of death. Confederate General Nathan Bedford Forrest (1821–1877), a former slave-trader who became a folk hero in the South for his amazing feats of cavalry warfare, and whom Union General W. T. Sherman regarded as the biggest menace to his campaign through the South, was found by a Congressional Commission to have allowed or encouraged the Fort Pillow massacre, whereby surrendered troops were murdered. In Forrest's official report of April 26 on the battle, no improprieties or summary executions were mentioned (see The Rebellion Record, *Vol. VIII, Document No. 139). After the war, Forrest helped establish the Ku Klux Klan.*

What follow are a few of the dozens of eyewitness accounts by white officers and "colored" troops.

THE following papers and affidavits were furnished the committee by General Mason Brayman, at Cairo, and are herewith submitted:

We have the honor of reporting to you, as the only known survivors of the commissioned officers of the 13th Tennessee cavalry, that, on the morning of the 12th day of the present month, at about the hour of daylight, the rebels, numbering from five thousand to seven thousand, attacked our garrison at Fort Pillow, Tennessee, numbering as it did only about five hundred effective men. They at first sent in a flag of truce demanding a surrender, which Major Booth, then commanding the post, (Major Booth, of the 6th United States. heavy artillery, colored) refused. Shortly after this Major Booth was shot through the heart and fell dead. Major William F. Bradford, then commanding the 13th Tennessee cavalry, assumed command of the fort, and under his orders a continual fire was kept up until about one o'clock p.m., when our cannon and the rifles of the sharpshooters were mowing the rebels down in such numbers that they could not make an advance. The rebels then hoisted a second flag of truce and sent it in, demanding an unconditional surrender. They also threatened that if the place was not surrendered no quarter would be shown. Major Bradford refused to accept any such terms, would not surrender, and sent back word that if such were their intentions they could try it on. While this flag of truce was being sent in the rebel officers formed their forces in whatever advantageous positions they were able to select. They then formed a hollow square around our garrison, placed their sharpshooters within our deserted barracks, and directed a galling fire upon our men. They also had one brigade in the trenches just outside the fort, which had been cut by our men only a few days before, and which provided them with as good protection as that held by the garrison in the fort. Their demand of the flag of truce having been refused, the order was given by General Forrest in person to charge upon the works and show no quarter. Half an hour after the issuance of this order a scene of terror and massacre ensued. The rebels came pouring in solid masses right over the breast-works. Their numbers were perfectly overwhelming. The moment they reached the top of the walls, and commenced firing as they descended, the colored troops were panic-stricken, threw down their arms, and ran down the bluff, pursued sharply, begging for life. But escape was impossible. The confederates had apprehended such a result, and had placed a regiment of cavalry where it could cut off all effective retreat. This cavalry regiment employed themselves in shooting down the negro troops as fast as they made their appearance. The whites, as soon as they perceived they were also to be butchered inside the fort, also ran down. They had previously thrown down their arms and submitted. In many instances the men begged for life at the hands of the enemy, even on their knees. They were only made to stand upon their feet and then summarily shot down. Capt. Theo. F. Bradford, of company A, 13th Tennessee cavalry, was signal-officer for the gunboat, and was seen by General Forrest with the signal flags. The general, in person, ordered Captain Bradford to be shot. He was instantly riddled with bullets, nearly a full regiment having fired their pieces upon him. Lieutenant Wilson, of company A, 13th Tennessee cavalry, was killed after he had surrendered, he having been previously wounded. Lieutenant J. C. Ackerstrom, company E, 13th Tennessee cavalry, and acting regimental quartermaster, was severely wounded after he had surrendered, and then nailed to the side of the house and the house set on fire, burning him to death. Lieutenant Cord Revelle, company E, 13th Tennessee cavalry, was shot and killed after surrender. Major William F. Bradford, commanding our forces, was fired upon after he had surrendered the garrison. The rebels told him he could not surrender. He ran into the river and swam out some fifty yards, they all the time firing at him, but failing to hit him. He was hailed by an officer and told to return to the shore. He did so. But as he neared the shore the riflemen discharged their pieces at him again. Again they missed. He ran up the hillside among the enemy with a white handkerchief in his hand in token of his surrender, but still they continued to fire upon him. There were several confederate officers standing near at the time. None of them ordered the firing to cease but when they found they could not hit him they allowed him to give himself up as a prisoner, and paroled him to the limits of the camp. They now claim that he violated his parole the same night and escaped. We have heard from prisoners who got away from the rebels that they took Major Bradford out in the Hatchie Bottom and there dispatched him. We feel confident that the story is true. We saw several negroes burning up in their quarters on Wednesday morning. We also saw the rebels come back that morning and shoot at the wounded. We also saw them at a distance running about hunting up wounded that they might shoot them. There were some whites also burning. The rebels went to the negro hospital, where about thirty sick were kept, and butchered them with their sabres, hacking their heads open in many instances, and then set fire to the buildings. They killed every negro soldier Wednesday morning upon whom they came. Those who were able they made stand up to be shot. In one case a white soldier was found wounded. He had been lying upon the ground nearly twenty-four hours without food or drink. He asked a rebel soldier to give him something to drink. The latter turned about upon his heel and fired three deliberate shots at him, saying, "Take that, you negro equality." The poor fellow is alive yet, and in the hospital. He can tell the tale for himself. They ran a great many into the river, and shot or drowned them there. They immediately killed all the officers who were over the negro troops, excepting one who has since died from his wounds. They took out from Fort Pillow about one hundred and some odd prisoners, (white,) and forty negroes. They hung and shot the negroes as they passed along toward Brownsville until they were rid of them all. Out of the six hundred troops (convalescents included), which were at the fort they have only about one hundred prisoners (all whites), and we have about fifty wounded, who are paroled.

Major Anderson, Forrest's assistant adjutant general, stated that they did not consider colored men as soldiers, but as property, and as such, being used by our people, they had destroyed them. This was concurred in by Forrest, Chalmers, and McCulloch, and other officers.

We respectfully refer you to the accompanying affidavit of Hardy N. Revelle, lettered "A", and those of Mrs. Rufin, lettered "B", and Mrs. Williams, lettered "C."

Respectfully submitted.

F. A. SMITH,
First Lieut. Co. D, 13th Tenn. Vol. cavalry

WILLIAM CLEARY,
Second Lieut. Co. B, 13th Tennessee Vol. Cavalry

GENERAL M. BRAYMAN
    A true copy.

C. B. SMITH,
Lieutenant and A. D. C.

Sergeant Benjamin Robinson, (colored) Company D, 6th United States heavy artillery, sworn and examined.

By Mr. Gooch:*

QUESTION. Were you at Fort Pillow in the fight there?
ANSWER. Yes, sir.
QUESTION. What did you see there?
ANSWER. I saw them shoot two white men right by the side of me after they had laid their guns down. They shot a black man clear over into the river. Then they hallooed to me to come up the hill, and I came up. They said, "Give me your money, you damned nig-

---

*Daniel Gooch of Massachusetts.

ger." I told them I did not have any. "Give me your money, or I
will blow your brains out." Then they told me to lie down, and I
laid down, and they stripped everything off me.

QUESTION. This was the day of the fight?

ANSWER. Yes, sir.

QUESTION. Go on. Did they shoot you?

ANSWER. Yes, sir. After they stripped me and took my money away
from me they dragged me up the hill a little piece, and laid me
down flat on my stomach; I laid there till night, and they took me
down to an old house, and said they would kill me the next morning. I got up and commenced crawling down the hill; I could not
walk.

QUESTION. When were you shot?

ANSWER. About 3 o'clock.

QUESTION. Before they stripped you?

ANSWER. Yes, sir. They shot me before they said, "come up."

QUESTION. After you had surrendered?

ANSWER. Yes, sir; they shot pretty nearly all of them after they surrendered.

QUESTION. Did you see anything of the burning of the men?

ANSWER. No, sir.

QUESTION. Did you see them bury anybody?

ANSWER. Yes, sir.

QUESTION. Did they bury anybody who was not dead?

ANSWER. I saw one of them working his hand after he was buried;
he was a black man. They had about a hundred in there, black and
white. The major was buried on the bank, right side of me. They
took his clothes all off but his drawers; I was lying right there looking at them. They had my captain's coat, too; they did not kill my
captain; a lieutenant told him to give him his coat, and then they
told him to go down and pick up those old rags and put them on.

QUESTION. Did you see anybody shot the day after the battle?

ANSWER. No, sir.

QUESTION. How did you get away?

ANSWER. A few men came up from Memphis, and got a piece of
plank and put me on it, and took me down to the boat.

QUESTION. Were any rebel officers around when the rebels were
killing our men?

ANSWER. Yes, sir; lots of them.

QUESTION. Did they try to keep their men from killing our men?

ANSWER. I never heard them say so. I know General Forrest rode
his horse over me three or four times. I did not know him until I

heard his men call his name. He said to some negro men there that he knew them; that they had been in his nigger yard in Memphis. He said he was not worth five dollars when he started, and had got rich trading in negroes.

QUESTION. Where were you from?

ANSWER. I came from South Carolina.

QUESTION. Have you been a slave?

ANSWER. Yes, sir.

Daniel Tyler, (colored) private, Company B, 6th United States heavy artillery, sworn and examined.

By Mr. Gooch:

QUESTION: Where were you raised?

ANSWER. In Mississippi.

QUESTION. Have you been a slave?

ANSWER. Yes, sir.

QUESTION. Were you in Fort Pillow at the time it was captured by the rebels?

ANSWER. Yes, sir.

QUESTION. When when you wounded?

ANSWER. I was wounded after we all surrendered; not before.

QUESTION. At what time?

ANSWER. They shot me when we came up the hill from down by the river.

QUESTION. Why did you go up the hill?

ANSWER. They called me up.

QUESTION. Did you see who shot you?

ANSWER. Yes, sir; I did not know him.

QUESTION. One of the rebels?

ANSWER. Yes, sir.

QUESTION. How near was he to you?

ANSWER. I was right at him; I had my hand on the end of his gun.

QUESTION. What did he say to you?

ANSWER. He said, "Whose gun are you holding?" I said, "Nobody's." He said, "God damn you, I will shoot you," and then he shot me. I let go, and then another one shot me.

QUESTION. Were many shot at the same time?

ANSWER. Yes, sir, lots of them; lying all round like hogs.

QUESTION. Did you see any one burned?

ANSWER. No, sir.

QUESTION. Did you see anybody buried alive?

ANSWER. Nobody but me.

QUESTION. Were you buried alive?

ANSWER. Yes, sir; they thought they had killed me. I lay there till about sundown, when they threw us in a hollow, and commenced throwing dirt on us.

QUESTION. Did you say anything?

ANSWER. No, sir; I did not want to speak to them. I knew if I said anything they would kill me. They covered me up in a hole; they covered me up, all but one side of my head. I heard them say they ought not to bury a man who was alive. I commenced working the dirt away, and one of the secesh made a young one dig me out. They dug me out, and I was carried not far off to a fire.

QUESTION. How long did you stay there?

ANSWER. I staid there that night and until the next morning, and then I slipped off. I heard them say the niggers had to go away from there before the gunboat came, and that they would kill the niggers. The gunboat commenced shelling up there, and they commenced moving off. I heard them up there shooting. They wanted me to go with them, but I would not go. I turned around, and came down to the river bank and got on the gunboat.

QUESTION. How did you lose your eye?

ANSWER. They knocked me down with a carbine, and then they jabbed it out.

QUESTION. Was that before you were shot?

ANSWER. Yes, sir.

QUESTION. After you had surrendered?

ANSWER. Yes, sir; I was going up the hill, a man came down and met me; he had his gun in his hand, and whirled it around and knocked me down, and then took the end of his carbine and jabbed it in my eye, and shot me.

QUESTION. Were any of their officers about there then?

ANSWER. I did not see any officers.

QUESTION. Were any white men buried with you?

ANSWER. Yes, sir.

QUESTION. Were any buried alive?

ANSWER. I heard that one white man was buried alive; I did not see him.

QUESTION. Who said that?

ANSWER. A young man; he said they ought not to have done it. He staid in there all night; I do not know as he ever got out.

Manuel Nichols, (colored) private, Company B, 6th United States heavy artillery, sworn and examined.

By Mr. Gooch:

QUESTION. Were you in the late fight at Fort Pillow?

ANSWER. Yes, sir.

QUESTION. Were you wounded there?

ANSWER. Yes, sir.

QUESTION. When?

ANSWER. I was wounded once about a half an hour before we gave up.

QUESTION. Did they do anything to you after you surrendered?

ANSWER. Yes, sir; they shot me in the head under my left ear, and the morning after the fight they shot me again in the right arm. When they came up and killed the wounded ones, I saw some four or five coming down the hill. I said to one of our boys, "Anderson, I expect if those fellows come here they will kill us." I was lying on my right side, leaning on my elbow. One of the black soldiers went into the house where the white soldiers were. I asked him if there was any water in there, and he said yes; I wanted some, and took a stick and tried to get to the house. I did not get to the house. Some of them came along, and saw a little boy belonging to company D. One of them had his musket on his shoulder, and shot the boy down. He said: "All you damned niggers come out of the house; I am going to shoot you." Some of the white soldiers said, "Boys, it is only death anyhow; if you don't go out they will come in and carry you out." My strength seemed to come to me as if I had never been shot, and I jumped up and ran down the hill. I met one of them coming up the hill; he said "stop!" but I kept on running. As I jumped over the hill, he shot me through the right arm.

QUESTION. How many did you see them kill after they had surrendered?

ANSWER. After I surrendered I did not go down the hill. A man shot me under the ear, and I fell down and said to myself, "If he don't shoot me any more this won't hurt me." One of their officers came along and hallooed, "Forrest says, no quarter! no quarter!" and the next one hallooed, "Black flag! black flag!"

QUESTION. What did they do then?

ANSWER. They kept on shouting. I could hear them down the hill.

QUESTION. Did you see them bury anybody?

ANSWER. Yes, sir; they carried me around right to the corner of the fort, and I saw them pitch men in there.

QUESTION. Was there any alive?

ANSWER. I did not see them bury anybody alive.

QUESTION. How near to you was the man who shot you under the ear?

ANSWER. Right close to my head. When I was shot in the side, a man turned me over, and took my pocket-knife and pocket-book. I had some of these brass things that looked like cents. They said, "Here's some money; here's some money." I said to myself, "You got fooled that time."

"The Returned Prisoners," Joint Commission on the Conduct and Expenditures of the War, Testimony by Surgeon A. Van Derkieft to the U.S. Senate Committee

(May 6, 1864)

[38TH CONGRESS, 1ST SESSION, REPORT NO. 67:18–20]

From the beginning of the war, Union prisoners of war in Confederate camps were treated so poorly that, when exchanges between armies could not be made, thousands died of disease or starvation. A Congressional Committee chaired by Benjamin F. Wade of Ohio interviewed returned prisoners at Annapolis, Maryland, and discovered horror after horror.

An estimated fifteen percent of Civil War soldiers were made prisoners; the Confederates held 200,000, the Union 220,000. After May 1863, the Confederates refused to exchange black prisoners of war, so the exchanges stopped and did not resume until the winter of 1864–65. Thirteen thousand Union prisoners of war died at the Confederates' Andersonville, Georgia, camp.

Surgeon B. A. Van Derkieft, sworn and examined.

By the chairman:[*]

QUESTION. Are you in the service of the United States; and if so, in what capacity?

ANSWER. I am a surgeon of volunteers in the United States service; in charge of hospital division No. 1, known as the Naval Hospital, Annapolis, and have been here since the 1st of June, 1863.

---

[*]B. F. Wade.

QUESTION. State what you know in regard to the condition of our exchanged or paroled prisoners who have been brought here, and also your opportunities to know that condition?

ANSWER. Since I have been here I think that from five to six thousand paroled prisoners have been treated in this hospital as patients. They have generally come here in a very destitute and feeble condition; many of them so low that they die the very day they arrive here.

QUESTION. What is the character of their complaints generally, and what does that character indicate as to the cause?

ANSWER. Generally they are suffering from debility and chronic diarrhœa, the result, I have no doubt, of exposure, privations, hardship, and ill treatment.

QUESTION. In what respect would hardship and ill treatment superinduce the complaints most prevalent among these paroled prisoners?

ANSWER. These men, having been very much exposed, and not having had nourishment enough to sustain their strength, are consequently predisposed to be attacked by such diseases as diarrhœa, fever, scurvy, and all catarrhal affections, which, perhaps, in the beginning are very slight, but, on account of want of necessary care, produce, after a while, a very serious disease. For instance, a man exposed to the cold may have a little bronchitis, or perhaps a little inflammation of the lungs, which, under good treatment, would be easily cured—would be considered of no importance whatever; but being continually exposed, and not having the necessary food, the complaint is transformed, after a time, into a very severe disease.

QUESTION. Is it your opinion, as a physician, that the complaints of our returned prisoners are superinduced by want of proper food, or food of sufficient quantity, and from exposure?

ANSWER. Yes, sir.

QUESTION. What is the general character of the statements our prisoners have made to you in regard to their treatment?

ANSWER. They complained of want of food, of bad food, and a want of clothing. Very often, though not always, they are robbed, when taken prisoners, of all the good clothes they have on. There is no doubt about that, for men have often arrived here with nothing but their pants and shirts on; no coat, overcoat, no cap, no shoes or stockings, and some of them without having had any opportunities to wash themselves for weeks and months, so that when they arrive here, the scurf on their skin is one-eighth of an inch thick; and we have had several cases of men who have been shot for the slightest offence. There is a man now here who at one time put his hand out of the privy, which was nothing but a window in the wall, to steady himself and keep himself from falling, and he was shot, and we have been obliged to amputate his arm since he arrived here. These men complain that they have had no shelter. We have men here now who say that for five or six months they have been compelled to lay on the sand. I have no doubt about the correctness of their statements, for the condition of their skins shows the statements to be true. Their joints are calloused, and they have callouses on their backs, and some have even had the bones break through the skin. There is one instance in particular that I would mention. One man died in the hospital there one hour before the transfer of prisoners was made, and as an act of humanity the surgeon in charge of the hospital allowed the friends of this man to take him on board the vessel in order to have him buried among his friends. This man was brought here right from the Richmond hospital. He was so much covered with vermin and so dirty that we were not afraid to make the statement that the man had not been washed for six months. Now, as a material circumstance to prove that these men have been badly fed, I will state that we must be very careful in feeding them when they arrive here, for a very light diet is too much for them at first.

QUESTION. You have accompanied us as we have examined some of the patients in the hospital to-day. Do their statements to us, under oath, correspond with the statements which they made when they first arrived here?

ANSWER. They are quite the same; there is no difference. Every man makes the same statement, and we therefore believe it to be true. All say the same in regard to rations, treatment, exposure and privations. Once in a while I have found a man who pretended to have been treated very well, but by examining closely I find that such men are not very good Union men.

QUESTION. You say that about six thousand paroled prisoners have come under your supervision and treatment?

ANSWER. Yes, sir.

QUESTION. State generally what their condition has been.

ANSWER. Very bad, indeed. I cannot find terms sufficient to express what their condition was. I cannot state it properly.

QUESTION. You have already stated that, as a general thing, they have been destitute of clothing.

ANSWER. Yes, sir; dirty, filthy, covered with vermin, dying. At one time we received three hundred and sixty patients in one day, and

fourteen died within twelve hours; and there were six bodies of
those who had died on board the transport that brought them up
here.

QUESTION. What appeared to be the complaint of which they
died?

ANSWER. Very extremely debility, the result of starvation and exposure—the same as the very weak man you saw here, [L. H. Parham.]

QUESTION. We have observed some very emaciated men here, perfect skeletons, nothing but skin and bone. In your opinion, as a
physician, what has reduced these men to that condition?

ANSWER. Nothing but starvation and exposure.

QUESTION. Can you tell the proportion of the men who have died
to the number that have lately arrived from Richmond?

ANSWER. If time is allowed me I can send the statement to the
committee.

QUESTION. Do so, if you please.

ANSWER. I will do so. I will say that some of these men who have
stated they were well treated, I have found out to have been very
bad to the Union men.

QUESTION. Are those men you have just mentioned as having been
well treated an exception to the general rule?

ANSWER. Yes, sir; a very striking exception.

QUESTION. Have you ever been in charge of Confederate prisoners?

ANSWER. Yes, sir.

QUESTION. State the course of treatment of our authorities towards
them.

ANSWER. We have never made the slightest difference between our
own men and confederate prisoners when their sick and wounded
have been in our hands.

QUESTION. You have treated both the same?

ANSWER. Yes, sir. When any one of their men, wounded or sick,
has been a patient in our hands, we have treated him the same as
we do our own men.

By Mr. Julian:

QUESTION. Have their sick and wounded been kept separate from
ours, or have they been kept together?

ANSWER. In Washington they were kept separate, but at Antietam,
where an hospital was established, in order to have the patients
treated where they were injured, the Union and confederate

patients were treated together and alike. At Hagerstown almost everybody is secesh. Well, the most I can say is, that some of the secesh ladies there came to me and stated that they were very glad to see that we had treated their men the same as ours.

QUESTION. It is sometimes said, by the rebel newspapers, at least, that they have given the same rations to our prisoners that they give to their own soldiers. Now, I want to ask you, as a medical man, if it is possible, with the amount of food that our prisoners have had, for men to retain their health and vigor, and perform active service in the field?

ANSWER. I do not believe that the rebels could fight as well or make such marches as they have done, upon such small rations as our prisoners have received.

QUESTION. Can the health of men be preserved upon such rations as they have given our prisoners?

ANSWER. No, sir; it cannot, not only on account of quantity, but quality. I have seen some specimens of their rations brought here by our paroled prisoners, and I know what they are.

QUESTION. As a general rule, what is the effect of treating men in that way?

ANSWER. Just what we hear every day—men dying from starvation and debility. Many of these men—mostly all the wounded men—are suffering from hospital gangrene, which is the result of not having their wounds dressed in time, and having too many crowded in the same apartment. We have had men here whose wounds have been so long neglected that they have had maggots in them by the hundred.

Wilderness Campaign Report of Confederate Lieutenant-General James Longstreet
(April 11–May 6, 1864)

[OR: SERIES 1, VOL. 36, PT. 1:1054–1055]

After Union Lieutenant-General U.S. Grant's Army of the Potomac crossed the Rappahannock in Virginia on May 4, Confederate General Lee blocked them in the Wilderness, a thick wood with bushes and creeks running through it. It was an unfortunate site for Grant's army to await its supply trains. In three days of battle in the woods, culminating in brush fires that killed some of the wounded, the Union suffered more than 17,000 casualties.

On May 6, the last date covered by this report submitted in 1865, James Longstreet (1821–1904), similarly to Stonewall Jackson, was wounded by his own men, shot in the throat and shoulder.

HEADQUARTERS FIRST ARMY CORPS,
March 23, 1865

Lieut. Col. W. H. Taylor, A. A. G.

COLONEL: On April 11, 1864, I received orders at Bristol from the Adjutant and Inspector-General to report with the original portion of the First Corps (Kershaw's and Field's divisions and Alexander's battalion of artillery) to General R. E. Lee, commanding Army of Northern Virginia. On the 14th I reached Charlottesville, and awaited there the arrival of my troops, which were somewhat delayed by want of transportation on railroad. As the troops arrived they were encamped at points between Charlottesville and Gordonsville. On the 22d, in obedience to orders received from the commanding general, I marched my command to Mechanicsville, and encamped in the near neighborhood thereof. On the 2d [May] Field's division was moved to the north of Gordonsville to meet an expected advance of a portion of the enemy by way of Liberty Mills. On the 4th was advised by the commanding general that the enemy appeared to be moving toward Stevensburg, and, as directed by him, started about 4 o'clock in the afternoon and marched to Brock's Bridge, on the border of Orange County, a distance of about 16 miles. Early on the morning of the 5th resumed my march on the [Orange plank] and Catharpin roads to Richards' Shop on Catharpin road. During the latter part of this day's march Rosser was skirmishing in my front with his brigade of cavalry.

At 12.30 A.M. on the 6th started for Parker's Store, on the plank road, in obedience to orders received from the commanding general, who also informed me that Generals Hill and Ewell had been heavily engaged the previous day. Arriving at Parker's Store about dawn, I was directed to move my column down the plank road to relieve the divisions of Heth and Wilcox, which were in position in face of the enemy on the right and left of the plank road, at right angles with it and about 3 miles below Parker's Store. Kershaw's division was in the lead, arriving in the rear of the line held by these two divisions, and when the head of my column had filed to the right, and had only time to deploy two regiments of Kershaw's old brigade, an advance was made by the whole line of the enemy, and the divisions of Heth and Wilcox broke and retreated in some confusion. With considerable difficulty, but with steadiness, opening their ranks to let the retreating divisions through, Kershaw formed his line on the right and Field on the left of the plank road. Having checked the advance of the enemy, I ordered a general advance by my line, which was made with spirit rarely surpassed, and before which the enemy was driven a considerable distance. The woods were dense and the undergrowth almost impossible to penetrate. This success was not purchased without the loss of many of the bravest officers and men of my corps. The circumstances under which they fought were most unfavorable. Thrown suddenly, while still moving by the flank, and when hardly more than the head of the column could face the enemy, into the presence of an advancing foe with their ranks broken each instant by bodies of our retreating men, they not only held their own, but formed their line, and in turn, charging the enemy, drove him back in confusion over half a mile to a line of temporary works, where they were re-enforced by reserves. About 10 o'clock Maj. Gen. M. L. Smith and the other officers sent out to examine the enemy's position, reported that the left of the enemy's line extended but a short distance beyond the plank road. Special directions were given to Lieutenant-Colonel Sorrel to conduct the brigades of Generals Mahone, G. T. Anderson, and Wofford beyond the enemy's left, and to attack him on his left and rear—I have since heard that the brigade of General Davis formed a part of this flanking force—the flank movement to be followed by a general advance, Anderson's brigade on the right and Wofford's on the left, Mallone being in the center. They moved by the flank till the unfinished railroad from Gordonsville to Fredericksburg was reached. Forming on this railroad facing to the north, they advanced in the direction of the plank road till they encountered the enemy in flank and rear, who was then engaging the brigades of Gregg, Benning, and Law in front. The movement was a complete surprise and a perfect success. It was executed with rare zeal and intelligence. The enemy made but a short stand, and fell back, in utter rout with heavy loss, to a position about three-quarters of a mile from my front attack.

I immediately made arrangements to follow up the successes gained, and ordered an advance of all my troops for that purpose. While riding at the head of my column, moving by the flank down the plank road, I came opposite the brigades which had made the flank movement, and which were drawn up parallel to the plank road, and about 60 yards therefrom, when a portion of them fired a volley, which resulted in the death of General Jenkins, and the severe wounding of myself. I immediately notified the commanding general of my being obliged to quit the field, and the command devolved on Major-General Field.

To the members of my staff I am under great obligations for their valuable services. They conducted themselves with their usual distinguished gallantry. Much of the success of the movement on the enemy's flank is due to the very skillful manner in which the move was conducted by Lieutenant-Colonel Sorrel.

I have the honor to forward the accompanying reports of subordinate commanders of corps.

I am, colonel, with great respect, your obedient servant,

J. LONGSTREET
Lieutenant-General

Battle at Cold Harbor, by Union soldier George E. Place, Co. B, 12th New Hampshire Volunteers
(June 1–3, 1864)

[HTR:206–208]

George E. Place (b. 1837) was a soldier ordered into the "battle" at Cold Harbor during the Wilderness Campaign, one of the strategic moves that Lieutenant-General U.S. Grant deeply regretted. It was a disaster for the Union forces, and Place was among the 15,000 killed or disabled during the mission. He begins his account on the afternoon of June 1 and continues it through his division's June 3rd advance, his wounding, his regiment's retreat, and his "harrowing" visit to the field hospital.

A CANNONADING was going on as we reached the field [on the afternoon of June 1]. We halted at least two miles from where the rebel guns were in action; yet an occasional shot came quite near us. One missile struck and buried itself in the ground about twenty feet from me, and not over six feet from where a comrade was standing. It was dug out, and proved to be a shot from a Whitworth rifle gun. Presently we moved on, and took up a position, "resting at will," in some pine woods where occurred that terrible enfilading fire from a concealed rebel battery. Colonel Barker was standing near me, and I heard him remark, that he thought he had experienced some heavy artillery firing at the battle of Bull Run, but none equaled the closeness of that fire, yet strange as it may appear, as far as I could learn, not a man of the regiment was hurt while in that position. The shot were evidently all solid, as I do not recollect hearing any explosion of shells. One shot struck a tree ten inches in diameter at about eighteen inches from the ground, not over four feet from where I was sitting, cutting it half off. I heard some of the boys express a wish that a charge would be ordered on that battery, as they would rather do that, than lie quietly there and be murdered in cold blood. After about half an hour we were ordered to advance, and so we got out of range. We moved on a few rods and halted again. While there, some movement on the picket line called out several volleys of musketry, and the bullets came spatting around quite thickly. "Sherb" Locke was sitting at my left; a bullet struck his tin dipper which was fastened to his haversack, making of it a shapeless mass. My elbow was so near the dipper as almost to touch it.

And now I will pass onto that fateful morning of the third of June. We are in line of battle, "close column by division." We are ordered to take the caps from our guns, and fix bayonet. We are now in the woods, and can see nothing of the rebels. Every thing is quiet. Ah! it is such occasions as this which try men's nerves. I made a study of the faces around me. Every face was more or less pale, but all had a determined look, except a New York recruit by the name of Hayes. He was trembling, and his face was pale as death. I encountered him not long afterwards in the field hospital. He was unharmed. I questioned him some, and was satisfied, from his evasive answers, that he had skulked out of the fight. I learned afterwards that he had deserted about that time—probably that night. Thus we stood, all ready for the charge; I know not how long, but it seemed a long time to me, for at such a time, with men's nerves strained to their utmost tension, a minute seems an hour. Finally, the Colonel drew his sword,—*"Forward march,"* and the regiment started. We had not gone ten feet, when a rebel battery on our left flank opened fire. I wondered how the rebels knew so soon that we had started, for being in the woods, they could not see us. The guns were so arranged that the iron storm swept past us about two rods in front. How it crashed and howled through those pine trees! For a moment, the regiment quailed and halted. As it did so, I turned and looked at Colonel Barker. I shall never forget the expression that came into his face as he beheld that halting. His eyes dilated, and it seemed as if I could almost see the fire flash from them. He flung his sword above his head and shouted with a voice that seemed as if the rebels must have heard, "Forward!" Instantly the regiment started again, yelling as it went. There was no more halting after that, until, swept down in killed and wounded, it lost all semblance of order, and could do no otherwise than fall back. The artillery discharge was immediately followed by the opening of musketry. I passed close by one of the vedettes in a rifle-pit, hugging to the ground as close as he could, and trembling like an aspen leaf. Past the vedettes, we immediately enter an open field. It is bare of vegetation. All over that field little puffs of dust are thickly rising, occasioned by the rebel bullets striking the ground. A line of breastworks runs zig-zag; one in front, the other on our left. We cannot see a man in these works, for a dense cloud of battle-smoke rests all along the line. From the works in front, and the works on our left, arose a musketry fire so heavy, it seemed almost like one continual crash of thunder, while artillery on our left poured in the shells. Just as we entered the field, a shell plunged into the ground at the left of our column, and immediately burst, throwing the dirt and pebbles all over us. Some small missile struck me just under the left eye, causing a sharp sting, and I felt the blood trickling down my face.

James Rollins was at my left, Charles Marden next to him, and the next beyond, Charles Bunker. Soon after we got into the field, Rollins threw up both hands, uttered a yell, and fell over on his face. I thought surely he was killed, but found him afterwards in the field hospital. A bullet had gone through the calves of both legs. I looked for Marden and Bunker to "dress" by, but they were missing; indeed, there was such a wide gap on my left (I was almost on the right of the column) that I thought I had fallen behind my columns, and hastened to catch up, only to find myself in Company A, who were in the front column. We were now so near the breastworks that I could see the flash of their musketry quivering through the bank of smoke that lay above them, like lightning through a cloud; and I was just thinking of the hand-to-hand struggle that would come when we reached the breastworks, when a bullet went through my right arm. My hand instantly flew open, and my gun dropped to the ground. All the fingers on that hand turned back to nearly a right angle with the back of my hand, and quivered, caused, probably, by a sudden contraction of the muscles. I thought for a moment, that my arm was broken, and I caught hold of my fingers and straightened them out. About this time, the regiment began to fall back. Just before I reëntered the woods a flank bullet grazed the small of my back. As I received that third blow, that old, familiar expression, "hit 'im agin, blue jacket, he's got no friends," passed across my mind. I reached the field hospital, and sat down among a group of wounded men, so as to get my wounds dressed. As I raised my eyes, I saw I was seated near an amputating table. The spectacle was too harrowing, and I arose to go away, but immediately grew faint, and had to sit down again. I was compelled to sit there nearly an hour before my condition would allow me to go away. Twice during the time I was there, a load of arms, legs, hands, and feet, was carried off on a shelter tent and dumped into a ravine.

Report on the Sinking of
the *Alabama* by the *Kearsarge,*
by Union Captain John A. Winslow
(July 30, 1864)

[RR-IX:224–226]

The Alabama, *which had sunk or taken at least sixty-five U. S. ships in the last two years, was in France for repairs after sailing from Brazil to Africa to the Indian Ocean to the China Sea and then back to Brazil before sailing to Europe. There, off the coast of France in the English Channel, the* Alabama *met the U.S.S.* Kearsarge, *which awaited it. The day before the pending battle, Confederate Captain Raphael Semmes (1809–1877) remarked, "The contest will no doubt be contested and obstinate, but the two ships are so evenly matched that I do not feel at liberty to decline it. God defend the right, and have mercy upon the souls of those who fall, as many of us must."*

"The Alabama *was built for speed rather than battle," observed* Alabama *officer John Macintosh Kell, and it lost the battle. Afterwards, Semmes complained that the* Kearsarge *was chain-armored: "It was the same thing as if two men were to go out and fight a duel, and one of them, unknown to the other, were to put on a suit of mail under his outer garment." Rather than allow the Union to try to salvage it and use it against the Confederacy, Semmes scuttled the* Alabama.

UNITED STATES STEAMER *Kearsarge,*⎫
English Channel, July 30, 1864 ⎰

SIR: In obedience to instructions of the department, I have the honor to make the following supplementary report of the action between the *Kearsarge* and *Alabama:*

On the morning of the nineteenth ultimo, the day being fine, with a hazy atmosphere, wind moderate from the westward, with little sea, the position of the *Kearsarge* at ten o'clock was near the buoy which marks the line of shoals to the eastward of Cherbourg, and distant about three miles from the eastern entrance, which bore to the southward and westward. At twenty minutes after ten o'clock, the *Alabama* was descried coming out of the western entrance, accompanied by the *Couronne,* (ironclad). I had, in an interview with the Admiral at Cherbourg, assured him that in the event of an action occurring with the *Alabama,* the position of the ships should be so far offshore that no questions could be advanced about the line of jurisdiction. Accordingly, to perfect this object, and with the double purpose of drawing the *Alabama* so far off shore that, if disabled, she could not return, I directed the ship's head seaward, and cleared for action, with the battery pivoted to starboard. Having attained a point about seven miles from the shore, the head of the *Kearsarge* was turned short around and the ship steered directly for the *Alabama,* my purpose being to run her down, or, if circumstances did not warrant it, to close in with her.

Hardly had the *Kearsarge* come round, before the *Alabama* sheered, presented her starboard battery, and showed her engines. On approaching her at long range of about a mile, she opened her full broadside, the shot cutting some of our rigging, and going over and alongside of us.

Immediately I ordered more speed, but in two minutes the *Alabama* had loaded and again fired another broadside, and following it with a third, without damaging us, except in rigging.

We had now arrived within about nine hundred yards of her, and I was apprehensive that another broadside (nearly raking as it was), would prove disastrous. Accordingly, I ordered the *Kearsarge* sheered, and opened on the *Alabama*. The position of the vessels was now broadside and broadside; but it was soon apparent that Captain Semmes did not seek close action. I became then fearful lest, after some fighting, he would again make for the shore. To defeat this, I determined to keep full speed on, and with a port-helm to run under the stern of the *Alabama* and rake her, if he did not prevent it by sheering and keeping his broadside to us. He adopted this mode as a preventive, and, as a consequence, the *Alabama* was forced, with a full head of steam, into a circular track during the engagement.

The effect of this manœuvre was such that, at the last of the action, when the *Alabama* would have made off, she was near five miles from the shore; and had the action continued from the first in parallel lines, with her head in shore, the line of jurisdiction would no doubt have been reached. The firing of the *Alabama* from the first was rapid and wild; toward the close of the action her firing became better. Our men, who had been cautioned against rapid firing without direct aim, were much more deliberate; and the instructions given to point the heavy guns below rather than above the water-line and clear the deck with the lighter ones, was fully observed.

I had endeavored with a port helm, to close in with the *Alabama*; but it was not until just before the close of the action that we were in position to use grape. This was avoided, however, by her surrender. The effect of the training of our men was evident; nearly every shot from our guns was telling fearfully on the *Alabama*, and on the seventh rotation on the circular track she winded, setting foretrysail and two jibs, with head in-shore. Her speed was now retarded, and, by winding her port broadside was presented to us, with only two guns bearing, not having been able, as I learned afterward, to shift over but one. I saw now that she was at our mercy, and a few more guns well directed brought down her flag. I was unable to ascertain whether it had been hauled down or shot away; but a white flag having been displayed over the stern, our fire was reserved. Two minutes had not more than elapsed before she again opened on us with the two guns on the port side. This drew our fire again, and the *Kearsarge* was immediately steamed ahead and laid across her bows for raking. The white flag was still flying, and our fire was again reserved. Shortly after this, her boats were seen to be lowering, and an officer in one of them came alongside, and informed us that the ship had surrendered and was fast sinking. In twenty minutes from this time the *Alabama* went down, her mainmast, which had been shot, breaking near the head as she sunk, and her bow rising high out of the water as her stern rapidly settled.

The fire of the *Alabama*, although it is stated she discharged three hundred and seventy or more shell and shot, was not of serious damage to the *Kearsarge*.

Some thirteen or fourteen of these had taken effect in and about the hull, and sixteen or seventeen about the masts and rigging. The casualties were small, only three persons having been wounded; yet it is a matter of surprise that so few were injured, considering the number of projectiles that came aboard. Two shot passed through the ports in which the thirty-twos were placed, with men thickly stationed around them, one taking effect in the hammock netting and the other going through the port on the opposite side, yet no one was hit, the captain of one of the guns being only knocked down by the wind of the shot, as supposed.

The fire of the *Kearsarge*, although only one hundred and seventy-three projectiles had been discharged, according to the prisoners' accounts, was terrific. One shot alone had killed and wounded eighteen men, and disabled a gun. Another had entered the coal-bunkers, exploding, and completely blocking up the engine room, and Captain Semmes states that shot and shell had taken effect in the sides of his vessel, tearing large holes by explosion, and his men were everywhere knocked down.

Of the casualties in the *Alabama* no correct account can be given. One hundred and fifteen persons reached the shore, either in England or France, after the action. It is known that the *Alabama* carried a crew, officers and men, of about one hundred and fifty into Cherbourg, and that while in the Southern ocean her complement was about one hundred and seventy; but desertions had reduced this complement. The prisoners state that a number of men came on board at Cherbourg, and the night before the action boats were going to and fro, and in the morning strange men were seen, who were stationed as captains of the guns. Among these there was one lieutenant (Sinclair), who joined her in Cherbourg.

The *Alabama* had been five days in preparation. She had taken in three hundred and fifty tons of coal, which brought her down in the water. The *Kearsarge* had only one hundred and twenty tons in; but as an offset to this, her sheet chains were stowed outside, stopped up and down, as an additional preventive and protection to her more empty bunkers.

The number of the crew of the *Kearsarge*, including officers and sick men, was one hundred and sixty-three; and her battery numbered seven guns—two eleven-inch and one thirty-pounder rifle, and four light thirty-two pounder guns.

The battery of the *Alabama* numbered eight guns—one heavy sixty-eight, of nine thousand pounds; one one hundred and ten pounder rifle; and six heavy thirty-two pounder guns.

In the engagement the *Alabama* fought seven guns and the *Kearsarge* five, both exercising the starboard battery, until the *Alabama* winded, using then her port side with one gun, and another shifted over.

The collateral events connected with this action have already been laid before the department.

I inclose a diagram showing the track which was described during the engagement by the rotary course of the vessels.

I have the honor to be, very respectfully, your obedient servant,

JOHN. A. WINSLOW,
Captain

HON. GIDEON WELLES,
     Secretary of the Navy, Washington, D. C.

Letter from Union Major-General W. T. Sherman to the Mayor and City Council of Atlanta
(September 12, 1864)

[MWTS:125–127]

Like him or not, Major-General William Tecumseh Sherman's moral bearing on the war was always deeply considered and clearly explained: "You cannot qualify war in harsher terms than I will. War is cruelty, and you cannot refine it; and those who brought war into our country deserve all the curses and maledictions a people can pour out." The Union had no general more effective than he at carrying out bold missions, and Sherman's "March to the Sea" was indeed devastating to property in the South and the Confederacy's war capabilities.

HEADQUARTERS MILITARY DIVISION OF THE MISSISSIPPI,}
in the field, Atlanta, Georgia, September 12, 1864 }

James M. Calhoun, *Mayor* E. E. Rawson *and* S. C. Wells, *representing City Council of Atlanta*

GENTLEMEN: I have your letter of the 11th, in the nature of a petition to revoke my orders removing all the inhabitants from Atlanta. I have read it carefully, and give full credit to your statements of the distress that will be occasioned, and yet shall not revoke my orders, because they were not designed to meet the humanities of the case, but to prepare for the future struggles in which millions of good people outside of Atlanta have a deep interest. We must have peace, not only at Atlanta, but in all America. To secure this, we must stop the war that now desolates our once happy and favored country. To stop war, we must defeat the rebel armies which are arrayed against the laws and Constitution that all must respect and obey. To defeat those armies, we must prepare the way to reach them in their recesses, provided with the arms and instruments which enable us to accomplish our purpose. Now, I know the vindictive nature of our enemy, that we may have many years of military operations from this quarter; and, therefore, deem it wise and prudent to prepare in time. The use of Atlanta for warlike purposes is inconsistent with its character as a home for families. There will be no manufactures, commerce, or agriculture here, for the maintenance of families, and sooner or later want will compel the inhabitants to go. Why not go now, when all the arrangements are completed for the transfer, instead of waiting till the plunging shot of contending armies will renew the scenes of the past month? Of course, I do not apprehend any such thing at this moment, but you do not suppose this army will be here until the war is over. I cannot discuss this subject with you fairly, because I cannot impart to you what we propose to do, but I assert that our military plans make it necessary for the inhabitants to go away, and I can only renew my offer of services to make their exodus in any direction as easy and comfortable as possible.

You cannot qualify war in harsher terms than I will. War is cruelty, and you cannot refine it; and those who brought war into our country deserve all the curses and maledictions a people can pour out. I know I had no hand in making this war, and I know I will make more sacrifices to-day than any of you to secure peace. But you cannot have peace and a division of our country. If the United States submits to a division now, it will not stop, but will go on until we reap the fate of Mexico, which is eternal war. The United States does and must assert its authority, wherever it once had power; for, if it relaxes one bit to pressure, it is gone, and I believe that such is the national feeling. This feeling assumes various shapes, but always comes back to that of Union. Once admit the Union, once more acknowledge the authority of the national Government, and, instead of devoting your houses and streets and roads to the dread uses of war, I and this army become at once your protectors and supporters, shielding you from danger, let it come from what quarter it may. I know that a few individuals cannot resist a torrent of error and passion, such as swept the South into rebellion, but you can point out, so that we may know those who desire a government, and those who insist on war and its desolation.

You might as well appeal against the thunder-storm as against these terrible hardships of war. They are inevitable, and the only way the people of Atlanta can hope once more to live in peace and quiet at home, is to stop the war, which can only be done by admitting that it began in error and is perpetuated in pride.

We don't want your negroes, or your horses, or your houses, or your lands, or any thing you have, but we do want and will have a just obedience to the laws of the United States. That we will have, and, if it involves the destruction of your improvements, we cannot help it.

You have heretofore read public sentiment in your newspapers, that live by falsehood and excitement; and the quicker you seek for truth in other quarters, the better. I repeat then that, by the original compact of Government, the United States had certain rights in Georgia, which have never been relinquished and never will be; that the South began war by seizing forts, arsenals, mints, custom-houses, etc., etc., long before Mr. Lincoln was installed, and before the South had one jot or tittle of provocation. I myself have seen in Missouri, Kentucky, Tennessee, and Mississippi, hundreds and thousands of women and children fleeing from your armies and desperadoes, hungry and with bleeding feet. In Memphis, Vicksburg, and Mississippi, we fed thousands upon thousands of the families of rebel soldiers left on our hands, and whom we could not see starve. Now that war comes home to you, you feel very different. You deprecate its horrors, but did not feel them when you sent carloads of soldiers and ammunition, and moulded shells and shot, to carry war into Kentucky and Tennessee, to desolate the homes of hundreds and thousands of good people who only asked to live in peace at their old homes, and under the Government of their inheritance. But these comparisons are idle. I want peace, and believe it can only be reached through union and war, and I will ever conduct war with a view to perfect and early success.

But, my dear sirs, when peace does come, you may call on me for any thing. Then will I share with you the last cracker, and watch with you to shield your homes and families against danger from every quarter.

Now you must go, and take with you the old and feeble, feed and nurse them, and build for them, in more quiet places, proper habitations to shield them against the weather until the mad passions of men cool down, and allow the Union and peace once more to settle over your old homes at Atlanta. Yours in haste,

W. T. SHERMAN,
Major-General commanding

Second Inaugural Address, President Lincoln
(March 4, 1865)

[ALGS]

With characteristic economy and generosity, Abraham Lincoln surveyed the past four years of war and directed the divided country to look ahead and "bind up the nation's wounds." The abolitionist and author Frederick Douglass, who was present at the President's second inaugural, admiringly observed that "the address sounded more like a sermon than a state paper."[5]

AT this second appearing to take the oath of the presidential office, there is less occasion for an extended address than there was at the first. Then a statement, somewhat in detail, of a course to be pursued, seemed fitting and proper. Now, at the expiration of four years, during which public declarations have been constantly called forth on every point and phase of the great contest which still absorbs the attention, and engrosses the energies of the nation, little that is new could be presented. The progress of our arms, upon which all else chiefly depends, is as well known to the public as to myself; and it is, I trust, reasonably satisfactory and encouraging to all. With high hope for the future, no prediction in regard to it is ventured.

On the occasion corresponding to this four years ago, all thoughts were anxiously directed to an impending civil war. All dreaded it—all sought to avert it. While the inaugural address was being delivered from this place, devoted altogether to *saving* the Union without war, insurgent agents were in the city seeking to *destroy* it without war—seeking to dissolve the Union, and divide effects, by negotiation. Both parties dep-

---

[5] See Ronald C. White, Jr.'s *Lincoln's Greatest Speech* for further discussion and background of the Second Inaugural Address.

recated war; but one of them would *make* war rather than let the nation survive; and the other would *accept* war rather than let it perish. And the war came.

One eighth of the whole population were colored slaves, not distributed generally over the Union, but localized in the Southern part of it. These slaves constituted a peculiar and powerful interest. All knew that this interest was, somehow, the cause of the war. To strengthen, perpetuate, and extend this interest was the object for which the insurgents would rend the Union, even by war; while the government claimed no right to do more than to restrict the territorial enlargement of it. Neither party expected for the war, the magnitude, or the duration, which it has already attained. Neither anticipated that the *cause* of the conflict might cease with, or even before, the conflict itself should cease. Each looked for an easier triumph, and a result less fundamental and astounding. Both read the same Bible, and pray to the same God; and each invokes His aid against the other. It may seem strange that any men should dare to ask a just God's assistance in wringing their bread from the sweat of other men's faces; but let us judge not that we be not judged. The prayers of both could not be answered; that of neither has been answered fully. The Almighty has His own purposes. "Woe unto the world because of offences! for it must needs be that offences come; but woe to that man by whom the offence cometh!" If we shall suppose that American Slavery is one of those offences which, in the providence of God, must needs come, but which, having continued through His appointed time, He now wills to remove, and that He gives to both North and South, this terrible war, as the woe due to those by whom the offence came, shall we discern therein any departure from those divine attributes which the believers in a Living God always ascribe to Him? Fondly do we hope—fervently do we pray—that this mighty scourge of war may speedily pass away. Yet, if God wills that it continue, until all the wealth piled by the bond-man's two hundred and fifty years of unrequited toil shall be sunk, and until every drop of blood drawn with the lash, shall be paid by another drawn with the sword, as was said three thousand years ago, so still it must be said "the judgments of the Lord, are true and righteous altogether."

With malice toward none; with charity for all; with firmness in the right, as God gives us to see the right, let us strive on to finish the work we are in; to bind up the nation's wounds; to care for him who shall have borne the battle, and for his widow, and his orphan—to do all which may achieve and cherish a just and lasting peace, among ourselves, and with all nations.

Correspondence Regarding Surrender between Union Lieutenant-General U. S. Grant of the Army of Potomac and Confederate General R. E. Lee, Commander of the Confederate States Armies

[OR: SER. 1, VOL. 46, PT. 3, 664–665]

President Lincoln had authorized his Lieutenant-General Ulysses S. Grant to negotiate with Confederate Commander Robert E. Lee on the surrender of the Confederacy's most important army, and Lee, foreseeing the destruction of his men, finally conceded defeat. Though Grant and Lee had met while serving in the Mexican War, Appomattox Courthouse (Clover Hill), Virginia, was their first meeting as equals. Grant then drafted the concluding terms of surrender on the spot.

HEADQUARTERS ARMIES OF THE UNITED STATES,
April 9, 1865

GENERAL R. E. LEE:
  Commanding C. S. Army:

GENERAL: Your note of yesterday is received. As I have no authority to treat on the subject of peace the meeting proposed for 10 A.M. to-day could lead to no good. I will state, however, general, that I am equally anxious for peace with yourself, and the whole North entertain the same feeling. The terms upon which peace can be had are well understood. By the South laying down their arms they will hasten that most desirable event, save thousands of human lives, and hundreds of millions of property not yet destroyed. Sincerely hoping that all our difficulties may be settled without the loss of another life, I subscribe myself,

  Very respectfully, your obedient servant,

U. S. GRANT,
Lieutenant-General, U. S. Army

April 9, 1865

LIEUT. GEN. U. S. GRANT,
  Commanding U. S. Armies:

GENERAL: I received your note of this morning on the picket-line, whither I had come to meet you and ascertain definitely what terms were embraced in your proposal of yesterday with reference to the surrender of this army. I now request an interview in accordance with the offer contained in your letter of yesterday for that purpose.

Very respectfully, your obedient servant,

R. E. LEE,
General

HEADQUARTERS ARMIES OF THE UNITED STATES,
Appomattox Court-House, Va., April 9, 1865

GENERAL R. E. LEE,
  Commanding C. S. Army:

GENERAL: In accordance with the substance of my letter to you of the 8th instant, I propose to receive the surrender of the Army of Northern Virginia on the following terms, to wit: Rolls of all the officers and men to be made in duplicate—one copy to be given to an officer to be designated by me, the other to be retained by such officer or officers as you may designate; the officers to give their individual paroles not to take up arms against the Government of the United States until properly exchanged, and each company or regimental commander sign a like parole for the men of their commands. The arms, artillery, and public property to be parked and stacked, and turned over to the officers appointed by me to receive them. This will not embrace the side-arms of the officers, nor their private horses or baggage. This done, each officer and man will be allowed to return to their homes, not to be disturbed by United States authority so long as they observe their paroles and the laws in force where they may reside.

Very respectfully,

U. S. GRANT,
Lieutenant-General

Farewell Address to His Army
by Confederate General R. E. Lee
(April 10, 1865)

[REL: 153–154]

Having surrendered on April 9, Lee, according to his son, remarked to his wait-ing soldiers of the Army of Northern Virginia, "Men, we have fought through the war together; I have done my best for you; my heart is too full to say more," and then "he bade them good-bye and told them to return home and become good citizens." Lee (1807–1870) became the president of Washington University in Virginia (renamed Washington and Lee after his death).

HEADQUARTERS, ARMY OF NORTHERN VIRGINIA,
April 10, 1865

AFTER four years' of arduous service, marked by unsurpassed courage and fortitude, the Army of Northern Virginia has been compelled to yield to overwhelming numbers and resources. I need not tell the survivors of so many hard-fought battles, who have remained steadfast to the last, that I have consented to this result from no distrust of them; but, feeling that val-our and devotion could accomplish nothing that could compensate for the loss that would have attended the continuation of the contest, I have deter-mined to avoid the useless sacrifice of those whose past services have endeared them to their countrymen. By the terms of the agreement, officers and men can return to their homes and remain there until exchanged. You will take with you the satisfaction that proceeds from the consciousness of duty faithfully performed; and I earnestly pray that a merciful God will extend to you His blessing and protection. With an increasing admiration of your con-stancy and devotion to your country, and a grateful remembrance of your kind and generous considerations of myself, I bid you an affectionate farewell.

R. E. LEE,
General

Last Public Address, President Lincoln
(April 11, 1865)

[ALGS]

With the Confederacy's capital, Richmond, taken, Confederate R. E. Lee's forces surrendered, President Abraham Lincoln spoke from the White House on the inevitable "reconstruction" of the South. Four days later he was dead.

WE meet this evening, not in sorrow, but in gladness of heart. The evacuation of Petersburg and Richmond, and the surrender of the principal insurgent army, give hope of a righteous and speedy peace whose joyous expression can not be restrained. In the midst of this, however, He from whom all blessings flow, must not be forgotten. A call for a national thanksgiving is being prepared, and will be duly promulgated. Nor must those whose harder part gives us the cause of rejoicing, be overlooked. Their honors must not be parcelled out with others. I myself was near the front, and had the high pleasure of transmitting much of the good news to you; but no part of the honor, for plan or execution, is mine. To Gen. Grant, his skilful officers, and brave men, all belongs. The gallant Navy stood ready, but was not in reach to take active part.

By these recent successes the re-inauguration of the national authority—reconstruction—which has had a large share of thought from the first, is pressed much more closely upon our attention. It is fraught with great difficulty. Unlike a case of a war between independent nations, there is no authorized organ for us to treat with. No one man has authority to give up the rebellion for any other man. We simply must begin with, and mould from, disorganized and discordant elements. Nor is it a small additional embarrassment that we, the loyal people, differ among ourselves as to the mode, manner, and means of reconstruction.

As a general rule, I abstain from reading the reports of attacks upon myself, wishing not to be provoked by that to which I can not properly offer an answer. In spite of this precaution, however, it comes to my knowledge that I am much censured for some supposed agency in setting up, and seeking to sustain, the new State government of Louisiana. In this I have done just so much as, and no more than, the public knows. In the Annual Message of Dec. 1863 and accompanying Proclamation, I presented *a* plan of reconstruction (as the phrase goes) which, I promised, if adopted by any State, should be acceptable to, and sustained by, the Executive government of the nation. I distinctly stated that this was not the only plan which might possibly be acceptable; and I also distinctly protested that the Executive claimed no right to say when, or whether members should be admitted to seats in Congress from such States. This plan was, in advance, submitted to the then Cabinet, and distinctly approved by every member of it. One of them suggested that I should then, and in that connection, apply the Emancipation Proclamation to the theretofore excepted parts of Virginia and Louisiana; that I should drop the suggestion about apprenticeship for freed-people, and that I should omit the protest against my own power, in regard to the admission of members to Congress; but even he approved every part and parcel of the plan which has since been employed or touched by the action of Louisiana. The new constitution of Louisiana, declaring emancipation for the whole State, practically applies the Proclamation to the part previously excepted. It does not adopt apprenticeship for freed-people; and it is silent, as it could not well be otherwise, about the admission of members to Congress. So that, as it applies to Louisiana, every member of the Cabinet fully approved the plan. The message went to Congress, and I received many commendations of the plan, written and verbal; and not a single objection to it, from any professed emancipationist, came to my knowledge, until after the news reached Washington that the people of Louisiana had begun to move in accordance with it. From about July 1862, I had corresponded with different persons, supposed to be interested, seeking a reconstruction of a State government for Louisiana. When the message of 1863, with the plan before mentioned, reached New-Orleans, Gen. Banks wrote me that he was confident the people, with his military co-operation, would reconstruct, substantially on that plan. I wrote him, and some of them to try it; they tried it, and the result is known. Such only has been my agency in getting up the Louisiana government. As to sustaining it, my promise is out, as before stated. But, as bad promises are better broken than kept, I shall treat this as a bad promise, and break it, whenever I shall be convinced that keeping it is adverse to the public interest. But I have not yet been so convinced.

I have been shown a letter on this subject, supposed to be an able one, in which the writer expresses regret that my mind has not seemed to be definitely fixed on the question whether the seceded States, so called, are in the Union or out of it. It would perhaps, add astonishment to his regret, were he to learn that since I have found professed Union men endeavoring to make that question, I have *purposely* forborne any public expression upon it. As appears to me that question has not been, nor yet is, a practically material one, and that any discussion of it, while it thus remains practically immaterial, could have no effect other than the mischievous one of dividing our friends. As yet, whatever it may hereafter become, that question is bad, as the basis of a controversy, and good for nothing at all—a merely pernicious abstraction.

We all agree that the seceded States, so called, are out of their proper practical relation with the Union; and that the sole object of the government, civil and military, in regard to those States is to again get them into that proper practical relation. I believe it is not only possible, but in fact, easier to do this, without deciding, or even considering, whether these States have ever been out of the Union, than with it. Finding themselves safely at home, it would be utterly immaterial whether they had ever been abroad. Let us all join in doing the acts necessary to restoring the proper practical relations between these States and the Union; and each forever after, innocently indulge his own opinion whether, in doing the acts, he brought the States from without, into the Union, or only gave them proper assistance, they never having been out of it.

The amount of constituency, so to speak, on which the new Louisiana government rests, would be more satisfactory to all, if it contained fifty, thirty, or even twenty thousand, instead of only about twelve thousand, as it does. It is also unsatisfactory to some that the elective franchise is not given to the colored man. I would myself prefer that it were now conferred on the very intelligent, and on those who serve our cause as soldiers. Still the question is not whether the Louisiana government, as it stands, is quite all that is desirable. The question is, "Will it be wiser to take it as it is, and help to improve it; or to reject, and disperse it?" "Can Louisiana be brought into proper practical relation with the Union *sooner* by *sustaining,* or by *discarding* her new State government?"

Some twelve thousand voters in the heretofore slave-state of Louisiana have sworn allegiance to the Union, assumed to be the rightful political power of the State, held elections, organized a State government, adopted a free-state constitution, giving the benefit of public schools equally to black and white, and empowering the Legislature to confer the elective franchise upon the colored man. Their Legislature has already voted to ratify the constitutional amendment recently passed by Congress, abolishing slavery throughout the nation. These twelve thousand persons are thus fully committed to the Union, and to perpetual freedom in the state—committed to the very things, and nearly all the things the nation wants—and they ask the nation's recognition and its assistance to make good their committal. Now, if we reject, and spurn them, we do our utmost to disorganize and disperse them. We in effect say to the white men, "You are worthless, or worse—we will neither help you, nor be helped by you." To the blacks we say "This cup of liberty which these, your old masters, hold to your lips, we will dash from you, and leave you to the chances of gathering the spilled and scattered contents in some vague and undefined when, where, and how." If this course, discouraging and paralyzing both white and black, has any tendency to bring Louisiana into proper practical relations with the Union, I have, so far, been unable to perceive it. If, on the contrary, we recognize, and sustain the new government of Louisiana the converse of all this is made true. We encourage the hearts, and nerve the arms of the twelve thousand to adhere to their work, and argue for it, and proselyte for it, and fight for it, and feed it, and grow it, and ripen it to a complete success. The colored man too, in seeing all united for him, is inspired with vigilance, and energy, and daring, to the same end. Grant that he desires the elective franchise, will he not attain it sooner by saving the already advanced steps toward it, than by running backward over them? Concede that the new government of Louisiana is only to what it should be as the egg is to the fowl, we shall sooner have the fowl by hatching the egg than by smashing it. Again, if we reject Louisiana, we also reject one vote in favor of the proposed amendment to the national Constitution. To meet this proposition, it has been argued that no more than three-fourths of those States which have not attempted secession are necessary to validly ratify the amendment. I do not commit myself against this, further than to say that such a ratification would be questionable, and sure to be persistently questioned; while a ratification by three-fourths of all the States would be unquestioned and unquestionable.

I repeat the question. "Can Louisiana be brought into proper practical relation with the Union *sooner* by *sustaining* or by *discarding* her new State Government?"

What has been said of Louisiana will apply generally to other States. And yet so great peculiarities pertain to each state, and such important and sudden changes occur in the same state; and withal, so new and unprecedented is the whole case, that no exclusive, and inflexible plan can safely be prescribed as to details and collaterals. Such an exclusive, and inflexible plan, would surely become a new entanglement. Important principles may, and must, be inflexible.

In the present *"situation,"* as the phrase goes, it may be my duty to make some new announcement to the people of the South. I am considering, and shall not fail to act, when satisfied that action will be proper.

Telegraph Message on the Assassination of President Lincoln, from Secretary of State Stanton to Union Major–General W. T. Sherman
(April 15, 1865)

[OR: SER. 1, VOL. 46, PT. 1: 220–221]

The war effectively over, John Wilkes Booth, an actor, assassinated the North and South's best hope for a calming, just peace. General Sherman, at the time he received this message, was negotiating "terms of capitulation" with Confederate General Joseph E. Johnston, the commander of the Army of Tennessee, the last major army in the South. Lincoln's successor, President Andrew Johnson, announced on May 10 that "armed resistance to the authority of this Government in the said insurrectionary States may be regarded as virtually at an end." The Civil War was over.

War Department,
Washington City, April 15, 1865—12.10 P.M.
(Sent 1.40 P.M.)

Major–General Sherman,
  Commanding:

President Lincoln was murdered about 10 o'clock last night in his private box at Ford's Theater in this city, by an assassin who shot him through the head with a pistol ball. About the same hour Mr. Seward's house was entered by another assassin, who stabbed the Secretary in several places, but it is thought he may possibly recover; but his son Frederick will probably die of wounds received from the assassin. The assassin of the President leaped from the box, brandishing a dagger, exclaiming, *Sic semper tyrannis!* and that now Virginia was revenged. Mr. Lincoln fell senseless from his seat, and continued in that state until twenty-two minutes after 7 o'clock, at which time he breathed his last.

General Grant was published to be at the theater, but fortunately did not go. Vice-President Johnson now becomes President, and will take the oath of office and assume the duties to-day. I have no time to add more than to say that I find evidence that an assassin is also on your track, and I beseech you to be more heedful than Mr. Lincoln was of such knowledge.

EDWIN M. STANTON,
Secretary of War

The Thirteenth Amendment to the Constitution
(December 6, 1865)

In January 1864, Senator John Henderson of Missouri proposed the Thirteenth Amendment to the Constitution, whereby slavery would be outlawed throughout the Union. In April 1864 the Senate approved it; the House of Representatives approved it on January 31, 1865; it became law on December 6, 1865, when twenty-seven of the thirty-six states ratified it. Kentucky did not ratify the amendment until 1976; Mississippi ratified it in 1995.

SECTION 1. Neither slavery nor involuntary servitude, except as a punishment for crime whereof the party shall have been duly convicted, shall exist within the United States, or any place subject to their jurisdiction.

SECTION 2. Congress shall have power to enforce this article by appropriate legislation.

A CATALOG OF SELECTED DOVER
BOOKS IN ALL FIELDS OF INTEREST

CONCERNING THE SPIRITUAL IN ART, Wassily Kandinsky. Pioneering work by father of abstract art. Thoughts on color theory, nature of art. Analysis of earlier masters. 12 illustrations. 80pp. of text. 5⅜ x 8½.   0-486-23411-8

CELTIC ART: The Methods of Construction, George Bain. Simple geometric techniques for making Celtic interlacements, spirals, Kells-type initials, animals, humans, etc. Over 500 illustrations. 160pp. 9 x 12. (Available in U.S. only.)   0-486-22923-8

AN ATLAS OF ANATOMY FOR ARTISTS, Fritz Schider. Most thorough reference work on art anatomy in the world. Hundreds of illustrations, including selections from works by Vesalius, Leonardo, Goya, Ingres, Michelangelo, others. 593 illustrations. 192pp. 7⅛ x 10¼.   0-486-20241-0

CELTIC HAND STROKE-BY-STROKE (Irish Half-Uncial from "The Book of Kells"): An Arthur Baker Calligraphy Manual, Arthur Baker. Complete guide to creating each letter of the alphabet in distinctive Celtic manner. Covers hand position, strokes, pens, inks, paper, more. Illustrated. 48pp. 8¼ x 11.   0-486-24336-2

EASY ORIGAMI, John Montroll. Charming collection of 32 projects (hat, cup, pelican, piano, swan, many more) specially designed for the novice origami hobbyist. Clearly illustrated easy-to-follow instructions insure that even beginning papercrafters will achieve successful results. 48pp. 8¼ x 11.   0-486-27298-2

BLOOMINGDALE'S ILLUSTRATED 1886 CATALOG: Fashions, Dry Goods and Housewares, Bloomingdale Brothers. Famed merchants' extremely rare catalog depicting about 1,700 products: clothing, housewares, firearms, dry goods, jewelry, more. Invaluable for dating, identifying vintage items. Also, copyright-free graphics for artists, designers. Co-published with Henry Ford Museum & Greenfield Village. 160pp. 8¼ x 11.   0-486-25780-0

THE ART OF WORLDLY WISDOM, Baltasar Gracian. "Think with the few and speak with the many," "Friends are a second existence," and "Be able to forget" are among this 1637 volume's 300 pithy maxims. A perfect source of mental and spiritual refreshment, it can be opened at random and appreciated either in brief or at length. 128pp. 5⅜ x 8½.   0-486-44034-6

JOHNSON'S DICTIONARY: A Modern Selection, Samuel Johnson (E. L. McAdam and George Milne, eds.). This modern version reduces the original 1755 edition's 2,300 pages of definitions and literary examples to a more manageable length, retaining the verbal pleasure and historical curiosity of the original. 480pp. 5⅜ x 8¼.   0-486-44089-3

ADVENTURES OF HUCKLEBERRY FINN, Mark Twain, Illustrated by E. W. Kemble. A work of eternal richness and complexity, a source of ongoing critical debate, and a literary landmark, Twain's 1885 masterpiece about a barefoot boy's journey of self-discovery has enthralled readers around the world. This handsome clothbound reproduction of the first edition features all 174 of the original black-and-white illustrations. 368pp. 5⅜ x 8½.   0-486-44322-1

STICKLEY CRAFTSMAN FURNITURE CATALOGS, Gustav Stickley and L. & J. G. Stickley. Beautiful, functional furniture in two authentic catalogs from 1910. 594 illustrations, including 277 photos, show settles, rockers, armchairs, reclining chairs, bookcases, desks, tables. 183pp. 6½ x 9¼. 0-486-23838-5

AMERICAN LOCOMOTIVES IN HISTORIC PHOTOGRAPHS: 1858 to 1949, Ron Ziel (ed.). A rare collection of 126 meticulously detailed official photographs, called "builder portraits," of American locomotives that majestically chronicle the rise of steam locomotive power in America. Introduction. Detailed captions. xi+129pp. 9 x 12. 0-486-27393-8

AMERICA'S LIGHTHOUSES: An Illustrated History, Francis Ross Holland, Jr. Delightfully written, profusely illustrated fact-filled survey of over 200 American light-houses since 1716. History, anecdotes, technological advances, more. 240pp. 8 x 10¾. 0-486-25576-X

TOWARDS A NEW ARCHITECTURE, Le Corbusier. Pioneering manifesto by founder of "International School." Technical and aesthetic theories, views of industry, economics, relation of form to function, "mass-production split" and much more. Profusely illustrated. 320pp. 6⅛ x 9¼. (Available in U.S. only.) 0-486-25023-7

HOW THE OTHER HALF LIVES, Jacob Riis. Famous journalistic record, exposing poverty and degradation of New York slums around 1900, by major social reformer. 100 striking and influential photographs. 233pp. 10 x 7⅞. 0-486-22012-5

FRUIT KEY AND TWIG KEY TO TREES AND SHRUBS, William M. Harlow. One of the handiest and most widely used identification aids. Fruit key covers 120 deciduous and evergreen species; twig key 160 deciduous species. Easily used. Over 300 photographs. 126pp. 5⅜ x 8½. 0-486-20511-8

COMMON BIRD SONGS, Dr. Donald J. Borror. Songs of 60 most common U.S. birds: robins, sparrows, cardinals, bluejays, finches, more—arranged in order of increasing complexity. Up to 9 variations of songs of each species.
Cassette and manual 0-486-99911-4

ORCHIDS AS HOUSE PLANTS, Rebecca Tyson Northen. Grow cattleyas and many other kinds of orchids—in a window, in a case, or under artificial light. 63 illustrations. 148pp. 5⅜ x 8½. 0-486-23261-1

MONSTER MAZES, Dave Phillips. Masterful mazes at four levels of difficulty. Avoid deadly perils and evil creatures to find magical treasures. Solutions for all 32 exciting illustrated puzzles. 48pp. 8¼ x 11. 0-486-26005-4

MOZART'S DON GIOVANNI (DOVER OPERA LIBRETTO SERIES), Wolfgang Amadeus Mozart. Introduced and translated by Ellen H. Bleiler. Standard Italian libretto, with complete English translation. Convenient and thoroughly portable—an ideal companion for reading along with a recording or the performance itself. Introduction. List of characters. Plot summary. 121pp. 5¼ x 8½. 0-486-24944-1

FRANK LLOYD WRIGHT'S DANA HOUSE, Donald Hoffmann. Pictorial essay of residential masterpiece with over 160 interior and exterior photos, plans, elevations, sketches and studies. 128pp. 9¼ x 10¾. 0-486-29120-0

THE CLARINET AND CLARINET PLAYING, David Pino. Lively, comprehensive work features suggestions about technique, musicianship, and musical interpretation, as well as guidelines for teaching, making your own reeds, and preparing for public performance. Includes an intriguing look at clarinet history. "A godsend," *The Clarinet,* Journal of the International Clarinet Society. Appendixes. 7 illus. 320pp. 5⅜ x 8½. 0-486-40270-3

HOLLYWOOD GLAMOR PORTRAITS, John Kobal (ed.). 145 photos from 1926-49. Harlow, Gable, Bogart, Bacall; 94 stars in all. Full background on photographers, technical aspects. 160pp. 8⅜ x 11¼. 0-486-23352-9

THE RAVEN AND OTHER FAVORITE POEMS, Edgar Allan Poe. Over 40 of the author's most memorable poems: "The Bells," "Ulalume," "Israfel," "To Helen," "The Conqueror Worm," "Eldorado," "Annabel Lee," many more. Alphabetic lists of titles and first lines. 64pp. 5 3/16 x 8¼. 0-486-26685-0

PERSONAL MEMOIRS OF U. S. GRANT, Ulysses Simpson Grant. Intelligent, deeply moving firsthand account of Civil War campaigns, considered by many the finest military memoirs ever written. Includes letters, historic photographs, maps and more. 528pp. 6⅛ x 9¼. 0-486-28587-1

ANCIENT EGYPTIAN MATERIALS AND INDUSTRIES, A. Lucas and J. Harris. Fascinating, comprehensive, thoroughly documented text describes this ancient civilization's vast resources and the processes that incorporated them in daily life, including the use of animal products, building materials, cosmetics, perfumes and incense, fibers, glazed ware, glass and its manufacture, materials used in the mummification process, and much more. 544pp. 6⅛ x 9¼. (Available in U.S. only.) 0-486-40446-3

RUSSIAN STORIES/RUSSKIE RASSKAZY: A Dual-Language Book, edited by Gleb Struve. Twelve tales by such masters as Chekhov, Tolstoy, Dostoevsky, Pushkin, others. Excellent word-for-word English translations on facing pages, plus teaching and study aids, Russian/English vocabulary, biographical/critical introductions, more. 416pp. 5⅜ x 8½. 0-486-26244-8

PHILADELPHIA THEN AND NOW: 60 Sites Photographed in the Past and Present, Kenneth Finkel and Susan Oyama. Rare photographs of City Hall, Logan Square, Independence Hall, Betsy Ross House, other landmarks juxtaposed with contemporary views. Captures changing face of historic city. Introduction. Captions. 128pp. 8¼ x 11. 0-486-25790-8

NORTH AMERICAN INDIAN LIFE: Customs and Traditions of 23 Tribes, Elsie Clews Parsons (ed.). 27 fictionalized essays by noted anthropologists examine religion, customs, government, additional facets of life among the Winnebago, Crow, Zuni, Eskimo, other tribes. 480pp. 6⅛ x 9¼. 0-486-27377-6

TECHNICAL MANUAL AND DICTIONARY OF CLASSICAL BALLET, Gail Grant. Defines, explains, comments on steps, movements, poses and concepts. 15-page pictorial section. Basic book for student, viewer. 127pp. 5⅜ x 8½. 0-486-21843-0

THE MALE AND FEMALE FIGURE IN MOTION: 60 Classic Photographic Sequences, Eadweard Muybridge. 60 true-action photographs of men and women walking, running, climbing, bending, turning, etc., reproduced from rare 19th-century masterpiece. vi + 121pp. 9 x 12. 0-486-24745-7

CATALOG OF DOVER BOOKS

LIGHT AND SHADE: A Classic Approach to Three-Dimensional Drawing, Mrs. Mary P. Merrifield. Handy reference clearly demonstrates principles of light and shade by revealing effects of common daylight, sunshine, and candle or artificial light on geometrical solids. 13 plates. 64pp. 5⅜ x 8½. 0-486-44143-1

ASTROLOGY AND ASTRONOMY: A Pictorial Archive of Signs and Symbols, Ernst and Johanna Lehner. Treasure trove of stories, lore, and myth, accompanied by more than 300 rare illustrations of planets, the Milky Way, signs of the zodiac, comets, meteors, and other astronomical phenomena. 192pp. 8⅜ x 11. 0-486-43981-X

JEWELRY MAKING: Techniques for Metal, Tim McCreight. Easy-to-follow instructions and carefully executed illustrations describe tools and techniques, use of gems and enamels, wire inlay, casting, and other topics. 72 line illustrations and diagrams. 176pp. 8¼ x 10⅞. 0-486-44043-5

MAKING BIRDHOUSES: Easy and Advanced Projects, Gladstone Califf. Easy-to-follow instructions include diagrams for everything from a one-room house for bluebirds to a forty-two-room structure for purple martins. 56 plates; 4 figures. 80pp. 8¾ x 6⅜. 0-486-44183-0

LITTLE BOOK OF LOG CABINS: How to Build and Furnish Them, William S. Wicks. Handy how-to manual, with instructions and illustrations for building cabins in the Adirondack style, fireplaces, stairways, furniture, beamed ceilings, and more. 102 line drawings. 96pp. 8¾ x 6⅜. 0-486-44259-4

THE SEASONS OF AMERICA PAST, Eric Sloane. From "sugaring time" and strawberry picking to Indian summer and fall harvest, a whole year's activities described in charming prose and enhanced with 79 of the author's own illustrations. 160pp. 8¼ x 11. 0-486-44220-9

THE METROPOLIS OF TOMORROW, Hugh Ferriss. Generous, prophetic vision of the metropolis of the future, as perceived in 1929. Powerful illustrations of towering structures, wide avenues, and rooftop parks–all features in many of today's modern cities. 59 illustrations. 144pp. 8¼ x 11. 0-486-43727-2

THE PATH TO ROME, Hilaire Belloc. This 1902 memoir abounds in lively vignettes from a vanished time, recounting a pilgrimage on foot across the Alps and Apennines in order to "see all Europe which the Christian Faith has saved." 77 of the author's original line drawings complement his sparkling prose. 272pp. 5⅜ x 8½. 0-486-44001-X

THE HISTORY OF RASSELAS: Prince of Abissinia, Samuel Johnson. Distinguished English writer attacks eighteenth-century optimism and man's unrealistic estimates of what life has to offer. 112pp. 5⅜ x 8½. 0-486-44094-X

A VOYAGE TO ARCTURUS, David Lindsay. A brilliant flight of pure fancy, where wild creatures crowd the fantastic landscape and demented torturers dominate victims with their bizarre mental powers. 272pp. 5⅜ x 8½. 0-486-44198-9

Paperbound unless otherwise indicated. Available at your book dealer, online at **www.doverpublications.com**, or by writing to Dept. GI, Dover Publications, Inc., 31 East 2nd Street, Mineola, NY 11501. For current price information or for free catalogs (please indicate field of interest), write to Dover Publications or log on to **www.doverpublications.com** and see every Dover book in print. Dover publishes more than 500 books each year on science, elementary and advanced mathematics, biology, music, art, literary history, social sciences, and other areas.